New Approaches to Materials Development for Language Learning

Olwyn Alexander (Ed.)

New Approaches to Materials Development for Language Learning

Proceedings of the 2005 joint BALEAP/SATEFL conference

PETER LANG

Oxford · Bern · Berlin · Bruxelles · Frankfurt am Main · New York · Wien

Bibliographic information published by Die Deutsche Bibliothek
Die Deutsche Bibliothek lists this publication in the Deutsche
Nationalbibliografie; detailed bibliographic data is available on
the Internet at ‹http://dnb.ddb.de›.

British Library and Library of Congress Cataloguing-in-Publication Data:
A catalogue record for this book is available from The British Library,
Great Britain, and from The Library of Congress, USA

ISBN 978-3-03910-909-8

© Peter Lang AG, International Academic Publishers, Bern 2007
Hochfeldstrasse 32, Postfach 746, CH-3000 Bern 9, Switzerland
info@peterlang.com, www.peterlang.com, www.peterlang.net

Printed in Germany

Contents

OLWYN ALEXANDER

Introduction

Materials development is a very practical theme for a BALEAP conference. This is partly a consequence of the fact that this conference was a joint venture with the Scottish Association for the Teaching of English as a Foreign Language (SATEFL) so there was a need for a theme with a broad appeal to a diverse audience. However, when BALEAP was established in 1972 as the Special English Language Materials for Overseas University Students Group, materials were 'the prime need' (Jordan 2002:71) and at the meeting in 1989 to change the name of the organisation to BALEAP there was 'general agreement over the continuing importance of materials-sharing to the organisation'.[1] Seventeen years later, faced with a much more diverse student population but with a great deal more understanding of their specific needs from research into genre and corpus linguistics, it seemed important to encourage the EAP community to come together specifically to share good practice in the development of new approaches to learning and teaching materials and to focus on how this good practice is underpinned by insights from research.

Materials development in EAP has come a long way since Hutchinson and Waters (1987:125) concluded their chapter on materials design by recommending it as 'the last resort, when all other possibilities of providing materials have been exhausted'. McGrath (2002:1) lists several book-length publications which attest to the 'acceptance of the appropriateness of materials as a field of serious study' and his own book and those edited by Tomlinson (1998, 2003) contribute to a lively research field. 'Materials' has tended to mean published materials such as coursebooks and their associated multimedia so that materials development was largely concerned with

---

1   Paul Fanning, personal communication, August 2006.

evaluation and adaptation. However, the past ten years has seen the increasing availability of electronic sources for materials development, ranging from a variety of genres on the Internet, through research papers and course materials held on local area networks, to corpora collected for specific research purposes. Materials development now includes analysis of these sources and creation of new learning tasks based on this analysis.

The EAP research community has also gained much more specific knowledge about what is involved in studying in further and higher education. Genre analysis and corpus linguistics have contributed enormously to our understanding of the types of texts and the kind of language that students will be required to deal with. Research into reading, writing, listening and speaking in academic settings has informed recent publications such as the University of Reading English for Academic Study series published by Garnet Education and the new editions of Study Reading/Writing/ Listening/Speaking/Tasks from Edinburgh, published by Cambridge University Press. Nevertheless, Harwood (2005) found that many of the EAP textbooks he surveyed did not reflect current research in applied linguistics. The gap between research or theory and practice has been discussed by Block (2000), and Tomlinson (1998:23) notes that many papers end by suggesting their research has implications for classroom practice without ever providing specific applications for this. While some developers make their materials freely available via websites e.g. Andy Gillett,[2] Sandra Haywood[3] and John Morley,[4] a great deal of good material based on sound research remains within the institution where it was created.

Jolly and Bolitho (1998:111) note the importance of materials writing for teachers' professional development, 'raising almost every issue which is important in learning to teach' and McGrath (2002:5) suggests that teachers

---

2   [http://www.uefap.com]
3   [http://www.nottingham.ac.uk/~alzsh3/acvocab/]
4   [http://www.phrasebank.manchester.ac.uk/]

need to possess the confidence and at least basic competences to (1) make informed decisions about the choice and use of materials and (2) develop materials when existing materials are found to be inadequate.

This conference with its practical theme was one way to enable researchers, teachers, writers and publishers to come together 'to pool resources and to take advantage of different areas of expertise' in materials design (Tomlinson 1998:343).

The 26 papers in this volume highlight most of the current issues confronting EAP practitioners. A number of underlying key themes run through the collection: the increasing diversity of the student population, socialisation of these students within their specific fields of study, genre analysis and corpus studies to understand these fields and design targeted teaching materials, the importance of critical thinking and academic literacy for learner autonomy, and writing as a key academic skill.

Section I concerns academic socialisation and needs analysis. Sandra Cardew uses the concept of citizenship tests to encourage students to think critically about their place within their academic discourse community. Erik Borg notes the contribution of genre analysis to the teaching of writing but shows the difficulties of applying those insights to emerging genres in fields such as Fine Arts and Design. Hania Salter-Dvorak argues for pragmatic training of students to enable them to be more than 'academic tourists' in their learning communities. Robert Berman uses a grounded theory approach to develop a questionnaire designed to establish the factors contributing to L2 undergraduates' academic success and Diana Ridley presents a needs analysis which investigated supervisor and research student views on the desirability and content of online thesis writing guidelines.

Section II covers curriculum and course design. Paul Fanning argues for the viability of EFL at undergraduate level, and shows how advanced language teaching materials can be adapted to meet the very particular needs of undergraduate education. Richard Bailey and Peter Sercombe present an alternative approach to course design in EAP which is holistically devised and content focused in order to address academic literacy requirements of international students. Ian Bruce addresses the diversity of approaches to genre classification and considers the genre constructs which might be used to design academic writing courses. John Wrigglesworth shows how genre-based pedagogy was used in the design and delivery of an English language support unit accompanying undergraduate and postgraduate degrees.

Section III focuses on modes of delivery. David Catterick explores the development of a conceptual tool which provides a frame of reference for the delivery and evaluation of individual academic coaching. Ann Smith shows how case-based teaching, now popular in many academic disciplines, can be used in an EAP context to develop learners' critical awareness, discussion skills and co-operative teamwork. Alison Stewart describes an academic writing course which used the concept of a community of practice to encourage a greater sense of mutual accountability for a writing assignment. Fred Tarttelin shows how students can be motivated to commit to substantial out-of-class extensive reading if the work contributes to other tasks and activities that are part of the assessment programme.

Section IV considers the possibilities for both teachers and students of finding and using sources in academic writing. Martin Millar addresses the issue of sourcing and selecting suitable materials for teaching by reflecting on past, present and future practice. Joan McCormack describes materials developed to provide a more integrated approach to the teaching of extended writing in the academic context. Lynn Errey evaluates the use of online discussion in an academic writing module to help students avoid plagiarism by seeing citation as embedded in academic writing culture. Cathy Benson, Jacqueline Gollin and Hugh Trappes-Lomax investigate reporting strategies in academic writing, using a corpus of academic texts, and offer practical suggestions for teaching and materials writing.

Section V concerns assessment. Siân Etherington investigated academic tutors' and students' understanding of and priorities within academic writing in order to both align pre-sessional testing more closely with authentic writing needs and to explore the development of student thinking about this area. John Slaght and Bruce Howell describe how the design of the University of Reading Test of English for Educational Purposes has evolved to fit in with pre-sessional course design principles and ensure that assessment complements the course rather than drives it. Andy Blackhurst demonstrates the comparability of IELTS tests delivered on paper and by computer.

Section VI covers online and blended learning. Paul Wickens argues that computer literacy needs to be brought fully into the academic literacy objectives of EAP and shows how traditional IT self-study training materials can be integrated into a situated task based framework. Bob Gilmour highlights some of the issues to consider in the design and development of an effective, online self-study site for English language materials within a Higher Education Institution. Lynne Hale and Gillian Lazar describe the conflicts and opportunities arising from a highly collaborative materials writing project to develop online academic writing materials. Fei-Yu Chuang and Hilary Nesi discuss the development of GrammarTalk, a set of interactive grammar materials designed to help Chinese EAP students improve their formal accuracy. Stella Harvey and Karen Nicholls describe the development and evaluation of two sets of online materials which build on the language, content, and context of the live lecture. Ian McGrath discusses the relationship between textbooks, technology and teachers, and in particular the impact of technology on teaching and learning.

Olwyn Alexander
October 2006

Bibliography

Block, D. (2000) 'Revisiting the gap between SLA researchers and language teachers'. *Links and Letters*, 7, 129–43.

Harwood, N. (2005) 'What do we want EAP teaching materials for?'. *Journal of English for Academic Purposes* 4/2, 149–61.

Hutchinson, T. and Waters, A. (1987) *English for specific purposes: a learning-centred approach*. Cambridge: Cambridge University Press.

Jolly, D. and Bolitho, R. (1998) 'A framework for materials writing' in Tomlinson, B. (ed.) *Materials development in language teaching.*

Jordan, R.R. (2002) 'The growth of EAP in Britain'. *Journal of English for Academic Purposes*, 1/1, 69–78.

McGrath, I. (2002) *Materials evaluation and design for language teachers*. Edinburgh: Edinburgh University Press.

Tomlinson, B. (ed.) (1998) *Materials development in language teaching*. Cambridge: Cambridge University Press.

—— (ed.) (2003) *Developing materials for language teaching*. London: Continuum.

Section I

Academic Socialisation and Needs Analysis

SANDRA CARDEW

1 Critical Thinking about Cultural and Academic Identity

The ability to think critically is seen as just one indication of membership of the academic community but what critical thinking means is largely tacit, unconscious and intuitive. It can be seen as a social practice embedded in a particular academic context. This paper draws parallels with the concept of cultural identity, which is often equally opaque and unconscious. It describes teaching materials designed to raise students' awareness of how the implicit can be made explicit, beginning with their personal experience as members of a particular cultural community. One way in which ideas about cultural identity are made explicit is through citizenship tests and this is the first focus of the materials. The aim is to transfer this process of reification to their role as students, able to think critically about their academic disciplines and their place within their academic discourse community.

Critical Thinking: definitions and problems

> Critical thinking is a defining concept of the Western university. Almost everyone is in favour of critical thinking but we have no proper account of it. Higher education, which prides itself on critical thought, has done no adequate thinking about critical thinking [...]. Its pedagogic strategy is to develop a mastery of the tacit epistemological rules within a cognitive field; the students ultimately have to demonstrate that they have the competence to participate in the conversation of the discipline. Its critical standards are internal, tacit, cognitive and under academic control. (Barnett 1997)

It may be true that higher education 'has done no adequate thinking about critical thinking' but there is a considerable critical thinking industry, especially highly developed in the USA and increasingly in the UK, producing teaching materials, web sites, training programmes, tests and academic papers. For example, a number of Cambridge colleges have piloted the use of the UCLES Critical Thinking Assessment A level, which tests reasoning and thinking skills, as an aid in filtering the large numbers of applications from students with very similar academic grades. There is no lack of proposed definitions of what critical thinking is and there are many taxonomies of critical thinking competencies. One fundamental question is whether it is an attitude, an approach, a 'disposition to enquiry' (Barnett 1997:4) or a value-neutral assembly of study strategies, such as those exemplified by the Ennis–Weir Critical Thinking Essay Test (Ennis and Weir 1985). It is likely, of course, that it is a combination of factors but this continuing lack of consensus leads to considerable confusion about what critical thinking is, among researchers, materials writers, teachers and thus students.

Another issue is whether teaching critical thinking is 'a surrender to an instrumental agenda' (Barnett 1997). There is a view, exemplified by writers such as Atkinson (1997), which sees it as having a policing, socialising, reductive function which excludes and marginalises minorities and women. In the EAP teaching context it is possible to argue that this is only problematic if EAP teachers see themselves as simply equipping students to play the academic game by teaching them the rules – enabling them to acquire mastery of the norms and modes of enquiry of their discipline – without also encouraging awareness of the necessary underlying critical disposition. For example, a problematic approach to plagiarism is primarily concerned with manipulating language and obeying rules – replacing words in the original with synonyms and producing well-formatted bibliographies – rather than developing an understanding of what plagiarism is and why it is unacceptable.

Cultural Identity and Critical Pedagogy

For students new to the academic community of a British university there is a need to make explicit the norms and conventions which are, in Barnett's words, 'internal, tacit and cognitive' (ibid:11). One recent attempt to do this is Rugg and Petrie's paradoxically titled book The Unwritten Rules of PhD Research which talks about

> things nobody bothers to tell you explicitly, either because they assume you know already, or because they are so familiar to them that they completely forget that other people don't know them, or because they don't think they are worth mentioning. (2004:x)

This could apply equally to the information sometimes given, or not given, in pre-departure briefings to those planning to spend time in an unfamiliar culture. It is often the most obvious and easily observable behaviour which is described but not the more subtle rules which govern people's interactions and relationships and the ways in which they are perceived. This idea led to the development of materials based on exploration of the concept of cultural identity, with the intention of drawing parallels with the assumptions of academic discourse communities. Obviously, no language teaching is contentless and often that content is determined by the textbook writer and, in academic disciplines, by the syllabus. I assumed that the notion of cultural identity would engage my students because it is a current issue in the UK and it interested me personally. The question of teacher-selected versus student-selected topics is one on which Sarah Benesch makes a striking point:

> [...] the traditional EAP literature overlooks the intellectual life of EAP teachers, assuming their job is to support the goals of the content course, even if those goals reduce academic life to listening, taking notes, memorising definitions and taking tests. I have not come across recommendations in the literature that EAP teachers find one area of study that interests them and promote that topic as an object of enquiry even though their intellectual engagement could be a great stimulus for students. (2001:84)

Most students are aware of the role that their subject tutors have as researchers but is this true of their EAP teachers? There are practical benefits in the students also seeing the latter as collaborators and even role models in research, as well as in the encouragement to staff of engaging with the reality of what their students are undertaking.

Benesch's ideas on critical pedagogy are not uncontroversial but the central notion of how identity is constructed is relevant to EAP students, as members of their own cultural communities and as members of the academic discourse community. EAP tutors and their students – the latter often seen, in Benesch's words, as 'underprepared, remedial or deficient' – can seem marginalised within their institutions. The aim is to help both groups to use critical thinking to influence change by questioning materials, pedagogic approaches and the academic community of which they are members.

Critical pedagogy encourages students to view institutional constraints on them in a way which is critical but not confrontational. Roz Ivanic makes the point that 'there is always tension and struggle at the interface between the institution and its members' (1988:106). There are clearly limits on the challenges which students, especially international students, can be expected to mount and some tutors may find this approach disconcerting. However, these same tutors cannot complain that students are too passive and then react negatively when their pedagogic practices or their assessment procedures are actively questioned. The practical value of this approach is that it addresses the fact that some students already engage in resisting behaviour, arriving late, not completing assignments or preparation, not participating in class. There may obviously be other causes but it is surely better to examine the possible underlying reasons and encourage students to take responsibility, work together and negotiate the changes they desire. For example, students' failure to complete a task may not be because they do not understand what is required but because they cannot see the relevance or relationship between the task and the course content and stated aims.

Materials: cultural identity and citizenship tests

The aim of the materials which were devised in the light of these considerations is to encourage students to develop their critical thinking skills through examining the concept of cultural identity. Students proceed from their individual membership of a cultural community to a critical analysis of various efforts to make identity explicit through citizenship tests. Throughout the tasks the underlying aim is to introduce the idea of implicit, unconscious 'rules' which can be made explicit and then examined and analysed. Everyone, the teacher included, is equally able to act as an informant on their cultural community.

The materials begin with a discussion of identity in a very general and individual way, asking the students to simply list all their 'identities' including nationality, gender, family roles, education, class, age. They may include 'student' and from this the teacher can develop, initially in a very basic way, the notion of academic identity and how it is recognised. Depending on their background the students may have a more or less explicit understanding of the expectations of membership of their target academic community. These might include its discourse structures (both written and spoken), its lexical choices, the key journals, conferences and publishers, how current research issues can be identified and its leading figures (both historical and current).

Clearly, it may not be appropriate to refer directly to any of this in the initial stage but an eventual awareness of these expectations is essential and needs to be addressed at some point. The teacher should also be sensitive to the fact that students are faced with the need to construct a *new* identity. International students, perhaps particularly graduates, often arrive having been very successful in their previous academic setting and face the shock of adjusting to a relatively novice status, in addition to all the other adjustments which are necessary. They need space to create a new voice, with programmes which balance authentic and realistic preparation with support and scaffolding in the early stages.

The materials include a worksheet which focuses on nationality and the introduction of citizenship tests in Britain. Students pool their ideas about the kinds of questions which should be asked and the underlying assumptions behind them, comparing these with the six topic areas suggested by the Life in the United Kingdom Panel

- British national institutions in recent historical context
- Britain as a multi-cultural society
- Knowing the law
- Employment
- Sources of help and information
- Everyday needs.

The Chairman of the Panel, Professor Sir Bernard Crick, has stated, 'We are not trying to define "Britishness"; we are trying to define what people need to settle in effectively' (BBC News, 25/02/2004). What the Panel appear to be attempting is to make assumptions explicit, for example, asking what makes a good neighbour, a topic which has generated a great deal of discussion in class. British newspapers have suggested their own sample questions and students are given the task of answering these. They are given time to research any they do not know and are also encouraged to ask British people to attempt them. When students do this they have been surprised that some are unable to answer, or answer wrongly, and this has led to fruitful discussion of the underlying rationale for the questions.

The next task is to work in small groups to consider whether the Panel's proposed topics would be an appropriate basis in all contexts and then devise a short questionnaire relevant to their own cultural community. This has been piloted with both mixed and mono-cultural groups with revealing results. Japanese participants, for example, have begun by assuming that there will be a high degree of unanimity among them because of their strong belief in the idea that Japan is a highly homogeneous society. In practice there have then been unexpected, but very productive, disagreements.

There is a variety of other tasks, depending on the time available. These include carrying out web-based research on citizenship tests in other countries such as the USA, Canada and Australia. These are then compared with the British proposals, considering the categories, the questions and the underlying principles, and what the priorities suggest about various cultures' view of what is important. For example, the Canadian citizenship test categories are

- Aboriginal people
- History
- Confederation/Government
- Rights and Responsibilities
- Languages
- Symbols
- Geography
- Economy
- Federal Government.

The proposed British tests have provoked considerable controversy so students have little difficulty in finding other material about them. They look at the web or in newspapers, with initial guidance from the teacher, and report back to the class. The area of research has been expanded to include the wider current national debate on national identity in Britain in the context of recent events in London. This has introduced the critical skill of distinguishing between fact, comment and opinion and of evaluating the status and reliability of web-based material in particular. This task has also served as an introduction to a variety of genres, including web-based message boards, leading to a discussion of whether there are identifiable cultural differences in humour. The BBC News website asked users, 'What question would you like to see included in the "Britishness" tests?' Suggestions ranged from the academic to the unanswerable, including;

What is the relationship between the Head of State (who is it?) and the government?
Is the euro currency good for Britain?
What is the favourite British pastime, is it:
a) moaning
b) moaning
c) moaning
Is Chelsea an English football club? (BBC News, 16/03/2005)

Discussion may be both oral and written. The focus of the materials is on the content and their classroom use is flexible. The tasks can be seen as a progression though research, presentation and discussion. The academic skills developed include reading, oral presentation and critical analysis of sources and writing. The transfer of these skills to academic texts can be slow and painstaking but it has been useful to begin with concepts which are related to personal experience, rather than introducing discipline-specific academic texts from the outset. It is, however, necessary to introduce the latter at a reasonably early stage. A concentration on genres broadly related to journalism is not necessarily the best preparation for a critical under-standing of the type of texts which students will have to deal with in their future studies. As a next stage students make oral presentations on a topic of their choice, related to their intended area of study. They are also required to provide a relevant follow-up text. This is then subject to the same kind of analysis as the earlier texts, with reference back to those where appropriate.

In this paper I have considered the interconnected concepts of cultural and academic identity as a route to the introduction or reinforcement of critical thinking skills. The materials are designed to introduce students to the approaches and strategies associated with critical thinking. The assumption is that even students unfamiliar with the notion of unconscious, tacit rules will be able to offer examples from their own experience of exactly these kinds of rules which govern culturally constrained behaviour. The aim is for the same process of reification to be applied to the requirements for member-ship of their target academic community. This may seem quite a leap but if students are to be helped to operate successfully within their target disciplines it seems reasonable to begin, in Clark and Ivanic's terms, with the autobiographical self before moving on to the authorial and discoursal. The purpose throughout is to raise students' awareness of the range of implicit rules and expectations within which we all operate, beginning with most deeply embedded assumptions about personal and socially constructed identities.

Bibliography

Atkinson, D. (1997) 'A critical approach to critical thinking in TESOL'. *TESOL Quarterly* 31/1, 71–94.

Barnett, R. (1997) *Higher education: a critical business.* Buckingham: Society for Research into Higher Education and Open University Press.

Bartlett, A., Holzknecht, S. and Cumming Thom, A. (1999) *To hit the ground running.* Canberra: Asia Pacific Press.

BBC News [http://newsvote.bbc.co.uk/mpapps/pagetools/print/news.-bbc.co.uk/1/hi/uk/3078690.stm] retrieved 16/03/2005.

Benesch, S. (2001) *Critical english for academic purposes: theory, politics and practice.* New Jersey: Lawrence Erlbaum Associates.

Bowell, T. and Kemp, G. (2002) *Critical thinking: a concise guide.* London: Routledge.

Browne, M.N. and Keeley, S.M. (1994) *Asking the right questions: a guide to critical thinking.* Upper Saddle River: Pearson Prentice Hall.

Clark, R. and Ivanic, R. (1997) *The politics of writing.* London: Routledge.

Ennis, R.H. and Weir, E. (1985) *The Ennis-Weir critical thinking essay test.* Critical Thinking Press and Software [http://faculty.ed.uiuc.edu/rhennis/Assessment.html] retrieved 18/03/1999.

Fisher, A. (2001) *Critical thinking: an introduction.* Cambridge: Cambridge University Press.

Gent, I.P., Johnston, B. and Prosser, P. (1999) 'Thinking on your feet in undergraduate computer science: a constructivist approach to developing and assessing critical thinking'. *Teaching in Higher Education* 4/4, 511–22.

Hyland, K. (2000) *Disciplinary discourses: social interactions in academic writing.* Harlow: Longman.

Ivanic, R. (1998) *Writing and identity: the discoursal construction of identity in academic life.* Amsterdam: John Benjamins Publishing.

Life in the United Kingdom Panel [www.ind.homeoffice.gov.uk] retrieved 16/03/2005.

OCR specification Advanced Subsidiary GCE in critical thinking [http://www.ocr.org.uk/resource/alevel/student/critcal.pdf]

Pennycook, A. (1997) 'Vulgar pragmatism, critical pragmatism and EAP'. *ESP* 16/4, 253–69.

Rugg, G. and Petrie, M. (2004) *The unwritten rules of PhD research.* Maidenhead: Open University Press.

Schulman M. (2004) *Thinking critically: world issues for reading, writing and research.* Ann Arbor: University of Michigan Press.

Sowden, C. (2003) 'Understanding academic competence in overseas students in the UK'. *ELT Journal* 57/4, 377–85.

Thompson, C. (1999) 'Critical thinking: what is it and how do we teach it?' in EAP programs, *HERDSA Annual International Conference.* Melbourne July 1999.

UCLES *Thinking skills assessment: background to TSA tests for Cambridge admissions.* [http://tsa.ucles.org.uk/background.html] retrieved 12/05/2004.

ERIK BORG

2 Academic Writing in Fine Arts Practice

Introduction

Advanced literacy involves the interaction of a writer with a social situation to achieve a goal through texts. What distinguishes advanced literacy from other forms of literacy is the high level of awareness of both goals and means within the situation that elicits the text. Learning advanced literacy is often described as a form of enculturation into a community of specialised practice, bringing with it an awareness of the written genres of the discourse community and how these genres are used to fulfil the purposes of the community. Enculturation is alternatively described as occurring through a process of cognitive apprenticeship (Atkinson 1997) or limited peripheral participation (Lave and Wenger 1991, Wenger 1998). Writing at PhD level provides a guided path of learning from the peripheral role of student to expert practitioner within the discourse community. Ethnographic descriptions of advanced literacy developing in this way have been written for fields such as applied linguistics (Berkenkotter and Huckin 1995), biology (Myers 1990), and sociology (Prior 1998), among others.

Along the path to advanced literacy, the student must develop an awareness of the genres of the discourse community, which are closely linked to participation in the community.

Full participation in disciplinary and professional cultures demands informed knowledge of written genres. Genres are the media through which scholars and scientists communicate with their peers. Genres are intimately linked to the discipline's methodology, packaging information in ways that conform to a discipline's norms, values and ideology. Understanding the genres of written communication in one's field is, therefore, essential to professional success. (Trosborg 2000:viii)

As Trosberg (2000) implies, the concept of enculturation to the expectations of the discourse community for written texts usually posits congruence between academic practice and professional practice. However, some disciplines focus on producing works in other semiotic modes, e.g. architecture, dance, design, fine arts. Dias, Freedman, Medway and Paré highlighted the difference between disciplines when they write, 'a law student writing a paper analyzing a case is being more of a lawyer than an architecture student is being an architect in writing on the origins of Gothic' (1999:83). This lack of congruence affects writing in Fine Arts practice.

This paper is based on an on-going study of writing and the development of advanced literacy in Fine Arts practice (FAP) and Design. The study looks at the enculturation to the academic writing practices of these two discourse communities as perceived by the participants in two PhD seminar groups (students and supervisors), one in FAP and one in Design. This report focuses on the FAP seminar and one student's learning of the expectations of the community.

Writing in Fine Arts Practice

Because of the close and crucial relationship between the discourse community, its goals and its writing, it is important to understand the 'goals, values and material conditions' (Swales 2004:73) of the participants in this study. In order to do this it is necessary to understand to some extent the perspective of the art world.

In interviews and the PhD seminars, the Fine Arts supervisor has suggested what the artist should intend at the current moment: 'The main aesthetic, if you like, of our time is to do with confronting expectations, lowering inhibitions, increasing sensitivity'. The artist should 'radicalise the moment' or 'destabilise the situation'. This view of art is shared by others in the Fine Arts community, as suggested by the selection in a poll of 500 art experts held in December 2004 (Higgins 2004), of Marcel Duchamp's Fountain (1917, a re-oriented urinal) as the most important artwork of the twentieth century.

The supervisor described writing as fundamentally similar to art creation: 'when [artists] sit down at the computer or at a desk, I think that's just the same, just a different zone, rather a different zone of your creativity.' As a student in art school, he found two models of thinking about art. One was an art historical model, in which the student artists would study lineages and influences, and situate themselves within that history. He rejected this model, as not reflecting the ferment of art school or the overlapping influences found there. The other model was one based on theory, in which the art would be created as a test or exemplification of a theory. This, the supervisor felt, led to a 'kind of blindness', in which students became 'totally confused and often inept when it came to actually saying, "Is it any good or not?"'

The alternative model he presented was drawn from Rosalind Krauss, who, in a work that is a seminal text for the supervisor, Sculpture in the Expanded Field, writes that postmodernism presupposes the acceptance of definitive ruptures and the possibility of looking at historical process from the point of view of logical structure (Krauss 1983:42). She then provides an alternative, logically-based (that is, neither historically-based nor theory-based) framework for the creation of sculpture, and, implicitly, other artworks.

The supervisor's approach to art creation, when applied to writing, may be antithetical both to some models of academic research (e.g. research frontiers or research projects) and to conceptualisations of genre that foreground linguistic description (e.g. Flowerdew 2002) or genre stability. The research that the art students engage in frequently involves juxtaposing different contexts of creation (e.g. science and art, social science and art). Further, their research may not be directly related to their artistic practice, but it nevertheless yields the content of the PhD thesis. These juxtaposed contexts result in genre hybridity or blending. However, despite the hybridity, the supervisor and many of the students have a core understanding of the limits of this hybridity. This understanding is conveyed through a process of enculturation that is less concerned with learning the specifics of writing than with learning to think like an artist.

Learning the Expectations of the Discourse Community

Disciplinary enculturation can be a rough school, as well as the nurturing community that seems implicit in the characterisation 'community' (Harris 1989), and novice members of the community can be bruised in the process. The example given here describes how a student, approximately a year into her full-time PhD, was shown some of the expectations of this community.

Doctorates in FAP require both a written text, the thesis, which is based on research, and an artistic submission. The Initial Project Application (IPA) provides the first description of the research programme. It is one link in a chain of genres (Swales 2004) leading to the thesis. In this case, the proposed title of the study was Therapeutic touch: the use of photo-based methodology as a healing practice within the context of healthcare. In her IPA, the student identified two somewhat contradictory themes that she wished to research. As suggested by her title and expressed in her IPA, she wanted both to document healing, and also to participate in healing through photography.

> It seems to me that using photography [...] has much to offer people who are giving and receiving healthcare in a manner that could be like a therapeutic touch.
>
> My proposition is that photography can address the widest possible concept of 'touch' in relation to the world of healthcare. That is, *photographic methods can be used to represent and document the healing properties of physical touch and generate well-being through the psychological state of being touched.* Together these can be treated as a form of therapeutic touch. [emphasis added]

These two themes comprise the representation and documentation of healing through touch and 'generating well-being' through the symbolic process of being touched by photography.

There is a well-established discipline of art therapy, which involves the use of art practice to help patients 'increase awareness of self, [or] cope with symptoms, stress, and traumatic experiences' (The American Art Therapy Association, n.d.). However, these are not the goals of the FAP discourse community. When the student selected a short reading from Cosden and Reynolds (1982) to discuss in the seminar group, the conflict between the two discourse communities became apparent. Writing in Arts in Psychotherap*y*, Cosden and Reynolds describe the use of photography (the process of taking pictures, processing the film and printing the pictures, and ultimately displaying them) as a means of helping people whom they called 'emotionally disturbed adolescents':

> the processes involved in taking pictures can help patients gain better control of their impulses, improve social interaction skills, develop more positive self-esteem, and accept praise and constructive criticism. (ibid:23)

This is reasonably consonant with the student's stated desire 'to generate well-being'. It is not, in the view of the supervisor or the other participants, art. As they read the portion of Cosden and Reynolds (1982) in the seminar, the participants seized on a passage, characteristic of the article, in which the dysfunctional behaviour of the adolescents is described. The participants are the supervisor, the presenting student, another student and myself:

> Supervisor: Yes, I identify with the narcissistic patient who takes roll after roll of himself.
> Presenter: unh hun
> Supervisor: with the aid of a tripod and a timed-release shutter, that would be my ideal practice-led research ...
> Second student: He's taking a piss
> Presenter: but, for example, when you take photographs, I mean
> Supervisor: I can dress myself up in different costumes
> EB: Cindy Sherman has already done that
> Supervisor: According to varying moods.

As can be seen, the passage from the article was mocked, but subsequently, the supervisor developed a more substantial point about the text:

it just could describe an artistic practice, that, but here, in here, in here it's a
therapeutic practice of some kind. Just context is different. I mean you could
take lots of little chunks of this and just change the context and you'd be talking
about artistic practice.

To the supervisor and other participants in the seminar, the
obsessive behaviour of the 'emotionally disturbed adolescents', as
described by Cosden and Reynolds (1982), seemed similar to accepted
artistic practices. This similarity was recognised by many of the
seminar participants, but not by the student who was presenting. When
she tried to use Cosden and Reynolds (1982) in thinking about her
research, trying to reposition it in a new hybrid genre, her supervisor
and more experienced students rejected the text.

On one level, there are similarities to Prior's (1998:202–4)
description of how one of his PhD participants, Sean, was deflected
from his original research hypothesis by his supervisor's mocking, or
to Casanave's description of local interaction, in which her participants constructed their professional identities in 'a world characterised
by tensions, ambiguities and uncertainties' (1995:101). Similarities
include a supervisor's denigration of a student's research intuition,
leading the student subsequently to fail to develop that idea.

In other ways, though, the case of these participants may have
been different. The mocking is still there, but ultimately the supervisor
is drawing on what he sees as fundamental values of the discourse
community. This core value may be described either as disruption/
disjunction, or innovation.

The seminar ended inconclusively for the presenter. The supervisor and supportive students contextualised their reaction, discussed
the role of innovation in FAP, and the discussion moved on. The
presenter continued to have difficulty bringing the two themes present
in her IPA into a balance that would find acceptance in reviews of her
progress.

In sociology, as described by Casanave (1995) and Prior (1998),
there is a much more limited charge to be new, or strikingly different;
in art, that is the purpose, that is the intention. In sociology, disciplinary enculturation involves 'learning the ropes', learning existing
patterns. Further, within English for Academic Purposes (EAP)

circles, creativity is somewhat neglected: 'the EAP discourse community is more concerned to show students how to follow conventions than to encourage them to be creative in research terms' (Allison 2004:194).

The Drive to be Creative

There is a tension between the regularities found in groups of text that are described in genre theory and the social context that elicits the texts. As Myers has written, because genre analysis 'focuses on the stereotypical and conventional, this framework is less useful in helping us understand how genres change' (2000:178). In order to help students, EAP focuses on the recurring. However, because genres respond to social context, both changes in texts as well as regularities are important. All discourse communities depend on innovation as well as convention, and these always exist with some degree of tension. Swales (1990) gives primary responsibility for maintaining disciplinary constraints on genre innovation to experts, established members of the discourse community, and in many discourse communities change develops from earlier, accepted knowledge, and an important element of advanced literacy in these disciplines is understanding earlier work in the field (Kaufer and Geisler 1989).

However, in art, as in some other disciplines such as design and architecture, innovation is central. Kaufer and Geisler (1989) describe novelty in most discourse communities as growing out of existing knowledge, and impossible without reference to this knowledge. However, writing about arts education, Stanley (2004) distinguishes between novelty and creativity. While novelty requires a knowledge of the past 'in order to quote it knowingly' (ibid:65), most art students want to create 'work that literally captivates their audience' (ibid:65).

Though the goal of captivating the audience may seem limited to the fine arts discourse community, Gunther Kress has argued that since genres reflect social relationships, in a time of social instability such as the present, genres will also be less stable. Contrasting critique with design, he identifies critique with the development of new knowledge from an accepted body of existing knowledge, while 'design is the essential textual principle for periods characterised by intense and far-reaching change' (1999:87). If Kress is correct, as I believe he is, we are currently in such a period, which will lead in turn to an increase in genre instability. This instability may lead to difficulties in teaching, and especially in learning, these less regular forms. This would be of relevance to the EAP discourse community.

Bibliography

Allison, D. (2004) 'Creativity, students' academic writing, and EAP: exploring comments on writing in an English language degree programme'. *Journal of English for Academic Purposes*, 3, 191–209.

Atkinson, D. (1997) 'A critical approach to critical thinking in TESOL'. *TESOL Quarterly*, 31/1, 71–94.

Berkenkotter, C. and Huckin, T.N. (1995) *Genre knowledge in disciplinary communication: cognition/culture/power*. Hillsdale, NJ: Lawrence Erlbaum Associates.

Casanave, C.P. (1995) 'Local interactions: constructing contexts for composing in a graduate sociology program' in Belcher, D. and Braine, G. (eds) *Academic writing in a second language: essays on research and pedagogy*, 83–110. Norwood, NJ: Ablex.

Cosden, C. and Reynolds, D. (1982) 'Photography as therapy'. *Arts in Psychotherapy*, 9, 19–23.

Dias, P., Freedman, A., Medway, P. and Paré, A. (1999) *Worlds apart: acting and writing in academic and workplace contexts*. Mahwah, NJ: Lawrence Erlbaum.

Flowerdew, J. (2002) 'Genre in the classroom: a linguistic approach' in Johns, A.M. (ed.) *Genre in the classroom: multiple perspectives*, 91–102. Mahwah, NJ: Lawrence Erlbaum.

Harris, J. (1989) 'The idea of community in the study of writing'. *College Composition and Communication*, 40, 11–22.

Higgins, C. (2004, 2 December) 'Work of art that inspired a movement ... a urinal'. *The Guardian*, 1, 3.

Kaufer, D.S. and Geisler, C. (1989) 'Novelty in academic writing'. *Written Communication*, 6, 286–311.

Krauss, R. (1983) 'Sculpture in the expanded field' in Foster, H. (ed.) *The anti-aesthetic: essays on postmodern culture*, 31–42. New York: New Press.

Kress, G. (1999) '"English" at the crossroads: rethinking curricula of communication in the context of the turn to the visual' in Hawisher, G.E. and Selfe, C.L. (eds) *Passions, pedagogies, and 21st century technologies*, 66–88. Logan, UT: Utah State University Press.

Lave, J. and Wenger, E. (1991) *Situated learning: legitimate peripheral participation*. Cambridge: Cambridge University Press.

Myers, G. (1990) *Writing biology: texts in the social construction of scientific knowledge*. Madison, WI: University of Wisconsin Press.

—— (2000) 'Powerpoints: technology, lectures, and changing genres' in Trosborg, A (ed.) *Analysing professional genres*, 177–91. Amsterdam: John Benjamins.

Prior, P. (1998) *Writing/disciplinarity: a sociohistoric account of literate activity in the academy*. Mahwah, NJ: Lawrence Erlbaum.

Stanley, N. (2004) 'Curriculum models and life choices: some issues for art students' in Bonaventura, P. and Farthing, S (eds) *A curriculum for artists* 64–7. Oxford and New York: University of Oxford and New York Academy of Art.

Swales, J.M. (1990) *Genre analysis: english in academic and research settings*. Cambridge: Cambridge University Press.

—— (2004) *Research genres: explorations and applications*. Cambridge: Cambridge University Press.

The American Art Therapy Association. (n.d.) *About art therapy* [http://www.arttherapy.org/aboutarttherapy/about.htm] retrieved 15/08/2005.

Trosborg, A. (2000) 'Introduction' in Trosborg, A. (ed.) *Analysing professional genres*, viii-xvi. Amsterdam: John Benjamins.

Wenger, E. (1998) *Communities of practice: learning, meaning, and identity*. Cambridge: Cambridge University Press.

HANIA SALTER-DVORAK

3 Academic Tourism or a Truly Multicultural Community? Why International Students Need Pragmatic Training for British Higher Education

> Currently, around 20% of our students come from outside the UK, from over 120 different countries. This makes the campus a truly multicultural community. International students can be found in all departments at both undergraduate and postgraduate level and are involved in every College activity.

This excerpt from a London university prospectus exemplifies 'the discourse of marketisation' (Fairclough 1995:143) and is familiar to us all. Yet evidence exists (Wright and Lander 2003, Volet and Ang 1998) that, while British universities boast of internationalisation, many international learners, especially South East Asians, risk being alienated from the learning culture. This may be due to lack of communicative competence, especially in terms of pragmatic competence, as well as the educational, cultural and social challenges they face in their new environment. Although they pass their courses, I view the university experience of such students as 'academic tourism' rather than membership of 'a truly multicultural community'. Arguably, international students have a right to be integrated into the learning community, as the literature on rights analysis and critical pedagogy suggests (Pennycook 1999, Benesch 2001). Universities, meanwhile, have both a duty and a commercial motive to promote this integration.

This paper argues that a strong hindrance to such integration is the students' inability to interact with native speakers of English (NS) and other non-native speakers (NNS) and presents a rationale for pragmatic training of international students, especially South East Asians. I begin with my research findings on attitudes of South East Asian students at British universities and present a case study of a

Chinese learner. I then identify linguistic needs for study and argue that the preparation provided for these learners at present is inadequate to meet their needs. Ideally, university-wide programmes designed by linguists and informed by research in pragmatics are needed to provide intercultural competence training for both students and university staff.

Attitudes and Perceptions of International Students

Recently I interviewed a number of South East Asian students at a London university about their linguistic needs for study. My respondents, all of whom expressed themselves with difficulty, identified lectures, making sense of written discourse, producing academic essays and participating in seminars. But more salient in their accounts were the following themes: they all found it difficult to converse with their fellow British students; many felt a sense of isolation; some were offended by the lack of knowledge people have about their countries; some felt that they were disliked in this country. When I probed deeper, one respondent reported that her British classmate had said to her, 'You don't say "really" or "did you?" when I speak. You should learn these words.' Another reported, 'My flatmates said "You have a laptop!" They thought Chinese people are poor, so how come I have laptop?' More disconcertingly, another said, 'British men are rude. A man in a shop called me "darling"'. These accounts, perhaps predictably, reveal a lack of communication strategies and feelings of isolation but they also suggest stereotypical views of NS which could impact negatively on motivation and self image, thereby providing real obstacles to academic success. This, when combined with lack of communicative competence, may lead to a vicious circle. By shunning contact, such learners appear shy or inarticulate. As a result, they do not make friends, avoid tutorials and appear not to participate fully in their courses, becoming invisible students. At times, it appears that they use English rather like Latin was used by scholars in the middle ages. Evidence exists that levels of depression among such students are high (Spencer-Oatey 2004). Yet, as Benesch points out, 'EAP has, for the most part, overlooked socio-political issues affecting life in and outside of academic settings' (2001:xv). The socio-political and the cultural, though, are inextricably linked to the linguistic.

Pragmatic Competence

Learners from different educational cultures require a complex set of skills to interpret information and to project themselves convincingly in their 'Socratic environment' (Scollon 1999:27). Following discussions, drawing inferences from prosody and identifying ideological positions all contribute to interpretation. Finding a juncture at which to join the discussion, phrasing a reply to a question and defending a position are elements of projecting the academic self. The language of academia, like much spoken language, is unpredictable in nature and contains multiple hybridised discourses. An academic lecture may often include humorous asides or colloquialisms, while conversations between students in a purely social setting may turn to discussing the intellectual content of the course.

Anyone who has had the experience of learning a foreign language will testify that interacting with NS represents 'the acid test' (Salter-Dvorak 2002:185). Verbal interaction entails decoding messages in terms of what Jacobson and Hymes (cited in Briggs 1986:42) have called 'referential' meaning, that which is understood literally, and 'indexical' meaning, that which is inferred. A response then needs to be crafted, in real time, which addresses both these aspects. The difficulty is that while referential meaning is covered by linguistic correctness of lexis and grammar, the more problematic indexical meaning is culture specific and is encoded in prosody, register and body language (Gumperz 1982:182). Thus learners need to build up pragmatic competence (PC) 'the ability to use language effectively in order to achieve a specific purpose and to understand language in context' (Thomas 1983:91). Relatively little is known about the psycholinguistic development of PC in L2 learners and so teaching it is problematic. Cultural and affective factors, too, render it a sensitive area. Despite this, there is strong evidence that its development is facilitated by instruction (Rose and Kasper 2001:8, Bouton 1994). An initial stage of PC is pragmatic awareness (PA), which comes from 'noticing' (Schmidt 1995) and 'consciousness raising' (Rose 1994). It is also known that interaction with competent speakers of the target language is crucial to the process of developing PC (Bardovi-Harlig and Dornyei 1988:233). L2 learners in Britain have a rich resource for such interaction and failure to exploit this can lead to negative stereotyping of NS (Salter-Dvorak 2002). This, in turn, may translate into pragmatically inept linguistic behaviour, thereby hindering PC (Robinson 1985:18).

Pragmatic Failure

Thomas (1983) divides pragmatic failure into the pragmalinguistic and the sociopragmatic. Pragmalinguistic failure results from lack of 'linguistic resources for conveying communicative acts' (Rose and Kasper 2001:2) such as routines. According to Thomas (ibid:93), inappropriate use of routine often accounts for failure in highly fluent learners' oral performance. The problem occurs when they appear unintentionally rude or subservient and are unaware of this. Often, the failure will be slight but the effect on the communicative event will be strong. My own research shows that it is often what is not said that hinders further communication (Salter-Dvorak 2002:188).

Sociopragmatic failure results from a lack of awareness of socio-cultural norms of the TL and refers to factors between interlocutors such as distance, social power and degree of imposition (Brown and Levinson 1987). We have evidence that NS ignore such mistakes or compensate for them (House 1993:250) which may mean NNS are unaware that there has been pragmatic failure (Bardovi-Harlig and Hartford 1993:300). The result is often a missed opportunity to continue the conversation, as shown by the following example from Wolfson's compliment corpus (1989a:230).

> American female student to her Chinese female classmate:
> A: Your blouse is beautiful.
> B: Thank you.
> A: Did you bring it from China?
> B: Yeah.

The Chinese student has understood the illocutionary force of the compliment but not its intended social function which is to open a conversation.

While experience tells us that it is possible to operate with two sets of norms, Johnstone argues that 'optimal rather than total convergence appears to be a more realistic and desirable goal' (1996:8). There is a difference between making learners aware of certain Anglo-Saxon standards of behaviour and attempting to enforce them. NNS may opt for pragmatic distinctness as a strategy of identity assertion. As Scollon and Scollon (1995:11), Thomas (ibid:110) and Wolfson (1989b) stress, these are highly sensitive issues which require a delicate approach on the part of the teacher. Learners need to be encouraged to make informed choices while taking into account their feelings.

Lucy: a case study of a Chinese student in British higher education

The following case study of Lucy, an 18-year-old student on an undergraduate foundation course at a London university, is a sample from my ethnographic interview data of learners' attitudes towards NS and misunderstandings they have experienced. Lucy has a proficiency level of IELTS 6.0 and has been in Britain for four months, living with an English host family. Although her ambition is to become a writer, Lucy has been sent to Britain by her parents to take a degree in Business.

Lucy begins by asserting that her experience of meeting British people has been 'lovely, I always meet someone friendly to talk to', yet as she discusses the differences between British and Chinese ways, darker sides are revealed. Some friends told her that London was 'quite a cruel place, not just the weather but the people'. Lucy recounts an exchange with her landlady who, on hearing that she has no plans for a particular Sunday, replies, 'It's up to you'. This expression in Chinese implies criticism and Lucy imitates her landlady's intonation, emphasising its censorious tone. Clearly, she has interpreted the phrase according to its illocutionary force in Chinese, transferring the only frame of reference available to her. While we do not know whether Lucy's interpretation is correct, this could be an example of pragmalinguistic failure. Her landlady may have used the phrase as a routine response to Lucy's non-committal statement but she has taken it as a criticism. As she continues, we see how this event is not isolated but contributes to a mistrust of her host family. If she is watching a TV programme they do not approve of, they make no comment, which she finds unnerving, 'I'd rather they say something, rather than you say nothing but you look at me in that way.' Is she reading too much into their silence?

As she describes her relations with strangers, Lucy provides a clear example of sociopragmatic failure. She explains how on Chinese New Year's Day she offered chocolates to strangers at her university, saying 'Have a nice day'. 'People here are quite serious, like sometimes I say "Have a nice day" and people look surprised, they don't think I should be so friendly.' But offering chocolates to strangers breaches social norms relating to distance and degree of imposition, while citing the Americanism 'Have a nice day', usually associated with service encounters, displays a lack of appropriacy.

In Lucy's view, culture is an essential part of language learning but this understanding is gleaned from distressing experiences, 'every time I feel sad, I will learn something' she says. Lucy's poignant examples of misunderstanding contrast starkly with the way she speaks, as she is fairly fluent and accurate, with an American accent. Her surface fluency and confident smile conceal anxiety and tension.

Discussion

Lucy seems atypical of Wen and Clement's (2003) model of a Chinese language learner in that she shows willingness to communicate with NS and does not appear afraid of taking risks. She conforms to the model through her acute sensitivity to the reactions of her interlocutors and their evaluation of her behaviour. Her distressing experiences seem to result from a mismatch between her behaviour and people's expectations. Her interpretations of her interlocutors' reactions arguably reinforce her stereotypes, corroborating the folk notions, friendly but quite cruel, she has collected from friends. This in turn leads to a feeling of isolation, affecting her motivation. Lucy's case clearly illustrates the view that lack of PC can cause misunderstanding and difficulty in everyday situations (Rose and Kasper 2001, Thomas 1983).

If Lucy is to participate fully in her university course, she needs to develop a schematic framework of cultural relativity, of how language and social conventions differ between cultures, together with a set of tools for analysing her communicative exchanges both in and out of class. Such a schematic framework, built on 'noticing' is the basis for creating PA and will prepare her for indexical meanings such as engaging in conversations in real time, using fillers and discourse markers, as well as strategies for starting, repairing and ending conversations.

Linguistic Preparation Received by International Learners for British Higher Education

Typically, international students attend language schools or university pre-sessionals to gain the required level of language proficiency. A survey of pre-sessional programmes offered by six London universities[1] at present shows that the preparation is driven by the tasks, such as essays and oral presentations, of target degree courses and tends to focus on grammatical and discourse competence. While social English and seminar skills sometimes feature, there is little focus on spoken interaction, or its relationship to culture. Yet successful interaction is central to the learning process. At university, discussing feedback, participating in seminars and collaborating on assignments are everyday activities. Criticality, which plays an important role in academic literacy, is built up largely through discussion and exchange of ideas. In the halls of residence, exchanges while doing the washing up may contribute as much to learning as independent reading. It is in the thick of such conversations that learners struggle because they have not been prepared. Ironically, the concept of communicative competence, which underpins learners' university preparation largely ignores the very dimension they need most – the pragmatic one.

University Institutional Discourse Surrounding Integration of International Students in British Higher Education

University institutional discourse surrounding integration is often based on a stereotypical deficit model of the learners, characterising South East Asians as passive, shy and lacking critical thinking skills. It also seems to be accompanied by a lack of curiosity regarding the

---

1   School of Oriental and African Studies, City University, Brunel University, Thames Valley University, Kings College and University College.

cultural heritage of these learners – educational, philosophical, linguistic and social – which could contribute towards making them feel more comfortable in the host learning institution. Such a deficit model is both disempowering and unrealistic because it fails to address the fact that successful integration is a dynamic, multi-faceted process involving all members of the university community – the overseas students, their British peers, their international colleagues, lecturers, administrative and house staff. It also implies a position of cultural superiority which sits uneasily with the rhetoric of inter-nationalisation often found in university publicity. Benesch (2001) exemplifies how rights analysis can lead to negotiation of the extent of adaptation required of international students, thus contributing to community building. This would require of the university a purposeful curiosity about the learners' educational culture and experience, and of the learners an awareness of the adaptations which are necessary for academic success and those which are optional and relate to cultural integration.

Conclusion

This paper has argued that if we are to welcome international students to our universities, we need to prepare them to interact effectively with their peers and lecturers so that they are integrated into the learning environment rather than condemned to academic tourism. As a minimum, the syllabus would involve training learners to follow referential meanings in conversation. I have argued, however, that the lexical represents the tip of the iceberg and that learners need to be provided with a schematic framework for making sense of their linguistic encounters in order to follow indexical meanings, i.e. pragmatic training. Such intercultural competence training, designed by those involved in teaching English to international students, should ideally be adapted and offered to all staff across the university community. One pedagogic model for this is the encounter project

(Salter-Dvorak 2002). Only then would the truly multicultural community, featured in the university publicity, be a serious proposition.

Bibliography

Bardovi-Harlig, K. and Dornyei, Z. (1998) 'Do language learners recognise pragmatic violations? Pragmatic vs. grammatical awareness in instructed L2 learning'. *TESOL Quarterly* 32/2, 219–33.

Bardovi-Harlig, K. and Hartford, B.S. (1993) 'Learning the rules of academic talk: a longitudinal study of pragmatic change'. *SSLA* 15, 279–304.

Benesch, S. (2001) *Critical English for Academic Purposes: theory, politics and practice.* New Jersey: Lawrence Erlbaum Associates.

Briggs, C.L. (1986) *Learning how to ask.* Cambridge: Cambridge University Press.

Bouton, L. (1994) 'Can NNS skills in interpreting implicature in American English be improved through explicit instruction? A pilot study'. *Pragmatics and Language Teaching* 5, 88–109.

Brown, P. and Levinson, S. (1987) *Politeness: some universals in language use.* Cambridge. Cambridge University Press.

Economist 27/5/03. 'Chinese students are flooding into British universities'.

Fairclough, N. (1995) *Critical discourse analysis.* London: Longman.

Gumperz, J. (1982) *Discourse strategies.* Cambridge: Cambridge University Press.

House, J. (1996) 'Developing pragmatic fluency in English as a Foreign Language: routines and metapragmatic awareness'. *SSLA* 18, 225–52.

Johnstone, B. (1996). 'Language, culture and self in language learning'. *Centre for Applied Linguistic Research, Thames Valley*

University, London: occasional papers on language and urban culture, 8, 2–18.

Kasper, G. and Schmidt, R. (1996) 'Developmental issues in interlanguage pragmatics'. *SSLA* 18, 149–69.

Pennycook, A. (1999) 'Introduction: critical approaches to TESOL'. *TESOL Quarterly* 33, 329–48.

Roberts, C. (1998) 'Language acquisition or language socialisation in and through discourse?' in Dörnyei, Z. and Skehan, P. *Working papers in Applied Linguistics*. London, TVU 4, 31–42.

Robinson, G.L.N. (1985) *Cross cultural understanding*. New York: Pergamon.

Rose, K.R. (1994) 'Pragmatic consciousness-raising in an EFL context'. *Pragmatics and Language Learning*, Monograph Series 5, 52–63. Urbana-Champaign: Division of English as an International Language, University of Illinois.

—— and Kasper, G. (2001) *Pragmatics in language teaching*. Cambridge: Cambridge University Press.

Salter-Dvorak, H. (2002) 'Changing consciousness of EFL learners through project work in the community' in *Revolutions of consciousness: local identities, global concerns in languages and intercultural communication*. Proceedings of the 1st IALIC Conference held at Leeds Metropolitan University, December 2000.

Schmidt, R. (1995) 'Consciousness and foreign language learning: a tutorial on the role of attention and awareness in learning' in Schmidt, R. (ed.) *Attention and awareness in foreign language learning* Technical Report 9, 1–63. Honolulu: Second Language Teaching and Curriculum Center, University of Hawaii.

Scollon, R. and Scollon, S.W. (1995) *Intercultural communication*. Oxford: Blackwell.

Scollon, S. (1999) 'Not to waste words or students: Confucian and Socratic discourse in the tertiary classroom' in Hinkel, E. (ed.) *Culture in second language teaching and learning*. Cambridge: Cambridge University Press.

Spencer-Oatey, H. (2004) 'Chinese students' adjustments to Britain: how are they coping and how can we help?' Paper presented at

'Responding to the needs of the Chinese learner in higher education Conference', University of Portsmouth, 2004.

Thomas, J. (1983) 'Cross cultural pragmatic failure'. *Applied Linguistics*, 4/2/19, 9.

Volet, S.E. and Ang, G. (1998) 'Culturally mixed groups on international campuses: an opportunity for intercultural learning'. *Higher Education Research and Development* 17/1, 5–23.

Wen, W.P. and Clement, R. (2003) 'A Chinese conceptualisation of willingness to communicate'. *ESL. Language, Culture and Curriculum*, 16/1, 18–38.

Wolfson, N. (1989a). 'The social dynamics of native and non-native complimenting behaviour' in Eisenstein, M. (ed) *The dynamic interlanguage: empirical studies in second language variation*, 219–36. New York: Plenum Press.

—— (1989b) *Perspectives: socio-linguistics and TESOL*. New York: Newbury House.

Wright, S. and Lander, D. (2003) 'Collaborative group interactions of students from two ethnic backgrounds'. *Higher Education and Development*, 22/3, 237–52.

4 International Undergraduate Students' Academic Acculturation in Canada: The Challenges Ahead

The increased internationalisation of all Canadian university campuses and recent Canadian immigration over the past 20 years have resulted in changes in policies relating to language admission requirements, heightened concern over the use of language proficiency testing in the selection of students for university admission and a proliferation of support programmes that are either available to or required of second language (L2) students as part of the undergraduate admission process, including both immigrants and international students. These programmes aim to prepare L2 students to use English at the university level and to help with the students' transition to both general academic and discipline-specific culture.

However, a review of literature on English for Academic Purposes (EAP) programmes across Canada (Berman 2002, Cheng and Myles 2002, Fox 2004) reveals little consensus on fundamental approaches, designs or procedures within these programmes and an absence of research to document their effectiveness. There is an urgent need for research regarding specific EAP programme outcomes at the university level, including how much time is required to support L2 students while they adjust to the demands of academic study, the factors that affect their transition to academic study and the specific role of EAP support (Atkinson 1999, Byram 1989, Kramsch 1991, Kramsch and Sullivan 1996). Given the increasing number of L2 students in undergraduate programmes, the varying nature of EAP approaches, and the lack of large-scale or comprehensive studies, research in the key factors that support the successful academic transition of L2 students to the demands of undergraduate study is of critical importance at this time (Hyland and Hamp-Lyons 2002,

Jordan 1997). A better understanding of the factors that contribute to L2 students' academic success will allow programme designers and teachers to develop more appropriate and effective EAP programmes. This paper reports on the development of a questionnaire designed to establish the factors contributing to L2 undergraduates' academic performance, as well as their transition to and engagement with undergraduate studies.

To create the questionnaire, interview data were first collected from volunteers at three universities. Those interviewed included 28 students, 13 in undergraduate studies and 15 in EAP programmes. The undergraduates came from a wide variety of majors, including Engineering, Economics, Business, Finance, Science and Arts. Among them, four were first-year students, five were second-year, one was third-year, and three were in their fourth year. In addition, interviews were conducted with eight discipline-specific professors and instructors and with one EAP instructor.

In order to recruit participants, announcements were posted in different places on the campuses. To ensure that participants understood the purpose of the study, the initial interview questions, together with a letter of information and a consent form, were sent to the respondents before the interviews. The interview questions were developed and honed collaboratively during research meetings and conversations over time by the three researchers and their research teams. L2 students were informed that these questions were the basis of a 'conversation' that would be allowed to develop as a natural and inevitable part of the interview process. In other words, not all interviews were the same. In exchange, students were promised to receive feedback on academic strategies, counselling (if requested) and an honorarium. All interviews were conducted in an informal setting and were audio-taped with the participants' consent. We used a range of questions as the basis of each interviews.

We began by asking for details of students' social and educational backgrounds (e.g. What is your first language? What other languages do you speak? How long have you been in Canada? Do you live alone, or with others? What languages do your roommates or housemates speak?). We then moved on to students' educational goals, and the role that English played in attaining them. Finally, we asked a number of questions more directly related to EAP:

- What type of English activity seems to help you the most?
- Of the English courses you have had, which one was the most helpful? Why?
- Assessing your language skills in terms of reading, writing, listening and speaking, what are your strengths and weaknesses?
- Which skills, if any, are you called upon to use frequently but feel that you have not learned well enough?
- Have you ever taken an English course that specifically prepared you to use English for academic purposes (i.e. EAP)? If yes, do you think that you are in a better position than other students you know who did not take a course? Explain. If no, do you think such a course would have helped you? How?

The data were analysed using a grounded theory approach (Strauss and Corbin 1994). In other words, the questionnaire was in part developed from the bottom up, grounded in and generated by the data. The raw interview data were analyzed in a 'zigzag process' (Cresswell 1998). Groups of interviews were analyzed using an 'open coding' approach (ibid:57), which allowed for initial categories to be identified. More interviews were then collected and analysis repeated to confirm or disconfirm the working categories accounting for the data. This process is known as the 'constant comparative' method (Strauss and Corbin 1994). When the categories became 'saturated', that is, no further information was provided by additional data collected from interview analysis, we generated the questionnaire items. In addition, findings from previous studies of factors influencing the academic acculturation process enabled the creation of further questionnaire items. A total of 59 items emerged.

Categories

We grouped the 59 items into seven major categories: learning and coping strategies, support, academic motivation, language and academic background, personal history, individual field of study, and EAP and English language support. Reported below are examples from the interview data that led to the identification of these categories.

Learning and coping strategies

Students indicated that their learning and coping strategies applied not only to learning regular academic subjects, as in the first three examples below, but also to the learning of English, as in the fourth.

> For me I just read the notes the prof gave us. It's usually Power-point slides, so just short sentences. You don't really read long sentences. When I am reading the textbook, I just focus on diagrams and tables. So I didn't read text a lot…
>
> I try not to take courses that require a lot of discussion. And I try not to take any course that requires essays.
>
> The white people tend to do assignments in the last minute. I am too scared to do my assignments just one day before.
>
> So I try to have a strong will not to hang out with […∙ people from my country], and try to be more sociable, and try to interview with Canadian people more.

Supporting systems

The following comments were made by students within the context of support received from roommates, friends, classmates, professors, teaching assistants, the university's writing centre, and other university support. For the purpose of questionnaire construction, we differentiated these sorts of social and academic support from EAP and English language support – the focus of the study – but obviously all forms of support are allied. All contribute to the success of these students' academic learning.

While some students reported trying to form relationships with Canadians, we noted that many students rely heavily on their compatriots for support. Whether this reliance was self-imposed or difficult to avoid was not always clear.

> I had to isolate myself first from the Chinese group... because everyone knows it's safer and easier to stay with your own group when you don't speak English, right?
> I've got lots of Chinese friends, and if we meet outside of anywhere, we have to talk Chinese.
> When I talk with classmates, because they are all Chinese... so we just use Chinese.

Academic motivation

Students' reasons for choosing a Canadian university included various educational and career goals, as well as a perceived lack of discrimination in Canada compared to other English speaking countries.

> I really appreciate any opportunities of staying here for a year and gain Canadian working experience.
> The probably reason why I want to study in Canada is that when I was working in [... my country], I really felt gender discrimination.

Motivation for taking EAP was largely instrumental in nature, which is not surprising since EAP is fundamentally a route into mainstream university studies.

> I have to speak... and be able to communicate with any people and be able to understand the prof in class.
> So improve my English before I enter the university is very necessary... maybe after I enter university I will have another reason.
> I don't pay the tuition to fail the course, I pay to pass it... I want to pass it, I want to go on.

Language and academic background

Students reported a wide spectrum of types of exposure to English, spanning a minimum of foreign high school exposure up to tertiary level coursework completed in Canada and other English language regions. There was a similar diversity in their academic backgrounds, both in terms of university-level coursework completed (or not) in their home countries and in Canada, and their major. Clearly, questions would be needed on the questionnaire to identify these differences.

Personal history

Many respondents were in their early twenties, from a relatively affluent background in their homelands, but by no means rich by Canadian standards. In fact, the following student could have been speaking for many others whose parents were making significant sacrifices for them to be able to study in Canada.

> When you are my parents, working in China, and this is me here and they spend money for my education… it's a serious economic pressure for them. So, for that reason I decide to work here as a part time worker to make some money to help, you know. But the working, or taking a job and taking five courses together, that's really tire. It's not good. It won't be good for the academic career.

Individual field of study

Students represented a wide variety of fields of study, both in terms of the faculties they were currently enrolled in or the faculty they were interested in entering. Reasons for their choices varied, including financial benefit and personal interest.

> Getting a degree and can do something earn money later. That's why I go for business and finance and accounting.

> Before, I wanted to be an engineer... because my dad is an engineer... but now I would like to help... I want to be a nurse... I like to take care of the old people.
> When I first came here I wanted to take drama. Still now I want to take drama [but have decided on] stage management... one of the programmes in drama.

English language requirements within courses varied both between universities and from course to course within universities. For example, at one university a science student reported that for him there was 'Not much writing or oral discussion, just lab reports, formulas.' On the other hand, a social science student at the same university reported a great deal of English language work, including 'presentation, oral reports, essay, [and] group work.'

EAP and English language support

Naturally, as the focus of the study and therefore of many of the interviewers' questions, a great deal of data referred directly to EAP and English language support.

> [Students who only use the TOEFL score to get into university] got lots of problems to study in the university... and now they out from university and learn to study in the college or somewhere because their English is not high enough and university won't accept them to study in the university no more.
> My writing skills have been improved a lot. At least now I know how to write a research paper, how to write an academic essay and uh... how to even write some summary.
> I know lots of people... dropped out from [EAP] and decided to take TOEFL just because it's easier, I have to say. I passed my TOEFL exam, but I still took [EAP]... I'll say I'm way better off.
> Yeah I'm really... definitely better because I always get better grade on the papers. That's what [EAP] taught me how to do it.
> [EAP teachers] give us lots of knowledge about how to study in the university, how to take the notes when we listen to the professor's thinking and how to organise our ideas and by writing and by explain to the professor what you want and what you need. My teacher told me if I really cannot follow what the teacher said, I can ask a question and stop them for a while.
> Group work is really help for me. In my country's education system, they would like every people's working alone and doing everything by themselves. I think they break the connection between the students... When I was working

with group, some people can find my weak side, and they can tell me how
should I improve.

From Categories to Questionnaire Items

Based on the seven major categories and 59 factors derived from the
interview data, we then designed the questionnaire items accordingly.
The 59 factors were organised in the following way to show
hypothesised factors that could contribute to or impede L2 students'
academic success in Canadian universities.

1. Learning and coping strategies

Academic
Critical/analytic skills
Time management
Assignments and studying
Asking for help
Reading ahead
Choices encouraging English use

Social
Time spent using L1
Time spent in autonomous play
Time spent using English socially
Home-stay
Working on campus
Familiarity with Canada

2. Supporting systems

Academic
Writing Centres
Professors/TAs (A)
Study Systems
Academic support systems

Social
Friends
L1 vs. L2 issues/choices
Family
Other social support

3. Academic motivation

Reasons for studying, or Goals	Working 'harder than L1s'
Seriousness/maturity	Sacrifices
Attitudes and beliefs	Expectations vs. reality
about Canada/Canadians	Family pressures
about English	Personality
about learning	Determination

*4. Language and academic
   background*

5. Personal history

Number of years in high school	Age
Previous tertiary-level experience	Gender
Type/extent of L1 writing	Country of origin
experience	Status: Visa/immigrant/refugee
English Experience in/beyond	Parents' educational level
school	Financial issues
Educational level	Programme costs
	Need to work

6. Individual field of study

7. EAP and English support

Field of study/Major	English proficiency upon arrival
English proficiency of instructors	Reading/Writing/Listening/
Requirements	Speaking
Course load	Group work, presentations
Factors in choice of field	

Patterns

Having grouped the interview data into seven categories, and taking into account the factors identified in the research literature, we further identified three *patterns* into which these seven categories could be placed: (1) Interpersonal and social relationships, (2) Student beliefs, assumptions and knowledge, and (3) Academic course and EAP characteristics, as represented in Chart 1.

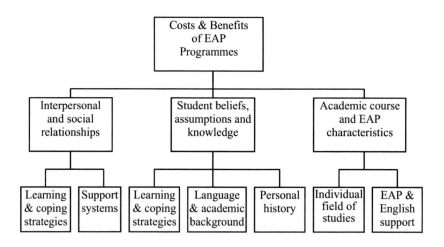

Chart 1. Overview of questionnaire specifications

The Draft Questionnaire

The questionnaire has now been distributed to international students at English medium universities across Canada with English language programmes, and we are analysing the substantial data that they have provided. Ultimately, we expect that the increased understanding of the factors that contribute to L2 students' academic success revealed by this grounded theory and multi-method approach (Caracelli & Greene 1997) will allow programme developers and teachers to create more appropriate and effective EAP programming.

Bibliography

Atkinson, D. (1999) 'TESOL and culture'. *TESOL Quarterly*, 33/4, 625–54.

Berman, R. (2002 May) 'Towards a common concept of English for Academic Purposes'. Paper presented at the Symposium, Concepts and Context in EAP: Preparing NNS of English for success in the academic community. Annual meeting of the Canadian Association of Applied Linguistics, Congress of the Social Sciences and Humanities. Toronto.

Byram, M. (1989) *Cultural studies in foreign language education*. Clevedon UK: Multilingual Matters.

Caracelli, V. and Greene, J. (1997) *Advances in mixed-method evaluation: the challenges and benefits of integrating diverse paradigms*. San Francisco, CA: Jossey-Bass.

Cheng, L., Myles, J. and Jun, Q. (2002, May) 'English for academic purposes: delineating the needs and the contexts of our NNS graduate students' in Cheng, L. and Myles, J. (Chairs). Concepts and Context in EAP: Preparing NNS of English for success in the academic community. Symposium presented at the Canadian Association of Applied Linguistics, Toronto.

Creswell, J.W. (1998) *Qualitative Inquiry and research design: choosing among five traditions*. Thousand Oaks, CA: Sage.

Fox, J. (2004) 'Test decisions over time: tracking validity'. *Language Testing* 21/4, 437–65.

Hyland, K. and Hamp-Lyons, L. (2002) 'EAP: Issues and directions'. *Journal of English for Academic Purposes*, 1/1, 1–12.

Jordan, R. (1997). *English for Academic Purposes*. Cambridge: Cambridge University Press.

Kramsch, C. (1991). 'Culture in language learning: a view from the United States' in De Bot, K., Kramsch, C. and Ginsberg, R. (eds) *Foreign language research in cross-cultural perspectives,* 217–40. Amsterdam: John Benjamins.
—— and Sullivan, P. (1996). 'Appropriate pedagogy'. *ELT Journal,* 50/3, 199–212.
Strauss, A.L. and Corbin, J. (1994). 'Grounded theory methodology: an overview' in Denzin, N.K. and. Lincoln, D.S. (eds) *Handbook of qualitative research.* Thousand Oaks, CA: Sage.

Diana Ridley

5 The Development of Online Thesis Writing Guidelines: Research Student and Supervisor Perceptions

In 2002, a report commissioned by the UK government recommended that generic skills development for doctoral students should be enhanced and extended alongside their subject specific research training (Roberts Review 2002). Consequently, in July 2003, funds were provided through the Research Councils UK for the enhancement of research training for both doctoral and postdoctoral researchers. Although the Roberts Review had focused on scientists and engineers, universities have generally applied the recommendation to research students across all disciplines. In response to the availability of this funding, I took the opportunity to propose the development of a package of online thesis writing guidelines at the University of Sheffield. In the first instance, the university requested a survey to establish needs and expectations with regard to an online university-wide resource. This paper reports on the findings. The study adds an online dimension to previous survey research into graduate student writing (Casanave and Hubbard 1992, Jenkins et al. 1993, Torrance et al. 1992, 1994).

The Survey

Research students and supervisors at the university were invited to participate in an online survey to share their views on the following:
- the desirability of online thesis writing guidelines
- the feasibility of any such provision
- the preferred mode of online delivery – credit or non-credit bearing
- the preferred content and type of activities.

The data collection involved two online questionnaires, one for research students and the other for supervisors. The response rate from research students was 17% (358 responses from a possible 2,115) and from supervisors, 24% (239 responses from a possible 1,000). There were both supervisor and research student respondents from all faculties and virtually all departments of the University. Of the 358 research student participants, 317 were registered as full time, 33 as part-time and eight did not say. With reference to nationality, there were 179 UK and 168 international student respondents. Eleven did not give their nationality. Of the 179 international students who participated, 29 were from countries where English is spoken as a first language.

Findings

As well as the multiple choice answers, there were a total of 109 supervisor and 258 research student comments on the questionnaires. The comments were coded into categories and these were divided into three overarching themes:
- views on the provision of guidelines and their feasibility
- opinions about the overall characteristics of the guidelines
- beliefs as to what the guidelines should include.

The findings are presented within this framework. Where relevant I also refer to the statistics generated from the multiple choice questions.

Theme 1: Views on the provision of guidelines

The questionnaires revealed a variety of viewpoints regarding the feasibility and usefulness of the proposed online thesis writing guidelines. The two tables below illustrate the number of respondents who believe they would make use of online thesis writing guidelines. Over 95% of both research students and supervisors responded positively, although 20.5% of supervisors would consider the needs of an individual research student before referring them.

Yes	No	It would depend on the individual research student	Blank	Total number of supervisor responses
182 (76%)	6 (2.5%)	49 (20.5%)	2 (1%)	239

Table 1. Supervisor responses to the statement 'I would refer my research students to access online thesis writing guidelines if they were available'.

Yes	No	Don't know	Blank	Total number of research student responses
341 (95%)	3 (1%)	13 (4%)	1 (0.25%)	358

Table 2. Research student responses to the statement 'I would access online thesis writing guidelines if they were available'

1.1   Guidelines are a good idea

Seven supervisors and 11 research students explicitly commented on the value of having some online thesis writing guidelines available.

> Good idea that is very much needed especially for those students who have been away from formal study for a while and for those who may have difficulty with English but also for all students. I am a bit wary of corralling students into

producing identikit styles and structures for PhDs but I am sure you are already aware of this problem. (Supervisor, East Asian Studies)
Would be great. Am hoping it is up soon so that I can use it. (Research student, Chemical and Process Engineering, Mexico)

1.2 Expectations of a 'good' thesis

Six research students made the point that they would like to feel more confident in their understanding of what is required to complete a successful thesis. Online thesis writing guidelines could assist research students with this. A Sociology research student suggested

> Thesis writing is a very individual performance but requires certain structures in order to fulfil general requirements. However, these appear to vary, according to the supervisor involved. In order to gain guidelines it might be advisable to approach as many supervisors as possible, to gain a 'consensus' of opinion as to what is acceptable and what is not. (Research Student, Sociology, UK)

1.3 The subject-specific nature of thesis writing

Sixteen supervisors and 11 research students made comments which emphasised the subject-specific nature of thesis writing and some suggested that it could be a challenging project to provide a generic set of materials that would be relevant for all research students. In connection with this view, the inclusion of subject-specific examples was mentioned as being very important. Indeed, the multiple choice responses confirmed this, as 86% (307) of research student respondents and 83% (199) of supervisor respondents considered this to be an important feature of any guidelines developed (Table 4). As one research student succinctly put it:

> The challenge, I believe, is striking the balance between information that is too general to be of any specific use and information that is too specific to one type of program (e.g physical sciences are a lot different from humanities). (Research student, Russian and Slavonic Studies, UK)

1.4 The role of the guidelines in relation to the supervision process

Five supervisors stressed that a package of online thesis writing guidelines should in no way be seen as a replacement for the crucial supervisor role of giving feedback on research student writing.

> Such guidelines may be additional support but should not be considered as alternatives for supervisor's advice. (Supervisor, Education)

Similarly, the importance of dialogue and face-to-face discussion between a research student and a supervisor were emphasised.

> Writing a thesis is an evolutionary process and requires face-to-face contact, support, discussion and supervision. (Supervisor, Sociological Studies)

Nevertheless, as other supervisor comments suggest, an online package of guidelines could be a means of raising awareness, amongst both research students and supervisors, of some of the difficulties that may arise when writing a thesis. They could also provide a helpful reference when research students and supervisors are trying to identify where a problem lies and then search for a solution.

1.5 Input into the guidelines

Four supervisors made the point that their decision to refer their research students to online thesis writing guidelines would depend on the quality of the materials. This point was implicitly made in other comments from both research students and supervisors, who urged that the guidelines should be written by active researchers and by those that have knowledge of thesis writing. Two supervisors argued that if supervisors were consulted as the materials were developed, it would be possible to ensure the relevance and accuracy of the guidelines for different fields.

> You will never achieve complete consensus in an area as subject to the whims of personal taste and experience as this but consulting widely might help to ensure that the guidelines reflect a broad consensus of opinion across faculties. (Supervisor, Modern Languages and Linguistics)

1.6   Summary of theme one

The proposed guidelines were generally perceived to be a valuable idea. They could help clarify what is expected for the successful completion of a PhD thesis. It is important that they are viewed as support for and not a replacement of supervisor–research student dialogue around drafts of writing. The importance of subject specificity is clear (Becher and Trowler 2001) and the guidelines should therefore include discipline-specific examples. Careful thought should be given to the knowledge and abilities of those producing any such materials and the availability of supervisor and research student consultants from different faculties to give feedback on the guidelines as they are developed.

Theme 2: Characteristics of the Guidelines

The second theme arising from responses to the questionnaires encompasses beliefs about the overall characteristics of an online thesis writing resource. Table 3 shows the opinions of supervisor and research student participants with regard to the purpose of the guidelines.

	A credit-bearing module	Non-credit bearing materials	Materials for either purpose	Blank	Total number of responses
Supervisor responses	24 (10%)	103 (43%)	107 (45%)	5 (2%)	239
Research student responses	12 (3%)	154 (43%)	186 (52%)	6 (2%)	358

Table 3. Supervisor and research student responses to the prompt 'I would prefer online thesis writing materials to be available as … '

These figures clearly show that a minority of respondents think that thesis writing online materials should be available only as a credit-bearing module. The majority of the respondents, 88% of supervisors and 95% of research students, feel the package should be accessible for more flexible consultation, with 45% of supervisors and 52% of research students stating that it should be possible to use the materials both for credit-bearing and non-credit bearing purposes.

2.1 Flexibility

A significant number of comments supported the notion of flexibility. The findings suggested that the proposed package of materials should be available for both credit-bearing purposes and for general reference and be accessible at any time in the research process. Use of the resource should be voluntary and content should be modular to enable targeted access.

There were a variety of opinions amongst both research students and supervisors as to the optimum stage in the PhD process to consult the materials. Some felt it would be useful early on in a doctoral programme as part of the entry requirements or the upgrading process. Others believed it would be most useful in the second or third year of the degree when there is more emphasis on writing up the thesis. These differences of opinion signal clearly that the guidelines should be a resource that could be consulted at a variety of different times to suit the needs and preferences of different departments and individual students. This view is supported by a supervisor comment below:

> My experience is that graduate students vary a lot in terms of the quantity and type of support that they need with their writing. For this reason, I think a flexible resource that different students can use in different ways would be very helpful. Some might just dip in to sort out the odd problem they have. Others might use it more systematically to develop their writing across a broad front. (Supervisor, English Language and Linguistics)

It was also emphasised, by both supervisors and research students, that the guidelines should not be compulsory and should not become a distraction.

2.2 Preferred features of online thesis writing guidelines

Table 4 shows the number and percentage of supervisor and research student respondents who would favour the different features suggested for an online resource. Participants were able to select more than one option when responding to this question on the questionnaire which is the reason that the percentage total is greater than one hundred.

	Number of supervisor responses	Number of research student responses
Tasks which can be done in relation to a research student's own research	174 (73%)	190 (53%)
Interactive tasks	94 (39%)	122 (34%)
Advice and suggestions without interactive tasks	158 (66%)	252 (70%)
Access to an online discussion board	111 (46%)	172 (48%)
Practical writing activities	112 (47%)	121 (34%)
Subject-specific examples of different types of writing	199 (83%)	307 (86%)

Table 4. Research student and supervisor preferences for different features of an online resource

As illustrated in Table 4, 174 supervisors (73%) and 190 research students (53%) stated that online thesis writing guidelines should include activities which a research student can complete in relation to his or her own research. Four supervisor comments reinforced this point. One supervisor stressed that because generic research training modules are often unpopular, it is crucial that thesis writing guidelines are perceived to be relevant to a student's own research. It was also suggested that there could be some integration of the guidelines into the upgrading process from an MPhil to a PhD. However, two other supervisors made a plea that research students should not be given extra work as they already have enough to cope with on a three-year

PhD programme. A comment from a research student encapsulates all these views by suggesting that the guidelines

> have lots of options so that students can tailor the work they can do to their own requirements (Research student, Biblical Studies, UK)

Overall, the responses showed that there were a higher number of research students and supervisors who favoured the inclusion of advice and suggestions about writing a thesis without interactive tasks (See Table 4). However, one supervisor mentioned the value of optional online self-assessed tasks. Another recommended the inclusion of some activities that a research student and supervisor could work on together so as to link the guidelines to the supervision process.

> I think there have to be practical writing activities and examples of writing, but tied into the subject and involving the supervisor. (Supervisor, Information Studies)

The point was also made that if the guidelines were to serve as a credit bearing module, some compulsory activities or interactive tasks would be essential for assessment purposes.

A number of respondents commented on the role of mentoring and workshops in establishing a support network for research students. Two research students mentioned that they would like advice from past students, one suggesting that it might be possible to pay post-doctoral students in the same department to give guidance on the thesis in terms of structure, content, presentation and language use. Others were keen on the idea of contact with a named tutor who has knowledge about thesis writing.

> It's a good idea to have online thesis writing guidelines but I think the best help is a personal help. (Research student, Chemical and Process Engineering, Mexico)

The figures in Table 4 indicate that 48% of research student respondents would favour access to an online discussion board. Their comments included a number of references to this possibility.

Have the option of emailing questions to someone who could advise on matters relating to thesis writing. This could be in the form of the discussion board but would want someone with experience and knowledge to be giving the answers. (Research student, Mechanical Engineering, UK)

Opportunity for online question and answer with tutors as well as other students – perhaps named tutor support – someone to e-mail. (Research student, Archaeology, UK)

A couple of part-time students commented on the difficulty of getting to workshops offered by departments as they are usually held during the day. As Deem and Brehoney (2000) emphasise, part-time students often find it more difficult to feel part of a research community. One participant suggested that an online facility could help compensate for this and reduce feelings of isolation. But it was emphasised that a discussion board needs moderating and that there must be checks on the quality of information.

2.3   Summary of theme 2

Thus, flexibility should be a key feature of any online thesis writing guidelines that are produced to ensure that they fulfill different needs for different research students. To enhance motivation to use the materials, it is important that they are perceived to be relevant to research students' own research projects. Therefore, it should be possible for a research student to complete any tasks by drawing on their own research topic. Interactive tasks and activities should be included but these should be optional unless a student is taking the course for credits. Many of the participants in the survey favour face-to-face contact with peers through workshops and also an online discussion board for frequently asked questions. This would need to be monitored by a tutor. It would also be helpful to research students to have a named tutor contact, other than their supervisor, with whom they could raise queries.

Theme 3: What should the guidelines include?

3.1 Examples of successful practice

Eighteen research students commented that they would like to see examples of recently submitted theses in their area. It was suggested that there could be links to exemplar theses in the library, or at least information on how to access theses in different fields. It was emphasised by one supervisor that the guidelines should advise research students of the importance of looking at previous successful theses in their area in order to get a feel for the basic principles. Some felt that examples of contents pages and different chapters in a thesis would be useful. Three supervisors also suggested that there should be examples of both good and poor practice in writing, the latter being anonymous and adapted or constructed.

> I hope that it will have more examples with excellent writing […] and also please give some comments. (Research student, Mechanical Engineering, China)

3.2 Study strategies

Twelve research students made reference to writers' block.

> How and where do you start?! (Research Student, Psychology, UK)

They also mentioned feeling overwhelmed, running out of steam and becoming too familiar with the topic. Others stated that they needed advice on finding their way through the literature. Supervisor comments emphasised that many research students need guidance in areas such as time management, planning their work and the management and back up of computer files. Five research students commented on how they were struggling with perfectionism and therefore finding it difficult to judge when they have done enough. These comments indicate that study strategies would be useful to serve as a reminder of effective practice at different stages in the research process.

3.3   Writing skills

There were a large number of research student comments and a smaller number of supervisor comments regarding the aspects of writing in which further support and guidance would be welcome. These comments fall into eight main areas.

- Structuring individual chapters and deciding on their content
- Cohesion and connection throughout the thesis
- The construction of effective arguments
- The writing style of a thesis
- Grammar
- Referencing conventions
- Writing summaries
- Critical engagement with the literature.

3.4   Computer literacy for thesis writing

There were 11 research student and six supervisor comments concerning various aspects of computer literacy for thesis writing. There was general agreement that there are a number of computer skills which are specific to thesis writing about which advice would be valuable. These include

- LaTex and Word templates appropriate for a PhD thesis
- Effective use of Endnote
- Automatic creation of a contents page and bibliography
- The management of long documents
- Tutorials on bibliographical databases
- The use of footnotes
- Scanning diagrams and pictures
- The use of sections and headings: numbers and font sizes.

3.5 Technical and structural requirements of the thesis: mandatory and recommended university guidelines

There were a notable number of comments from both research students (55) and supervisors (9) in connection with university expectations of the PhD thesis and the submission process. There was a request for consistency across the university faculties in relation to

- Thesis length
- Margin width and line spacing
- Formatting (e.g. whether the text should be right justified)
- Maximum and minimum font sizes
- Layout of contents pages
- Layout of headings and subheadings
- The resolution of scanned photos
- The use of colour in diagrams
- The presentation of figures and tables
- The layout of footnotes
- Binding.

A supervisor requested that it should be made clear which regulations are mandatory and which are recommended. If there are no requirements with regard to a particular technical issue, for example, font size for headings, this should also be specified. One research student suggested that each department should have a standard PhD thesis template for students to download. It would also be helpful, when there are no university-wide regulations regarding the aspects listed above, if departments could ensure they have recommendations on these issues. It was clear from the responses that many research students would like more explicit guidance on university and departmental expectations.

3.6 Summary of theme 3

In terms of the content of proposed online thesis writing guidelines, the elements below were recommended by the participants in the survey:

- Examples of effective writing practice with links to exemplar theses from different departments

- Advice on study strategies such as dealing with writers' block, planning, time management and organisation of the literature.
- Guidance on writing skills
- Computer literacy advice for thesis writing
- Information on technical and structural requirements for the PhD thesis.

Conclusion

The findings from the survey therefore suggest that good quality and relevant core materials covering generic approaches to writing a thesis would be valuable bearing in mind the following points. Any online thesis writing resource developed should offer support for supervisor-research student dialogue and not act as a replacement. Guidelines should be flexible and multi-purpose having the potential to serve as support for a face-to-face thesis writing module, a stand-alone online thesis writing research training module and a general reference package for all research students. They should be accessible at any time in the research process and have a modular presentation to enable selective access. To enhance their motivation to use the materials, research students should perceive them to be relevant. They should include subject-specific extracts to illustrate how generic principles can be realised in specific contexts. Electronic links to exemplar theses would be helpful. Tasks and activities should enable users of the resource to relate the guidelines to their own research and thesis. Generally speaking, it was found that participants in the survey would like advice and guidance on different aspects of writing a PhD thesis with the option of interactive activities or writing tasks. Alongside the guidelines, tutorial support should be available, both as a face-to-face option and as part of an online discussion board. During the production of the materials, supervisor and research student consultants should comment on their relevance, accuracy and ease of use. Those responsible for producing the resource should have knowledge of PhD thesis writing and be actively involved in research.

March 2006

An online thesis writing resource is now available at the University of Sheffield, UK. It is available to research students as a course on WebCT Vista which is the Managed Learning Environment supported by the university. The resource provides advice and guidance on the planning of the research project and writing the thesis. It includes interactive tasks where students examine extracts from student texts and reflect on issues in relation to their own research topic.

The guidelines are used by some as a stand-alone resource for reference. The resource also provides supplementary materials for research students attending a face-to-face thesis writing research training module. WebCT Vista tracking data shows that sustained usage is greater amongst the latter group which supports the generally accepted view that online learning is most successful when embedded into a course structure. The resource is evaluated on a regular basis and amendments and developments are being incorporated in the light of user feedback.

Bibliography

Becher, T. and Trowler, P.R. (2001) *Academic tribes and territories: intellectual enquiry and the culture of disciplines* (2nd ed.) Buckingham: The Society for Research into Higher Education and Open University Press.

Casanave, C.P. and Hubbard, P. (1992) 'The writing assignments and writing problems of doctoral students: faculty perceptions,

Diana Ridley

pedagogical issues and needed research'. *English for Specific Purposes*, 11/1, 33–49.

Deem, R. and Brehony, K.J. (2000) 'Doctoral students' access to research cultures: are some more unequal than others?' *Studies in Higher Education*, 25/2, 149–65.

Jenkins, S., Jordan, M.K. and Weiland, P.O. (1993) 'The role of writing in graduate engineering education: a survey of faculty beliefs and practices'. *English for Specific Purposes*, 12/1, 51–67.

Roberts, G. (2002) *SET for success: the supply of people with science, technology, engineering and mathematics skills*. London: HM Treasury.

Torrance, M., Thomas, G.V. and Robinson, E.J. (1992) 'The writing experiences of social science research students'. *Studies in Higher Education*, 17/2, 155–67.

—— (1994) 'The writing strategies of graduate research students in the social sciences'. *Higher Education*, 27/3, 379–92.

Section II

Curriculum and Course Design

PAUL FANNING

6 The Problem of Undergraduate EFL

Demand for EFL Degrees

Until the recent internationalisation of higher education, British universities experienced no real demand for undergraduate courses in English as a foreign language (EFL). However, the number of international students today, many receptive to the idea of undergraduate EFL through familiarity with it in their country of origin, plus the potential income from such students, would seem to be compelling reasons for having EFL degrees in Britain. The only foreseeable difficulty might be some negative perceptions of the subject arising from its 'servicing' history (Skeldon and Swales 1983). In fact, though, undergraduate EFL can provoke other criticisms that the more conventional language degrees seem to escape. It is these criticisms that constitute the problem to be discussed here. After setting them out, I wish to present some counter-arguments and consequent ideas for learning materials.

The Nature of the Problem

The criticisms to which degree-level EFL is prone centre on its perceived quality and its efficiency. Quality criticisms concern both the amount of learning and the suitability of EFL as a degree subject. With respect to the first it is suggested that learners eventually outgrow what EFL has to offer, so that any further study will become 'too easy' for degree level. This stage is likely to be reached particularly soon with university students, as many begin at Cambridge Proficiency level (traditionally regarded as the ultimate competence). The other quality criticism, the suitability of EFL degree content even for learners who still have some way to go to proficiency level, perhaps derives from the fact that EFL does not usually involve the standard intellectual content of more traditional English degrees, such as a literary canon, or the history of English, or transformational-generative grammar.

On the efficiency side, EFL at university level is questioned in the belief that Literature or Linguistics can achieve the same effect equally well or better. It is asked why a university should run two separate programmes when it could achieve the economy of scale of putting all students interested in English, native and non-native speakers alike, into the same lectures and seminars.

The Counter-Arguments

The question of whether one can design an EFL course to challenge the most advanced of non-native speakers raises the thorny Second Language Acquisition (SLA) issue of the limits of second language competence. Clearly, if second languages can be mastered as fully as first languages, then there must be a point at which EFL learners become too advanced for an EFL course; and conversely if there is no such possibility, then degree EFL might still have value.

There is in fact one type of non-native speaker who might outgrow EFL. However, they form a minority, and would be easy to exclude from an EFL degree by means of an objective criterion. These exceptional learners are those who have undertaken their secondary education in a wholly English-medium environment. They differ from other adult learners in at least three ways. Firstly, their English immersion begins before puberty, so that, if one accepts Long's (1990) link between starting age and ultimate attainment, they will have a realistic chance of achieving native-like competence.[1] Secondly, their English-medium education will have given them important cultural understanding. Thirdly, they will have what Cummins (1983) calls Cognitive Academic Language Proficiency (CALP). This includes not just literacy (reading and writing), but also language and concepts of formal study, and facility with decontextualised language. It is mainly learned precisely at secondary school. For Cummins CALP is an essential component of full language proficiency. Thus university English learners who have *not* had their secondary schooling in English will probably have CALP as part of their university learning need.

Apart from the few with English-medium secondary schooling, however, there seems to be no type of adult EFL learner who can achieve native speaker competence (Hyltenstam and Abrahamsson 2003). It might be argued that even if advanced adult learners can never be perfect in English, they can nevertheless reach such a level of competence that their motivation to learn more will be minimal. However, our experience suggests that some learners do have a motivation to keep going virtually forever, for such reasons as perfectionism or love of English.

A question that needs resolving if one aims to teach learners at such rarified levels is whether or not to use the term 'post-proficiency'. It could be argued that 'proficiency' describes all levels beyond a minimum competence. However, we prefer 'post-proficiency', both because it emphasises the undergraduate nature of our course, and because it encourages a distinction between advanced students who may never have seen a typical proficiency syllabus before and those who have. What post-proficiency students still have to learn is what they still do not know and/or cannot do in English. It is likely to be different for each learner, and hence very hard to produce a general syllabus for (anything suitable for such a syllabus would probably already be part of a typical proficiency syllabus!).

---

1   Explanations of this difference between younger and older language learners range from notions of 'brain plasticity' (Penfield and Roberts 1959) to a claimed loss by adults of access to Universal Grammar (Bley-Vroman 1989).

Individualised learning thus has to be an important element of our course.

The other quality criticism of undergraduate EFL, its unsuitability as a degree subject, can be avoided without necessarily incorporating literary or theoretical linguistic content. One can instead look for ideas to Modern Foreign Languages (MFL), with which, as indicated earlier, there is anyway an affinity. Doing this ought to come naturally, provided one is not overly influenced by the word 'English' in the degree title. The lead that MFL can give is explored in depth below.

In response to the efficiency criticism, three points can be made. Firstly, international students may not *want* to take a standard Literature or Linguistics degree. In my own institution there have been plenty of students who, having registered for these other subjects in the expectation that they would resemble English degrees in their own country, were shocked by the difference and only too happy to switch to a more EFL-orientated programme. Secondly, and perhaps partly explaining the students' shock, the tutors in these other areas tend not to understand the language learning needs and aspirations of international students. They are not, in short, EFL specialists. Thirdly, these other subjects only partially meet the needs of EFL students. Literature study tends to provide immersion learning – good for fluency but not for accuracy (Harley and Swain 1984, Swain 1991). Linguistics, on the other hand, tends to provide lots of linguistic understanding, but the grammar is usually not of the right type (theoretical rather than descriptive), and analysed without an accompanying communicative involvement in its message.

Alignment with MFL

MFL degrees are quality-controlled by national (QAA) guidelines for Languages and Related Studies. There are five key areas:
- Language Skills
- Language Related Skills (tools and metalanguage for describing and analysing target language)
- Subject Related Skills
- Intercultural Awareness and Understanding
- Graduate Skills (e.g. analysis, criticism, argument, independent learning).

In addition, it is possible to expand area 2 to include Language Learning Awareness, wherein students are directed to think analytically about not just what they are learning but also how.

The content of an undergraduate EFL course is easily mapped out from the above six targets. The rest of this paper illustrates activities that can be performed under each heading, and the appendix has some sample materials.

Language skills

If a degree course were simply to work through language development exercises in class, much as might be done in a standard proficiency course, then the quality criticisms might again be justified. However, there are a number of ways in which advanced language learning can be adapted for higher education.

Some language study can, if carefully managed, be undertaken independently – outside class tackling topics of the students' own choosing. This does not just compensate for inadequate class contact time, but also promotes the graduate skills of independent and lifelong learning, and provides the individualisation required for the post-proficiency variation of student need mentioned above. An experiment with a portfolio assignment for these purposes is described in the first of the specimen materials in the appendix.

In addition to using portfolios, we teach grammar analytically. An emphasis on naturalistic language-learning is rejected because students already receive plenty of that just by being students in a British university (particularly as the EFL course forms only half of a Joint Honours degree). If there were no formal language study, many students would see little reason to take EFL at all. Moreover, formal study is particularly suited to university students. Even if Krashen (1985) and others are right about its uselessness for acquisition, it retains educational value. The analysis the students do is not so much working through somebody else's pedagogical description as working out language features for themselves, so that QAA objective 5 is again incidentally catered for. Two such analysis projects, one using computer concordances, are described in the Appendix.

Further, incidental language analysis takes place in the context of other activities, such as arguing about issues in contemporary British society, or criticising SLA theories in light of personal SLA experience. The *Question Time* activity in the Appendix is an example.

Linguistic description

This QAA requirement does not require the heavy theorising of formal linguistics, but it does emphasise learning *about* language in addition to just learning it. It has led to our explicitly teaching basic metalinguistic terminology in year 1 (a module entitled Language Awareness that is taken by MFL and EFL students together), as well as to occasional later forays into such areas as Phonology and Collocation. Concordance analyses – already mentioned as a language acquisition tool – also present obvious language description opportunities. When this is the purpose, the students are closer to language teachers than learners, and need something different from the activity types suggested by such writers as Tribble and Jones (1990). Likewise, they can benefit from cross-linguistic comparisons for teachers of the type provided by Swan and Smith (2000).

Subject-related skills and (inter)cultural awareness

The first of these involves any non-linguistic academic input relating to the target-language civilisation, including history, geography, macro-economics, sociology, politics, drama, literature or business. It is valued not just for its own educational sake, but also, of course, because as cultural input it assists the learning of the target language, and (hopefully) educates students about the cultural nature of their own world views (Byram 1997). In MFL this input might be wholly divorced from the language work, but in most EFL circles integration would be considered normal.

The exact cultural content in an EFL degree will to some extent depend on tutors' own knowledge and preferences,[2] but current affairs and literature can be useful and reliable default sources. They are areas that tutors and students are likely to be comfortable with, they can be complex and open to critical analysis, and they often (as in the *Question Time* activity) involve extensive cultural knowledge. They can be accessed via spoken and written authentic texts that either determine specific subtopics or are determined by them. Written texts can be short (literary extracts, short stories, newspaper articles), or book-length. Spoken texts are easily obtainable from radio and TV, whether as soaps, news, documentaries or studio discussions. Mac-Donald (2000) describes a course where students analysed short stories determined by a topic syllabus. Another approach is to set carefully-chosen projects requiring Internet and library research.

Generic skills

It will already be clear that generic skills need not be targeted separately. Instead students can be encouraged to identify and debate issues whilst conducting language analysis or reflecting on an episode of *Eastenders*; they can analyse and criticise arguments in a news-

2   It is impossible to teach everything. As Kelly (2000:91) points out, 'the potential cultural content vastly exceeds the ability of any single degree to encompass all [...] domains beyond the most rudimentary level'.

paper feature article; they can generalise from data produced by a concordancer; and they can learn independently during a portfolio assignment.

Language learning awareness

This can be divided into general and personal awareness. The former would include study of those SLA topics whose understanding would promote students' own EFL proficiency, e.g. error types, learning strategies, input and output theory, noticing, and vocabulary acquisition. Because tutors are themselves likely to have had academic training in such topics, the teaching could be more wholly authentic. Personal learning awareness, on the other hand, could involve a reflective element, e.g. reviewing an independent learning experience, identifying personal learning styles, or evaluating learner training texts such as Gethin and Gunnemark (1995) against personal experience. They could even include writing critiques of published learning material.

Literature for Language Teaching

It may have been noticed that literature is recommended above as a post-proficiency resource despite earlier questioning of literature degrees for language teaching. Of course much has been written about the value of literature for EFL (see for example, Collie and Slater 1987, Carter and McRae 1996). Its value in an EFL degree requires it to be handled differently from in a literature degree (Maley 1989). Some possible differences are as follows:

English Literature	EFL
Views literary texts as a means of initiating students into a particular way of thinking.	Views literary texts as rich sources of information about the target language and culture.
Presents literary concepts such as tone and irony as aspects of writers' artistic and professional expertise.	Uses literary concepts such as tone and irony for developing linguistic competence (e.g. lexical connotation).
Investigates deeper meanings and issues evoked by setting, plot and characters.	Uses setting, plot and character to demonstrate British culture as well as raise issues.
Presents works and writers as part of a wider literary context.	Chooses literary texts for their motivational and cultural value rather than literary importance.

Literature in English Literature and EFL degrees

It should be noted that these objectives are priorities in their particular approach, and not exclusive to it: aspects may appear in either approach. The EFL priorities enable identification of important EFL language points that might not be considered at all in a class of native speakers. For example, the phrase 'Blackpool by the Med' as a description of Majorca in David Lodge's Paradise News (p. 5) might merit no more than a passing acknowledgement of its pithiness in a literary appreciation, but requires extensive cultural explanation with EFL students.

Conclusion

The problem that I have been discussing might be summed up as the opposition likely to arise to the idea of mounting a degree for non-native speakers of a country's official language. The main question that a university might ask is why an existing course in that language (targeting native speakers) cannot suffice instead, thus guaranteeing not just efficiency of provision, but also academic respectability. It is commonly assumed that EFL teachers are trained in nothing but language teaching, whereas English Literature or Linguistics teachers (lecturers) bring an extra, more intellectual dimension.

The answer to these concerns is that EFL degrees bring something special that learners cannot derive from courses targeting native speakers. And intellectual rigour can be achieved without trying to mimic what is done in those other courses. The UK's QAA guidelines for Languages and Related Studies provide a blueprint for the necessary intellectual rigour. One way of working with them has been the main focus of this paper.

Appendix (Sample Materials)

A. Portfolio assignment

Students submit:
- Twelve completed and corrected sets of grammar and vocabulary exercises, chosen according to personal need and interest.
- A short reflection on the experience of doing the exercises (their selection, strengths and weaknesses, effectiveness, future implications).

B. Concordance research assignment

Student groups give short oral analyses of forms and meanings in grammar or vocabulary concordances that they have themselves composed using university software according to instructions received in class.

C. *'Question time'*

Students are assisted during a single 3-hour session to understand a recorded TV panel discussion of a selected British current affairs issue (e.g. the pensions crisis). The students must:
- Understand and predict answers to the selected discussion question
- Prematch meanings with words and idioms from the discussion
- Take notes on each speaker's contribution
- Compare understandings
- Contribute understandings to a class discussion
- Complete a follow-up writing task (summary and critique of the panel's discussion of a second question).

D. *Analytic grammar*

Students answer questions that help them appreciate aspects of model sentences. For example, in the following *as* sentences, (a) some verbs express actions done by a WRITER, some the READER; (b) Reader, but not writer, verbs follow *will/can/may be*; (c) Prepositions differ according to verb type.

- As (has been) explained in Chapter 6, ...
- As is illustrated in Table 1, ...
- As will be seen from the map, ...
- As can be found in Diagram 5, ...
- As may be determined from the above section, ...
- As was explained at the start of this section, ...
- As will be realised from this data, ...
- As has been already suggested. ...

Bibliography

Bley-Vroman, R. (1989) 'What is the logical problem of foreign language learning?' in Gass, S. and Schachter, S. (eds) *Linguistic perspectives on Second Language Acquisition*, 41–68. Cambridge: Cambridge University Press.

Byram, M. (1997) *Teaching and assessing intercultural communicative competence*. Clevedon, Multilingual Matters.

Carter, R. and McRae, J. (eds) (1996) *Language, literature and the learner*. Harlow: Longman.

Collie, J. and Slater, S. (1987) *Literature in the language classroom*. Cambridge: Cambridge University Press.

Cummins, J. (1983) 'Language proficiency and academic achievement' in Oller, J. (ed.) *Issues in language testing research*. Rowley MA: Newbury House.

Gethin, A. and Gunnemark, E. (1995) *The art and science of learning languages*. Oxford: Intellect.

Harley, B. and Swain, M. (1984) 'The interlanguage of immersion students and its implications for second language teaching' in Davies, A., Criper, C. and Howatt, A (eds) *Interlanguage*, 291–311. Edinburgh: Edinburgh University Press.

Hyltenstam, K. and Abrahamsson, N. (2003) 'Maturational constraints in SLA' in Doughty, C. and Long, M., *The handbook of Second Language Acquisition*, 539–88. Oxford: Blackwell.

Kelly, M. (2000) 'Mapping culture in language degrees' in McBride, N. and Seago, K. (eds) *Target culture – target language?* 81–92. London, CILT.

Krashen, S. (1985) *The input hypothesis: issues and implications*. London: Longman.

Long, M. (1990) 'Maturational constraints on language development'. *Studies in Second Language Acquisition* 12, 251–85.

MacDonald, M. (2000) 'Strangers in a strange land: fiction, culture, language' in McBride, N. and Seago, K. (eds) *Target Culture – Target Language?* 137–55. London: CILT.

Maley, A. (1989) 'Down from the pedestal: literature as a resource' in Carter, R., Walker, A. and Brumfit, C.J. (eds) *Literature and the learner: methodological approaches* 10–24. Basingstoke/London: MEP/British Council.

Penfield, W. and Roberts, L. (1959) *Speech and brain mechanisms.* New York: Atheneum Press.

Skeldon, P. and Swales, J. (1983) 'Working with service English timetables'. *English Language Teaching Journal.* 37/2, 138–44.

Swain, M. (1991) 'French immersion and its offshoots: getting two for one' in Freed, B. (ed.) *Foreign language acquisition: research and the classroom,* 91–103. Lexington MA: Heath.

—— and Smith, B. (2000) *Learner English* (2nd ed.) Cambridge: Cambridge University Press.

Tribble, C. and Jones, G. (1990) *Concordances in the classroom.* Harlow: Longman.

RICHARD BAILEY AND PETER SERCOMBE

7 A Contextual Approach to Course Design

International Students and Widening Access

The composition of the international student cohort has significantly altered in recent years. Traditionally, many international students entering higher education in Britain have had high levels of secondary socialisation, in that they already had a first degree and came to the UK as graduates to follow post-graduate courses. Increasingly, students are coming from more diverse backgrounds, as a consequence of wider access, and a significant difference between now and say ten years ago is that they are frequently self-selected, younger and targeting undergraduate study (Cortazzi and Jin 2004).

At Northumbria University the vast majority of our pre-sessional students come from mainland China with most of the rest coming from other Asian countries and a few from the near East. Most students arrive without a formal English entry qualification and are tested using the University of Northumbria proficiency test, before being placed in an English language class suitable to their level of proficiency. The course under discussion provides for students with a level of English that can be equated with IELTS 5.0. The majority of these students are aiming at undergraduate study in Northumbria's Business School, with the remainder mostly seeking to study courses in Social Science.

There are several issues that concerned us about general purpose EAP provision in the pre-sessional university context. Firstly, in study skills approaches to course design and pedagogy there is little concern with or attention given to coherence of content input. In many published EAP materials, study skills approaches are typically atomised and decontextualised. The importance of content knowledge and its relation to disciplinary understanding is largely outside the remit of the EAP course. A further concern is the relevance and transferability of what is done in the support context to the target disciplinary context and this remains largely under-researched. Furthermore, EAP at Northumbria has until relatively recently been predicated on a deficit model, i.e. what students have been deemed to lack, rather than building on the experience and knowledge students already have and how these can be used to enhance their capabilities in terms of content, approaches to study and language in the HE context. The needs of international students seeking entry to undergraduate study are likely to be broader than a study skills/remediation paradigm admits. The focal issue becomes how to prepare students for the demands of first-year undergraduate study.

A Contextual Approach: concept and rationale

We feel a holistic approach with an emphasis on content can provide coherence and structure. There are three models of content-based instruction (CBI): adjunct, sheltered and theme-based (Scarcella and Oxford 1992). Although similar to these, our approach does not identify specifically with any of these models. We consider CBI as an approach that is adaptable to context (Prabhu 1990). Our course stems from the in-house adaptation of particular content in sociology and has been developed solely by staff in Northumbria's English Language Department. We would distinguish it from special purposes EAP (ESAP) on the one hand and point out that it has not been a team-teaching initiative. The former is more specific in focus and context while the latter involves input from subject lecturers, which was not the model used in this case. A broader aim is to apply educational principles to our EAP provision, to focus on learning appropriate to the exigencies of first-year undergraduate study and the aptitudes required for this, through the conduit of sociology.

We suggest a theme-based approach so we can immerse students in a discipline; different disciplines have different approaches to knowledge and investigation and students need to learn these to be academically literate in that area (Ballard and Clanchy 1988). We recognise that the discipline is social science but this is what most of our students are going on to study. By focusing on content rather than language we can turn students' attention to learning in a broad social science discipline rather than giving them context free skills which they have to transfer themselves. In this model language is taught implicitly, subservient to content.

Our model involves a shift of emphasis, providing the learner with an experience that can foster appropriate attitudes and behaviours towards the learning and literacy requirements of the target context. Intrinsic is a shift towards the notion of the universality of learning processes rather than an inventory of deficits (Biggs 1999). We create a context where teaching, learning and content come together to develop academic proficiency. In this context, we consider a task-based approach to be the most effective methodology for achieving this goal (Prabhu 1987, Waters and Waters 1992, 2001). Taken together we feel this represents a move away from the dominant perception of the pre-sessional course as a remedial pre-requisite as was prevalent in our institutional context until 2002, and may remain so in other institutions where pre-sessional EAP is taught.

The approach to language development being suggested is more commonly associated with first language (than second language) learning pedagogy. Overall we espouse a whole language approach. The idea is that language learning is more successful when not explicitly taught in compartmentalised and disengaged ways, but where acquisition predominates (cf. Krashen 1982). Actively engaging with content develops abilities in reading fluency and vocabulary development, quality of expression and writing, speaking and listening in more authentic ways. This enhances self-awareness and confidence in learners. In a theme-based approach the continuous and connected nature of content and study is the focus, bearing in mind that there is nevertheless a need to talk and write about it. Language form and function are addressed as the need arises, rather than being specifically targeted in advance.

In addition there is an emphasis on learning theory. In fore-grounding content we are not espousing a transmission model of teaching and learning. The emphasis is on constructivism (cf. Piaget 1968, and Vygotsky 1962), taking account of students' own life experience, and the development of their critical faculties. Learning focuses on the learners' attitudes to study and their personalities by attempting to facilitate independent thinking, creativity, engagement: essential ingredients for affective learning. Constructivism stresses the active, developmental and inter-relatedness of learning. This permeates all aspects of teaching and learning, including assessment. The choice of sociology as the theme is directly linked to an emphasis on broad educational considerations in two principal ways. Firstly, the subject introduces ways of life, norms and values and social organisation in modern Britain, enriching students' understanding of the host cultures and society. This is juxtaposed with learners' own social backgrounds and fosters understanding and integration (cf. Noels et al. 1996). Secondly, learners develop the facility to question and problematise accepted knowledge in this context (and more universally). This can be transferred to other contexts, such as the norms and values of their own society. Students draw on this knowledge and this constitutes an integral part of learning experience as, in theory, this influences the capacity for self-awareness, understanding and critical reflection. This has a bearing on personal development and intellectual maturation. Based on qualitative feedback we have received and a questionnaire survey, we feel that not only is there a noticeable increase in language proficiency and effective study know-how of students but also levels of confidence, participation and critical reasoning: in short, students' overall academic literacy capabilities.

How the Course is Implemented

We use a standard GCSE/A level sociology text (Browne, K. [1998] *An Introduction to Sociology*. Cambridge: Polity Press 2nd edition). This text was selected according to a number of criteria. Firstly, it provides a source for and introduction to the epistemological and methodological basis for study in the social sciences. Secondly, the text is appropriate to the language proficiency level of the students (the readability level is around 13 according to the Gunning-Fog index). The text is also a good source of generic academic vocabulary and familiarises students with the academic register of English in meaningful ways and provides for greater authenticity in terms of the learning and teaching context. The subject matter (e.g. the family, the media, population, education) is within the scope of understanding of the students and can easily be related to their life experiences: an affective ingredient. In addition and linked to this is the enquiring nature of sociology which encourages students to question assumptions and stereotypical views as well as adopting a critical and problematising approach to knowledge in general.

What follows is a broad outline of the salient aspects of how the course is implemented and teaching and learning conceived. Delivery is organised around language skill areas for pedagogical focus and timetabling purposes on a weekly basis, although classes are not skills based, rather they are integrated around content. All the teaching and learning materials have been developed in conjunction with sociological themes included in the syllabus, so that students develop their comprehension of content knowledge; in this respect, content drives the learning.

Students are introduced to the themes (a chapter in the core text) at the beginning of a given week via a series of guided questions. This sets the scene for the one main weekly lecture, which is preceded by a preparatory session on new vocabulary that is used in the lecture. Lectures recycle vocabulary from the course book and from previous lectures, as well as representing ideas from previous weeks, so there is a coherent link between theme and lexis. There are several weekly sessions on listening to lectures, which involve follow-up seminars, guided note-taking listening to parts of a recorded version of the lecture to focus on intensive aspects of listening skills. In conjunction with these are classes that deal with training in speaking, to prepare students to deliver a short presentation at the end of the semester to defend their major piece of written work.

Regular post-reading questions are assigned on material from the sociology course textbook; in addition, explicit direction is given towards other materials including a range of supplementary Internet and book-based sources, to encourage the development of extensive reading skills, to increase exposure to (academic) vocabulary, engagement with sociological thinking and current issues. Reading classes focus on main topics and students are given guided tasks on these, including summaries of readings, and the interpretation of non-lexical text such as tables, charts and graphs. These tasks comprise a variety of activities that students complete usually in pairs or groups and include

- producing definitions of key words and concepts
- completion exercises based on recall of parts of the text
- guided note-taking from parts of the main text on key sub-topics
- reading and speaking on topical issues in groups as a fluency task, describing topics from home contexts or comparing British issues with those from their own countries
- paraphrasing segments of a chapter, with an underlying focus on synthesising and reformulation.

The integrated nature of reading and writing is emphasised in class work and self-directed learning. The majority of writing tasks are based on text(s) and content. There is an emphasis on developing micro or pre-writing skills through class-work as a preliminary for the extended writing assignment (Bailey 2003). In academic writing students need to be familiar with grammatical form and function but also with the features of particular discourse patterns and conventions. This involves an understanding of texts at the level of discourse and socio-cultural awareness of the relationship between readers and writers in terms of culturally specific forms of organisation and textual patterning. We feel that the essentially organic nature of adjusting to studying in the disciplines is encapsulated in what we do more than in the artificial and atomised nature of a study skills approach. This has been borne out by a student questionnaire with a 5-point attitude scale, which revealed that 33 out of 34 students felt that the course had raised their awareness and understanding of the expectations of academic study at a British university.

The following account illustrates the task-based nature of the work done in the classroom focused around the text and the weekly themes. Under the theme of power and politics, for example, class-room tasks on language knowledge include presenting the appropriate tense forms in a narrative account of the background to the British political system, and the coherent organisation of the discourse of a passage paraphrased from the core text, on pressure groups. In this activity, there is a requirement to locate cohesive devices and determine the position of words and phrases removed from the passage. Another task focuses on discourse elements in written text, such as positioning cohesive markers, elliptical features, substitution and synonymy. Another task involves reading a text and mapping it, in terms of rhetorical structure and discourse organising words and phrases, for summary and paraphrase. In addition, nonverbal material such as charts and graphs are incorporated into these activities. Text-responsible writing exercises accompany this, predominantly class-room based work (see Leki and Carson 1997 for further detail). Exercises within the text are used for role-play and guided fluency activities.

The essay is the predominant genre in student writing in humanities and social science areas and the default genre in student writing in higher education (Womack 1993). From the third week of the course, students begin preparing a 2000-word essay, on a sociology topic. Input each week parallels incrementally the part of the essay that students are working on. Draft copies of essays are submitted at pre-specified points in the semester for written and oral feedback from writing tutors, on the basis of which students are expected to review and revise their work. The strength of a theme-based course is the time and scope available for developing pre-writing skills and abilities around related themes with an emphasis on synthesising and recasting information from sources which can be integrated into, and assessed through, a more extended and autonomously managed writing task. Students have the experience and resource of being immersed in content knowledge and background, epistemologies, methodologies and modalities appropriate to an area of study. This contrasts with the literature-based mini-project where the emphasis is on generic conventions of essay writing and less on the incorporation and use of content knowledge.

Tutorial support is provided on a one-to-one basis, at regular intervals to reflect on academic progress, which prepares students for final assessments and for their subsequent undergraduate experience. Course assessment involves the following: a set of notes, from the last lecture of the semester, a 2000-word essay, an oral summary of the essay – including rationale, main arguments and details of sources used, and a 2-hour exam to test reading and writing skills under exam conditions. The summative reading task is based on a pre-prepared text that students bring to the exam while the writing task is both process and product oriented. Students undertake an exam essay in which content knowledge is combined with personal knowledge and experience.

Our approach is supported by qualitative and quantitative research into student and teacher feedback. Our survey reveals that 94% of students felt the course is improving their general academic English and the same percentage felt that the course is helping them to understand useful ideas. In addition, 89% of students felt a theme-based approach is an effective way to organise teaching and learning. We also sought the opinions of EAP tutors, who have been positive about their experience of engaging with and teaching a theme-based course, enjoying the stimulation of dealing with academic content. One tutor said that 'from a teacher's point of view it is fun and challenging, innovative, and creates more opportunity to reflect on teaching styles'. Another commented that 'It is integrated and real. It feels more important. The identity of the teacher is reinforced and this is reassuring for learners. The focus is taken away from artificial examples to language with real academic use'.

Conclusion

In this article we have argued in favour of and provided a rationale for a theme-based concept for course design in the preparation of international students for university study, predominantly targeting undergraduate social science degree courses. The focus is on content and the ways in which it is used and expressed in order to foreground disciplinarity in the pre-sessional context and to foster academic literacy. Results in assessment and feedback from questionnaires suggest this revised approach to the delivery of EAP has provided benefits to students that a more traditional skills based approach may not necessarily achieve.

Bibliography

Bailey, R. (2003) *Holistic activities for developing academic writing skills in the classroom.* European Association for the Teaching of Academic Writing (EATAW), Central European University, Budapest. Conference proceedings on CD ROM.

Ballard, B. and Clanchy, J. (1988) 'Literacy in the university: an "anthropological" approach' in Taylor, G. et al. (eds) *Literacy by Degrees.* Buckingham: The Society for Research in Higher Education. Open University Press.

Benesch, S. et al. (eds) (1988) *Ending remediation: linking ESL and content in higher education.* TESOL papers.

Biggs, J. (1999) *Teaching for quality learning at university.* Buckingham: The Society for Research in Higher Education. Open University Press.

Browne, K. 2nd edition (1998) *An introduction to sociology.* Cambridge: Polity Press.

Cortazzi, M. and Jin, L. (2004) 'Changing practices in Chinese cultures of learning'. Paper presented at the *Responding to the*

Needs of the Chinese Learner conference. University of Portsmouth.

Krashen, S. (1982) *Principles and practice in second language acquisition*. Oxford: Pergamon.

Leki, I. and Carson, J.G. (1997) 'Completely different worlds: EAP and the writing experiences of ESL students in university courses'. *TESOL Quarterly*, 31, 39–69.

Noels, K., Pon, G. and Clément, R. (1996) 'Language, identity and adjustment: the role of linguistic self-confidence in the acculturation process'. *Journal of Language and Social Psychology*, 15 246–64.

Piaget, J. 8th edition (1968) *Le langue et la pensée chez l'enfant*. Neuchâtel: Delachaux et Nestlé.

Prabhu, N.S. (1987) *Second language pedagogy: a perspective*. Oxford: Oxford University Press.

—— (1990) 'There is no best method – why?' *TESOL Quarterly*, 24/2, 161–76.

Scarcella, R. and Oxford, R. (1992) *The tapestry of language learning: the individual in the communicative classroom*. Boston: Heinle and Heinle.

Vygotsky, L. (1962) *Thought and language*. Cambridge, MA: MIT Press.

Waters, A. and Waters, M. (1992) 'Study skills and study competence: getting the priorities right'. *ELT Journal*, 46/13, 264–73.

—— (2001) 'Designing tasks for developing study competence and study skills in English' in Flowerdew, J. and Peacock, M. (eds) *Research perspectives on English for Academic Purposes*, 375–89. Cambridge: Cambridge University Press.

Womack, P. (1993) 'What are essays for?' *English in Education* 27/2, 42–5.

IAN BRUCE

8 Defining Academic Genres: An Approach for Writing Course Design

Introduction

This paper addresses the issue of using genre as a basis for designing courses that teach the writing skill, and in particular, academic writing. The paper has two overall aims. The first is to address the issue of the diversity of approaches to genre classification of written discourse by identifying two broad approaches. The second aim is to consider the genre constructs around which it may be possible to design academic writing courses. The paper has four sections:

- The problem: diversity of approaches to genre
- A possible solution: the social/cognitive genre distinction
- A model for cognitive genre
- Social and cognitive genre knowledge and materials development

The Problem: the diversity of approaches to genre

It seems that, for the teaching of the writing skill, genre-based courses have three major strengths: first, they make it possible to focus on units of language above sentence level; secondly, they can provide a focus on the organisational or procedural elements of written discourse, and thirdly, they make it possible to retain linguistic components as functioning features of a larger unit of discourse, thereby avoiding atomistic approaches to language teaching. As Paltridge (2001:6) observes:

> [a] genre-based approach to language program development aims to incorporate discourse and contextual aspects of language use that are often underattended to in programs based only on the lower-level organisational units of language, such as structures, functions, or vocabulary.

However, the central problem in using a genre-based approach to course design is identifying the discourse entities that are most appropriate for a particular syllabus or course. The lists in Table 1 provide some indication of the range of terminology and variety of approaches to discourse classification that have been proposed. The separation into two different columns is merely to show terms used to classify whole discourses and those to classify parts of discourses.

Whole discourses	Parts of discourses
genre (Hasan 1989, Swales 1990, Bhatia 1993, Fowler 1982) text genre (Pilegaard and Frandsen 1996, Werlich 1976) macro-genres (Martin 1994, 1995, 1997) discourse types (Virtanen 1992)	genre (Swales 1990) elemental genre (Feez 2002) text type (Biber 1989, Pilegaard and Frandsen 1996, Werlich 1976, Virtanen 1992) rhetorical functions (Lackstrom, Selinker and Trimble 1973, Jordan 1997) rhetorical modes (Silva 1990) macro-functions (Council of Europe 1996) macro-genres (Grabe 2002) séquences (Adam 1985, 1992) discourse patterns (Hoey 1979, 1983, 1995, 2001) macrostructures (Van Dijk 1980)

Table 1. Diversity of approaches to text classification

Any review of theory or research related to classifying texts in terms of such categories as genre and text-type needs to address the fact that terminology is used in very different ways by different writers. However, this is not simply a terminological problem of naming or designation. It is a problem that arises out of fundamental disagreement about the very nature of the object of enquiry – what it is that is being investigated and classified. For some, discourse classification is largely a social phenomenon, something that is directly reflected in the overall conventionally recognised purpose and structure of texts, for example: editorials, postcards, research articles. For others, discourse classification is a communicatively or rhetorically motivated, cognitive phenomenon, for example: argument, explanation, recount, description. In this case, the phenomenon is reflected only indirectly, if at all, in the overall structure of whole texts.

A Possible Solution: social genres and cognitive genres

In providing a framework for my own research (Bruce 2003), I propose that the different systems of classification of extended discourse (both written and spoken) fall into two broad categories: 'social genres' and 'cognitive genres'. The actual investigation that I carried out related to the latter category of cognitive genres.

Social genres are socially recognised constructs according to which whole texts are classified in terms of their overall social purpose. Thus, for example, personal letters, novels and academic articles are examples of social genres. These are created to fulfil different types of socially recognised and understood purpose. Drawing on the current literature, creating a social genre in an academic setting appears to involve at least knowledge relating to:

- context – involving specialist knowledge of a field
- epistemology – 'disciplinary assumptions about the nature of knowledge' (Lea and Street 1998:162)
- stance – addressivity and audience, including conventions relating to formality (Adam and Artemeva 2002)
- the recognised staging of texts, such as schematic structure (Hasan 1989) or systems of moves and steps (Swales 1990).

The term cognitive genre is used here to refer to the overall cognitive orientation of a segment of writing in terms of its realisation of one particular rhetorical purpose. This is reflected in the way in which information is internally organised and related. Different types of rhetorical purpose (such as, to recount sequenced events, to explain a process, to argue a point of view) are each realised by employing a different cognitive genre. The designation 'cognitive' is used because of the types of internal, organisational knowledge that such units of discourse employ and also because of the apparent automatic nature of the use of such knowledge by proficient language users. Fundamental to this internal organisation is the role played by various types of relationship between propositions.

A particular example of a social genre (e.g. a personal letter) may draw upon a range of different cognitive genres in relation to the different sections of the overall message as it unfolds, for example: recounting events, presenting an argument, providing an explanation.

The choice of the terms social and cognitive has been made in order to establish unequivocally that each relates to a different object of enquiry. While some may prefer the two constructs to be described using existing terminologies, it is felt that this would only further serve to perpetuate the current genre confusion. For example, current terms, such as 'communicative' relating to social purpose and 'rhetorical' relating to discourse organisation, could possibly be used to refer to this distinction. However, these are insufficiently distinguished in their use by applied linguists and EAP practitioners. This lack of focus on the social and cognitive aspects of discourse is admitted by Swales (1990). While acknowledging that the exercise of genre skills involves two types of knowledge: content knowledge and general, rhetorical structures – what Carrell (1988) terms formal schemata – Swales suggests that it may be difficult to maintain this distinction when examining genre as 'the nature of genres is that they coalesce *what* is sayable with *when* and *how* it is sayable' (p. 88). However, failure to give due consideration to the cognitive, rhetorical dimension as an important organisational influence in discourse structure results in approaches to genre that focus solely on matching content staging to linguistic features, an approach already found to be inherently flawed (Paltridge 1993, 1997). Given this issue along with the current multiplicity of approaches to discourse categorisation and their use of competing and often overlapping terminologies, it is, therefore, crucial to establish the nature of the knowledge types to which any classificatory terminologies apply.

Cognitive Genres in Academic Prose: a model

In my own research, I proposed models for the four cognitive genres that occur most commonly in academic English prose. I termed these 'rhetorical types'[1] (Bruce 2003, 2005). Establishing the rhetorical type model involved the following steps:

- a review of cognitive categorisation theories
- proposal of a provisional model
- a corpus study leading to refinement of the model
- testing the model in the survey and analysis of writing responses to four tasks.

The organisation of the Rhetorical type model (see Table 2 following) is based on three principles from categorisation theory:

- categorisation is in response to purpose or intentionality (Barsalou 1983); therefore, certain types of rhetorical or communicative purpose each activate a prototypical discourse pattern (rhetorical type), which is, in effect, a type of highly complex category
- complex knowledge is hierarchically organised, from higher level general to lower level specific structures (Miller 1984, Rumelhart and Ortony 1977); thus, complex categories, such as rhetorical types may be described in terms of different systems of intermeshing procedural (organising) knowledge, which relate hierarchically (from general higher level to more specific lower level structures)
- creating and identifying categories is in relation to knowledge and memory of prototypes (Rosch 1975, 1978); therefore,

---

1   In following sections, the terms cognitive genre and rhetorical type are synonymous. Rhetorical types merely refer to the specific cognitive genres that occur in academic prose for which I propose a model.

discourse that relates to a single or communicative purpose may be realised by a prototypical pattern.

The first idea from categorisation theory is that categories are formed in relation to intention and purpose. The types of communicative purpose for the model were identified by drawing on two existing taxonomies of text types – the corpus-based text types of Biber (1989) and the pedagogic text types of Quinn (1993). However, their use in the rhetorical type model involves a reinterpretation of the term text type to include extralinguistic as well as linguistic information. Biber's corpus study reveals that one (social) genre category of written texts can employ more than one text type. Biber put forward a typology of eight text types, and, in his corpus study, he found that academic prose texts employed four of the eight text types. The types of communicative purpose of the four proposed rhetorical types are:

- the presentation of data or information that is essentially non-sequential (report rhetorical type)
- the presentation of information with the orientation on means (explanation rhetorical type)
- a focus on the organisation of data in relation to (possible) outcomes/conclusions/choices (discussion rhetorical type)
- presentation of data or information that is essentially sequential or chronological (recount rhetorical type).

Drawing on the second idea from categorisation theory that units of complex knowledge are hierarchically organised – higher level general and more specific lower level structures – the rhetorical type model employs the following classificatory systems for its organisational knowledge: (see Table 2).

- gestalts called 'image schemata' (Johnson 1987)
- discourse patterns (Hoey 1983, 1996, 2001)
- 'interpropositional relations' (Crombie 1985).

Gestalts

At the upper levels of the model, a certain rhetorical purpose will engage a general gestalt pattern in order to broadly structure the content knowledge that is being represented. This is based on the idea that, by the use of metaphor (metaphorical projection), gestalts can be used to structure different types of knowledge in the way that Lakoff proposes in his spatialisation of form hypothesis (Lakoff 1987:283). For example, non-sequential knowledge, such as the information contained in certain types of graph or tables of numbers is structured by a whole–part schema. Sequential information such as describing a process or recounting events is structured by source–path–goal schema.

Discourse patterns

Gestalts (image schemata) refer to the organisation of concepts or ideas (in effect, at the pre-writing stage). In relation to the organisation of the written text, they lead to the engagement of the discourse patterns that Hoey proposes, for example, general–particular, problem–solution. These provide approaches to the organisation of text in terms of topic and paragraph structure.

Interpropositional relations

The types of rhetorical purpose proposed also lead to selection from a specific set of lower-order, cognitive categories termed interpropositional relations, for example, reason–result, condition–consequence, chronological sequence. These always have two parts as they involve the relationship of more than one proposition (Crombie 1985). Because these organising categories involve related propositions, they have a direct effect on linguistic organisation and linguistic selection. For example, in English the reason member of a reason–result relation may be introduced by because + clause or because of + noun phrase. The specific choice of language to realise a relation will be determined, in part, by expectations which relate to the social genre engaged and in part by other considerations such as individual preference for specific types of stylistic variety.

Report rhetorical type: static descriptive presentation

Rhetorical Focus	Presentation of data or information that is essentially non-sequential
Gestalt Structure	Whole–part structure, of which the part has an up–down structure
Discourse Pattern	Preview – Details
Interpropositional Relations	Amplification; Reason–Result, Grounds–Conclusion; Simple Contrast, Comparative Similarity, Concession–Contraexpectation, Condition–Consequence

Explanation rhetorical type: means–focused presentation

Rhetorical Focus	The presentation of information with the orientation on means.
Gestalt Structure	Source–path–goal schema; link schema
Discourse Patterning	Preview – Details
Interpropositional Relations	Means–Purpose, Means–Result, Amplification, Concession–Contraexpectation

Discussion rhetorical type: choice/outcome–focused presentation

Rhetorical Focus	Focus on the organisation of data in relation to (possible) outcomes/conclusions/choices
Gestalt Structure	Container schemata (more than one)
Discourse Pattern	Generalisation – Examples and Matching
Interpropositional Relations	Grounds–Conclusion, Reason–Result, Means–Purpose, Means–Result, Concession–Contraexpectation

Recount rhetorical type: sequential presentation

Rhetorical Focus	Presentation of data or information that is essentially sequential or chronological
Gestalt Structure	Source–path–goal schema
Discourse Pattern	General – Particular
Interpropositional Relations	Means–Purpose, Means–Result, Amplification. Chronological Sequence, Grounds–Conclusion, Reason–Result

Table 2. Summary of the rhetorical type model (Bruce 2003)

An example of report rhetorical type analysed in terms of the model can be found in Bruce (2005).

Social Genre and Cognitive Knowledge and Materials Development

This section provides a brief discussion about the inclusion of social genre and cognitive genre knowledge into different types of courses that have a central focus on academic writing.

Social genre knowledge appears to be complex, multi-faceted and, it seems, not simply able to be described merely in terms of textual analysis. Biber proposes that (social) genre categories are 'defined primarily on the basis of external format, related to differences in purpose and situation' (Biber 1989:39) Furthermore, Luke in discussing genre from a sociological perspective, emphasises that (social) genres are 'sites for the contestation of difference' (1996:318), which is not reflected in a 'finely grained synchronic analysis of texts' (ibid:333). A focus on social genre knowledge, therefore, needs to be within the context of a discipline-specific learning situation and should include aspects of textual and extra-textural knowledge. This would take place in a specialist EAP course where the target group of writers share the same disciplinary interest and concerns, and the social genres that are central to the subject can be identified and analysed. In such a setting the disciplinary social genres may be deconstructed with regard to both (a) social genre knowledge and (b) their use of cognitive genre structures (which I have operationalised as rhetorical types).

This dual approach to EAP course construction is also proposed by Paltridge (2002:83) in his article which says that 'EAP programmes need to focus on both genre (social genre) and text type (cognitive genre) in their course of instruction' and that 'students need to have an understanding of both genre and text type and how they interact with each other in EAP settings'.

In more general academic writing courses, where the target group of writers have different disciplinary interests, there needs to be a primary focus on cognitive genre knowledge (see Bruce 2005). This does not mean that cognitive genres (such as rhetorical types) have to be introduced within a course unit devoid of social context and social purpose. The issue is rather one of the central pedagogic focus. For example, a pedagogic focus on a segment of discourse realising a rhetorical type could be located within a larger authentic text relating to a social genre. The rhetorical type approach to cognitive genres can be used for both selecting authentic text segments and as a means for deconstructing and reconstructing the texts in ways that highlight the different levels of organisational or procedural knowledge.

Awareness of gestalt structure and discourse patterns provides frameworks for the future planning of the structure of a piece of written discourse. Furthermore, the organisation of linguistic elements around interpropositional relations can ensure awareness of a wider range of ways of signalling meaning relationships and cohesion than the more conventional sentence-level approaches to grammar and syntax.

Conclusion

A proficient, academic writer is someone who has a clear under-standing of the conventions and the resources of the field of writing in which they are engaged. The writer is able to use this knowledge in innovative and effective ways to craft a message appropriate to the discipline and the target audience. The effectiveness of the writing emerges from their use of the means by which academic discourse is constructed. However, to get to this point the writer has to know what these means are and have them at his or her disposal.

Bibliography

Adam, C. and Artemeva, N. (2002) 'Writing instruction in English for academic purposes (EAP) classes: introducing second language learners to the academic communit' in Johns, A. (ed.) *Genre in the classroom: multiple perspectives* 179–96. Mahwah, NJ: Lawrence Erlbaum.

Adam, J. (1985) 'Quels types de texts?'. *Le Français dans le Monde*, 192, 39–43.

—— (1992) *Les textes: types et prototypes*. Paris: Nathan.

Barsalou, L.W. (1983) 'Ad hoc categories'. *Memory and Cognition*, 11/3, 211–27.

—— (1991) 'Deriving categories to achieve goals' in G.H. Bower (ed.) *The Psychology of Learning and Motivation*, 27, 1–64. San Diego, CA: Academic Press.

Bhatia, V.K. (1993) *Analysing genre: language use in professional settings*. London: Longman.

Biber, D. (1988) *Variation across speech and writing*. Cambridge: Cambridge University Press.

—— (1989) A typology of English text. *Linguistics*, 27, 3–43.

Bruce, I.J. (2003) 'Cognitive genre prototype modelling and its implications for the teaching of academic writing to learners of English as a second language'. Unpublished doctoral dissertation: University of Waikato, Hamilton, New Zealand.

—— (2005) 'Syllabus design for general EAP courses: a cognitive approach'. *Journal of English for Academic Purposes*, 4/3, 239–56.

Chafe, W. (1994) *Discourse, consciousness, and time*. Chicago: The University of Chicago Press.

Council of Europe (2001) *Common European framework of reference for languages: learning, teaching, assessment*. Cambridge: Cambridge University Press.

Crombie, W.H. (1985) *Process and relation in discourse and language learning*. Oxford: Oxford University Press.

—— (1987) *Free verse and prose style: an operational definition and description.* London: Routledge, Kegan and Paul.

Feez, S. (1998) *Text-based syllabus design.* Sydney: National Centre for English Language Teaching and Research, Macquarie University.

Fowler, A. (1982) *Kinds of literature: an introduction to the theory of genres and modes.* Cambridge, MA: Harvard University Press.

Grabe, W. (2002) 'Narrative and expository macro-genres' in Johns, A. (ed.) *Genre in the classroom: multiple perspectives*, 249–67. Mahwah, NJ: Erlbaum.

Hasan, R. (1989) 'The identity of a text' in Halliday, M.A.K. and Hasan, R. *Language, text and context*, 97–118 Oxford: Oxford University Press.

Hoey, M. (1979) 'Signalling in discourse' in *Discourse Analysis Monograph No. 6.* Birmingham: English Language Research, University of Birmingham,

—— (1983) *On the surface of discourse.* London: George Allen and Unwin.

—— (1994) 'Signalling in discourse: a functional analysis of a common discourse pattern in written and spoken English, 26–45'' in Coulthard, M. (ed.) *Advances in written text analysis.* London: Routledge.

—— (2001) *Textual interaction: an introduction to written discourse analysis.* London: Routledge.

Jordan, R.R. (1997) *English for academic purposes: a guide and resource book for teachers.* Cambridge: Cambridge University Press.

Johnson, M. (1987) *The body in the mind: the bodily basis of meaning, imagination, and reason.* Chicago: University of Chicago Press.

Lackstrom, J.E., Selinker, L. and Trimble, L.P. (1973) Technical rhetorical principles and grammatical choice. *TESOL Quarterly*, 7, 127–36.

Lakoff, G. (1987) *Women, fire and dangerous things: what categories reveal about the mind.* Chicago: Chicago University Press.

Lea, M.R. and Street, B. (1998) 'Student writing in higher education: an academic literacies approach'. *Studies in higher education*, 23, 157–72.

Luke, A.N. (1996) 'Genres of power? Literacy education and the production of capita' in Hasan, R. and Williams, G. (eds) *Literacy in Society*, 308–38. London: Longman.

Martin, J.R. (1994) 'Macro-genres: the ecology of the page'. *Network*, 21, 29–52.

—— (1995) 'Text and clause: fractal resonance'. *Text*, 15, 5–42.

—— (1997) 'Analyzing genre: functional parameter' in Christie, F. and Martin, J.R. (eds) *Literacy in society*, 3–39. London: Cassell.

Miller, C.R. (1984) 'Genre as social action'. *Quarterly Journal of Speech*, 70, 151–67.

Murphy, G.L. and Medin, D.L. (1985) 'The role of theories of conceptual coherence'. *Psychological Review*, 92, 289–316.

Paltridge, B. (2001) *Genre and the language learning classroom*. Ann Arbor: University of Michigan Press.

—— (2002) 'Genre, text type, and the English for academic purposes (EAP) classroom' in Johns, A. (ed.) *Genre in the classroom: multiple perspectives*, 73–90. Mahwah, NJ: Lawrence Erlbaum.

Pilegaard, M. and Frandsen, F. (1996) 'Text type' in Verschueren, J., Ostaman, J.-O., Blommaert, J. and Bulcaen, C.C. (eds) *Handbook of Pragmatics*, 1–13. Amsterdam: John Benjamins.

Quinn, J. (1993) 'A taxonomy of text types for use in curriculum design'. *EA Journal*, 11/2, 33–46.

Rosch, E. (1975) 'Cognitive representations of semantic categories'. *Journal of Experimental Psychology: General*, 104, 192–233.

—— (1978) 'Principles of categorisation' in Rosch, E. and Lloyd, B.B. (eds) *Cognition and categorization*, 27–47. Hillsdale, NJ: Erlbaum.

Rumelhart, D.E. and Ortony, A. (1977) 'The representation of knowledge in memory' in Anderson, R.C., Spiro, R.J. and Montague, W.E. (eds) *Schooling and the acquisition of knowledge*, 99–135. Hillsdale, NJ: Erlbaum.

Silva, T. (1990) 'Second language composition instruction: developments, issues and directions in ESL' in Kroll, B. (ed.) *Second language writing: research insights for the classroom*, 11–23. Cambridge: Cambridge University Press.

Swales, J. (1990) *Genre analysis: English in academic and research settings.* Cambridge: Cambridge University Press.

Van Dijk, T.A. (1980) *Macrostructures: an interdisciplinary study of global structures in discourse, interaction and cognition.* Hillsdale, NJ: Erlbaum.

Virtanen, T. (1992) 'Issues of text typology: narrative – a basic type of text?' *Text*, 12, 292–310.

Werlich, E. (1976) *A text grammar of English.* Heidelberg: Quelle and Meyer.

JOHN WRIGGLESWORTH

9 Using a Genre-based Approach to Curriculum Design in EAP: Assumptions, Applications, and Reactions

Introduction

The advantages of a genre-based pedagogy are becoming familiar to university-based language teachers in the UK. Almost all practitioners will at some time teach discourse level text structure to their students. Most practitioners will be familiar with the work of Swales (1990) and Bhatia (1993). Many will be aware of the developments of genre in Systemic Functional Linguistics (SFL) perhaps through theoretical accounts such as Hyland (2004) or in an applied form in textbooks such as *EAP Now!* (Cox and Hill 2004). Absorbing all these ideas and putting them together into a course is, however, no easy task.

This paper looks at the method of weaving together the various ideas surrounding genre and discourse structure that informed a particular academic English unit. Swales' (1990) formulation of a discourse community was used to design a needs analysis. Martin's (1999) definition of genre – a staged, goal-oriented, social process – was used to develop a syllabus to meet these needs. The syllabus was taught using a genre-based learning and teaching cycle. The ideas of theme/rheme and given/new were exploited to show how the packaging of content-information could be explained to students at a clause, paragraph and whole-text level. Thus thinking about syllabus through the notions of genre helped teachers to encourage students to make links between the grammar they already know, the things that they need to put in an essay, and the discipline that they study. This paper provides an introduction to some of the ideas from genre theory and SFL that were used to develop the syllabus, explains the pedagogic teaching cycle used to enact the syllabus and reviews some of the reactions to using the syllabus from teachers.

Context

The context of the current paper was the development of an under-graduate academic English unit for international students at a new, UK university. The unit was designed to provide compulsory academic English language support to approximately 200 students on the university's successful English Plus degrees, such as International Trade and English or Communication Studies and English. For International Trade, content units include Physical Distribution and Export Marketing. For Communication Studies, content units include Business Communication and Communication in the Workplace. Final-year undergraduates on all English Plus courses have one major unit in common: the Student Special Project (SSP). The SSP requires students to conduct empirically grounded research and write up a report on a topic related to International Trade or Communication. The academic English unit focuses on English for General Academic Purposes rather than Occupational Purposes (Dudley-Evans and St. John 1998) and is intended to equip the students with the language they need to succeed in UK higher education.

Discourse Community

When thinking through the academic English needs of the under-graduates, we used the concept of discourse community as defined by Swales (1990) as a heuristic device. The concept may have been criticised for its lack of linguistic rigour (see Borg 2003 for a summary) but the discussion surrounding the concept's application to our situation proved fruitful.

Swales offers six criteria for a discourse community. I will briefly define and apply the first three and the sixth criteria before looking at the text-based criteria, the fourth and fifth. First, a discourse community must have an agreed set of common public goals. A group of students working for a unit on an undergraduate degree have a common set of goals imposed on them, certainly in the assessment and marking criteria. However, academic units must also have specific learning objectives. Outcomes for the SSP include the identification and implementation of an empirically-based research project followed up with a written report. The genre of such a report is thus a valid target of an EAP course.

The second and third criteria look at communication. The discourse community must have mechanisms for intercommunication between members. The lectures, seminars and tutorials provide a foundation for formal intercommunication along with written formative feedback. There are also many less formal forums where students meet, such as the coffee shop. However, it is not compulsory for students to employ these mechanisms and it is possible for a student to communicate solely with a lecturer, a point that affects Swales' third criterion: the discourse community *uses* the mechanisms of intercommunication. Whether these criteria are fulfilled or not seems to depend on a variety of situational variables including the curriculum, students and lecturers but as EAP tutors we can take part. The needs analysis for the EAP unit tapped into this intercommunication by interviewing SSP tutors about the purpose of the whole report and its sections (Hyland 2004) and looking at examples of good quality student work and the feedback it received. Swales' sixth criterion looks at the changing membership of the discourse community. Undergraduate degrees have a regular and predictable change in membership as students graduate. The extent to which the discourse community of a final-year undergraduate matches that of the one students join when they enter the world of work will depend on a number of factors particularly discipline – compare a student who takes a job in the city after completing a History BA with a student who takes employment as a dental technician after a Dental Technology degree. However, the responsibility of aligning the outcomes of a unit or assessment with a student's future needs is assumed to be the responsibility of the discipline-specific department.

The remaining two criteria bring in text-based features. The fourth criterion says that a discourse community has a set of genres by which it gets things done. As Kusel (1991) and Dudley-Evans (1995) have argued, these may be peculiar to a particular university department, as commonalities cannot be assumed from discipline to discipline or university to university. By contrast, the discipline that students study probably does contain lexical items and abbreviations, which are unique to the subject (Swales' fifth criteria) but common across universities, although this set of terms may not extend to those used to describe assessment types.

In summary, applying Swales' criteria to the needs of our undergraduate students allowed us to better understand the students' context and discourse community. Students are preparing assessments to pass a degree course, but the purposes of the assessments are those of a discipline-specific discourse community. The next section discusses the purposes of the assessment texts and the stages they pass through, which was conceptualised using a socially defined approach to genre.

Genre

Genre has been defined in a variety of ways (Swales 1990, Bhatia 1993, Hyland 2004). To link the texts that students are expected to use to the academic discourse community requires a socially located approach to genre. The work within SFL provides such an approach:

> For us genre is a staged, goal-oriented social process
> - social because we participate in genres with other people
> - goal-oriented because we use genres to get things done
> - staged because it usually takes a few steps to reach our goals. (Rose and Martin 2003, *my bullet points*)

Genres are thus characterised by particular social criteria, for example, as being by someone, for someone, somewhere, at some time, and for a particular purpose. As communicative purposes become more complex so do the genres required to achieve them. The discourse community will see a text as being an example of a particular genre. An example of how a genre is laid out in this approach may help here. An exposition is identified as having a particular purpose: to persuade by arguing one side of an issue. To achieve this, it moves through a series of stages:

Thesis ^ Justification of Argument ^ Summary (^ = followed by).

Table 1 summarises an exposition as it was presented (with examples) to students.

Exposition to persuade by arguing one side of an issue.	
Position Statement	states the author's position on the issue to be argued and previews the arguments that will follow.
Justification of argument	states the arguments to be presented. An argument is comprised of a series of points and elaborations (support with evidence).
Summary	the final stage restates the author's position and sums up the arguments raised.

Table 1. Purpose and stages of an exposition

Paltridge (1994) contrasts this definition of genre with text-types, which are defined by text-internal criteria, for example:

Situation– problem– solution–evaluation

Thus, as genre, a letter arguing for traffic calming measures on a side street contains a sender's address, date, receiver's address, salutations, exposition, signature; as text-type it contains a situation – problem – solution – evaluation. Genre thus provides an account of context and an explanation of form. Expositions therefore enact a particular, but relatively simple, social context.

The types of extended, complex texts that are assessed as part of a university degree (documented essays, research reports, case studies, dissertations, critical reviews, document analyses) generally comprise series of these simple genres. Martin and Rose (2003) call complex texts macro-genres in contrast to micro-genres such as expositions. For example, a macro-genre such as a research report may contain several micro-genres (its chapters), and can be set out as follows:

> Abstract ^ Introduction ^ Literature Review ^ Methodology ^ Results ^
> Discussion ^ Conclusion ^ References ^ Appendices

The introduction section to a research report probably contains the stages outlined by Swales (1990). These stages may themselves contain micro-genres such as a recount of events, perhaps to give a historical context for a business case study. The stages can be set out as follows:

> General statement about field ^ Statements about particular topic ^ Establishing
> niche ^ (Aims) ^ (Thesis Statement) ^ (Definitions) ^ Report Preview
> Stages marked in brackets are optional.

Genres can thus be nested, one inside another, to achieve complex communicative purposes.

The critical next step in understanding genre is to match the stages of the genre to academic language. For example, students could be introduced to two ways of providing a definition. First, the familiar pattern, word–category–detail–use:

> Marketing is the management process which identifies, anticipates, and supplies
> customer requirements efficiently and profitably. (Chartered Institute of
> Marketing in Cannon 1992:3)

Alternatively, apposition:

> Marketing, a management process which …

So, from recognising the discourse community, selecting the macro-genres it employs and the micro-genres they use, we have moved to establishing the language features that can be brought to the students' attention. In constantly maintaining the link to a wider context, the teacher is given a rationale for teaching language features and maintains the focus on the communicative purpose of the text.

Content Information

Genre maps out the stages of a text and matches them to social purpose. Arguably, the stages are defined on grounds of their content rather than language (Paltridge 1994).

The content of a text must, of course, be packaged for the reader. Martin and Rose (2003) term the flow of information 'periodicity' and describe it in terms of waves. The smallest wave is the 'theme' of a clause, the starting point or thing that the clause is about, which is often simply the subject:

<u>Max</u> was eating rice.

A marked theme, such as a circumstantial adjunct, is often used to show a shift in time or place:

<u>At three o'clock</u>, he left the restaurant.

The rest of the clause is the 'rheme' and this often contains new information that will be picked up and developed in the following clause. A mid-level wave comes at the beginning of a paragraph in the topic sentence, or 'hyper-theme'. The largest wave of information comes in the introduction to a text, the 'macro-theme'. The process of packaging information not only focuses students on paragraph construction and coherence but also on reader expectations and the content of the discipline.

The flow of information was developed throughout the syllabus as a strand (see Figure 1 below). The work on recounts provides an accessible entry point packaging a chronology of events using a biography of a key figure. Clause themes refer to the figure (He studies … He completed …). Marked themes, such as circumstantial adjuncts of

time, show jumps (boundaries to the packaging) in the story (In
1948 ...). Different genres (argument, for example) exemplify different thematic developments and so a sensitivity to theme can be developed throughout a course. The work on theme in packaging information thus nicely complements the use of genre.

Table 2 below shows a schema of the different levels of the
syllabus design. Whether the teacher wishes to remain consistent to
the approach and use SFL terminology at the clause level or deploy
more familiar terms from pedagogical grammar is a further issue.

The discourse communities that our students form on the course
and the one they aspire to are those of final-year undergraduates and
MA / MBA students. Both share, as a significant macro-text, an
empirically-grounded research report. The format of a research report
is laid out in many business research books (see Saunders et al. 1997).
The course replicated the process of putting together such a report by
asking the students to complete a group project (Jordan 1997). Table 3
below shows how the micro-genres were covered over the two
semesters. Teaching most of the genres took more than one week (as
shown in brackets). Semester 1 was essentially a literature review
course, with three weeks named as such, as they focused on structural
points about the review and key skills such as quotation and citation.
At the beginning of Semester 2, students collected data using a
questionnaire to test hypotheses derived from the literature review.
The syllabus was arranged so that the teaching of a genre took place a
week before the students would be required to use it in the
independent construction phase of the teaching cycle (described in the
next section).

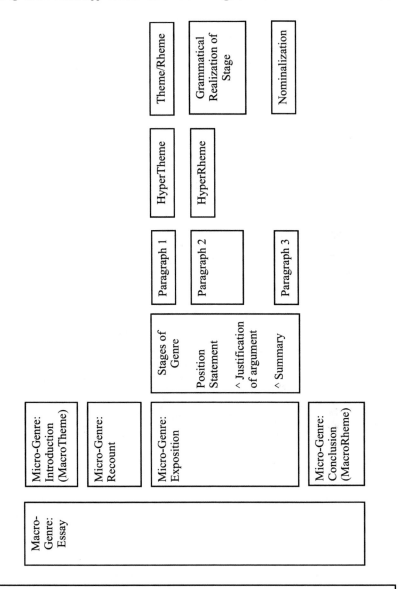

Table 2. Representation of the levels of syllabus design

Semester 1	Semester 2
Research Report (1)	Questionnaires (3)
Narrative (2)	Methodology
Recount (2)	Results
Literature Review (3)	Conclusion
Explanation (2)	Introduction
Exposition (2)	Abstract
Discussion (2)	Academic style *

* not a genre

Table 3. Micro-genres used in the syllabus

Teaching

The teaching and learning cycle (Rothery 1996) is well established in SFL accounts of classroom interaction (Martin 1999, Feez 2002, Macken-Horarik 2002, Ellis 2004). Figure 1 below shows the stages that the students pass through in the cycle. The first stage accesses content knowledge and vocabulary and the second provides models of the target genre, its purpose and stages.

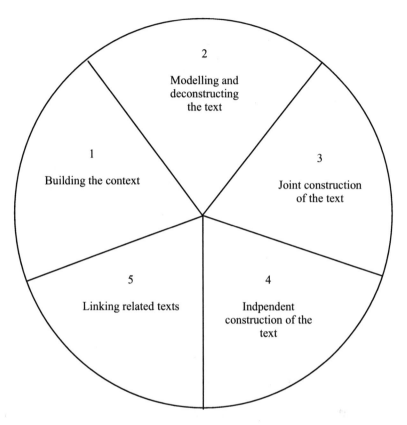

Figure 1. A teaching and learning cycle (From Feez 2002)

In the third stage, joint construction (or negotiation) of the text, students work together to produce a text in the target genre drawing on their shared knowledge. Then, in the fourth stage, students move on to independent construction of a text perhaps through a series of drafts. It is this stage that is timed to coincide with the students completing that part of the project work. The final stage offers students a chance to compare the target genre to others and recycle what they have learned earlier in the course. The teaching and learning cycle does not represent a revolution in classroom pedagogy; indeed, much of its strength is that it allows tried and tested classroom techniques to be subsumed within it.

Applying the learning and teaching cycle to our own course was relatively straightforward. The timetabling of a two-hour and a one-hour class formed spaces which seemed to fit the requirements of Stages 1 and 2 (two-hours) and Stage 3 (one-hour). Independent construction took place outside the classroom but was supported by a computer-based virtual learning environment (WebCT), which was used to transfer drafts and address problems on a discussion board. The process of drafting and redrafting a text improved the quality of the work but also reduced instances of plagiarism (the possibility of being detected by a peer seems to have acted as a deterrent).

Reactions

A number of features of the course emerged as challenges to the teachers. Three – choice of genre, terminology, and ability of students to analyse genre – are discussed below.

The decision regarding which genres to teach was a key consideration. The hierarchy of macro- and micro- genre helped here as macro-genres could be selected from the types of text students need for assessment purposes, and these could be matched with the micro-genres that they contain. However, other genres were added for pedagogical reasons. Narratives, for example, were used as they are familiar to students (starting with what they know) and can be exploited to highlight appraisal and evaluation in a text, issues which were recycled when covering a literature review. Once a set of genres has been chosen there is the problem of finding texts which exemplify them. The search becomes more time-consuming as the course is made more discipline-specific and the variety of examples is increased. A system whereby students had to find and label genres from their own reading, used as part of assessment, failed to produce a bank of materials, as the students tended to download simple genres such as recipes from the Internet. Nevertheless, developing sets of examples has proved worthwhile as a basis for future courses.

Genre analysis, and SFL in general, tends to be terminologically dense. Labels such as those given to a narrative (Abstract ^ Orientation ^ Complication ^ Evaluation ^ Resolution ^ Coda) were seen as overly technical by some teachers – 'we are not teaching linguistics' – who wished to simplify. However, metalanguage is seen by some practitioners as empowering and generative (Maken-Horarik 2002). The course retained SFL terminology and, so far, no students have complained about its use.concerns arose at the beginning of the course about how successfully students could identify the stages of a genre. Once students had the texts, sensitive classroom exploitation was required to get beyond the veil of content that they first encountered. Questions that first highlighted the meaning of a text and then went on to focus on picking out the stages helped. Similarly, activities such as sequencing slips of paper with parts of the text on them worked well. Concerns about how well students could analyse and label a text proved unjustified.

Conclusion

This paper has looked at one approach to using genre pedagogy on a university course. It has described how the idea of a discourse community can be employed along with those of macro- and micro-genres to tease out communicative purposes and develop a genre-based syllabus. The syllabus was combined with a learning and teaching cycle embedded within project work. Finally, problems with selection, terminology and student analysis were addressed.

The advantages that flow from an application of these ideas have been stressed rather than an analysis of their theoretical underpinnings. The developers of this course continue to benefit from both the struggle with, and the application and misapplication of, genre theory and Systemic Functional Linguistics.

Bibliography

Bhatia, V.K. (1993) *Analysing genre: language use in professional settings*. London: Longman.

Borg, E. (2003) 'Key concepts in ELT: discourse community'. *ELT Journal*, 57/4, 398–400.

Butt, D., Spinks, S. and Yallop, C. (2000) *Using functional grammar: an explorer's guide*. Sydney: Macquarie University.

Cox, K. and Hill, D. (2004) *EAP Now! English for academic purposes: student's book*. New South Wales: Pearson Longman, Australia.

Dudley-Evans, T. and St. John, M.J. (1998) *Developments in English for specific purposes: a multi-disciplinary approach*. Cambridge: Cambridge University Press.

Ellis, E.A. (2004) 'Supporting genre-based literacy pedagogy with technology – the implications for the framework and classification of pedagogy' in Ravelli, L.J. and Ellis, R.A. (eds) *Analysing academic writing: contextualised frameworks*, 210–52. London: Continuum.

Feez, S. (2002) 'Heritage and innovation in second language education' in Johns, A.M. (ed.) *Genre in the classroom: multiple perspectives*, 43–71. Mahwah, New Jersey: Lawrence Erlbaum Associates.

Hyland, K. (2004) *Genre and second language writing*. Ann Arbor, Michigan: The University of Michigan Press.

Jordan, R.R. (1997) *English for academic purposes: a guide and resource book for teachers*. Cambridge: Cambridge University Press.

Macken-Horarik, M. (2002) '"Something to shoot for": a systemic functional approach to teaching genre in secondary school science' in Johns, A.M. (ed.) *Genre in the classroom: multiple perspectives*, 17–42. Mahwah, New Jersey: Lawrence Erlbaum Associates.

Martin, J.R. (1999) 'Mentoring semogenesis: 'genre-based' literacy pedagogy' in Christie, F. (ed.) *Pedagogy and the shaping of consciousness: linguistic and social processes*, 123–55. London: Continuum.

—— and Rose, D. (2003) *Working with discourse: meaning beyond the clause*. London: Continuum.

Paltridge, B. (1994) 'Genre analysis and the identification of textual boundaries'. *Applied Linguistics*, 15/3, 288–99.

Rothery, J. (1994) *Exploring literacy in school English*. Sydney: Metropolitan East Disadvantaged Schools Program, NSW Department of School Education.

Saunders, M., Lewis, P. and Thornhill, A. (1997) *Research methods for business students*. London: Pitman.

Swales, J.M. (1990) *Genre analysis: English in academic and research settings*. Cambridge: Cambridge University Press.

Section III

Modes of Delivery

DAVID CATTERICK

10 Teaching or Coaching? Reflecting on Roles and Objectives in One-to-one EAP

Background

Part-time English for Academic Purposes (EAP) courses are typically populated by international students who see targeted language and study skills support as a means of reaching a strategic goal such as giving an academic presentation or writing an assignment, leading to the ultimate goal of gaining a degree. While most EAP teaching traditionally occurs in group settings, at the University of Dundee there was recently a growth in demand for one-to-one provision from non-native English speaking (NNS) academic members of staff. This paper explores the development of a conceptual tool and presents feedback about the resulting instruction from the members of staff. The conceptual tool, the one-to-one continuum, spans the spectrum of two very different approaches: group instruction and academic coaching. In practical terms this means consciously situating the various frame factors (roles, objectives, materials, dynamics and length) along the one-to-one continuum between the poles of group instruction and academic coaching to create an appropriate teaching context.

The Frame of Reference

Before considering the tool, it is important to understand the challenge which resulted in its creation, namely the absence of an adequate frame of reference for one-to-one instruction. A frame of reference is

> [a] mental map used by a decision maker to make sense of events. Frames are both windows on the world and lenses to bring the world into focus. ('Strategic Leadership and Decision Making', n.d.)

Many EAP teachers have a well-developed frame of reference for group instruction simply by virtue of the fact that the majority of EAP teaching takes that form but they frequently have a much less-developed mental map for one-to-one instruction. The author's own frame of reference for group instruction comprised five distinct factors. The difference in the two frames of reference became clear when the five factors were compared for each mode of instruction. The following chart shows the clear gap.

	Group instruction	One-to-one EAP
Factor 1: Objectives	prescribed	
Factor 2: Materials	prepared	
Factor 3: Participant roles	predefined	?
Factor 4: Session dynamics	predictable	
Factor 5: Course length	predetermined	

Figure 1. Frame of reference factors

Research Context

In order to fill the gap, a review of literature on the topic of one-to-one instruction was undertaken. The most reflective and revealing data seemed to come from US-based research on the conduct of tutorials in

Writing Centers. This research seemed promising as it was a context similar to that of one-to-one EAP instruction. What became clear was that the practitioners in this context also seemed to be struggling to find an 'adequate frame for tutorials with NNSs' (Thonus 2004:239). Thonus herself points to ongoing challenges connected particularly with NNSs accessing the Writing Center services. She specifically focuses on the challenges connected with locus of control, tutor roles and student-tutor discourse (2004:228 and 236–7).

Though one-to-one teaching is well-established in the world of ELT, research on the topic is quite scant. Wilberg (2002) in his introduction to one of the few books specifically focusing on one-to-one language training even goes so far as to suggest that one-to-one teaching 'is the least discussed subject in language teaching theory' (2002:iii). Where studies do exist, they tend to question the effectiveness of one-to-one instruction in content areas with which the tutor has little or no familiarity (Shaw 1996). Shaw's doubts are based on evidence from his own experiences in tutoring situations and he concludes that the type of input he provided was unlikely to positively influence the student's language.

With the literature review failing to inform the frame of reference, the author decided to develop his own conceptual framework to serve as a decision-making tool for one-to-one EAP.

Definition of Terms

Before examining the development of the tool, some of the terms used in this paper need to be defined.

One-to-one teaching

One-to-one teaching in EAP can be seen as an instructional approach broadly similar in style to group teaching but with different dynamics (given the absence of the group) and more specific objectives (remediation or addressing very individualised needs to allow for more accelerated learning). It would seem that this instructional approach is very much the default one, with the EAP teacher typically taking the techniques from the group classroom and applying them to a single learner context while consciously compensating for differences in group dynamics and the more limited strategies available.

Academic coaching

Academic coaching (as distinct from peer or executive coaching) is a term the author uses to mean a one-to-one collaborative partnership between client and coach in which the coach provides targeted support in order to enhance the specific academic and/or professional skills of the client in the context of a clearly-identified goal (or goals).

Differences Between One-to-one Teaching and Academic Coaching

In order to fully grasp the theoretical differences between one-to-one teaching and academic coaching, we need to be able to conceptualise the relationship between them. One-to-one teaching and academic coaching do not form a duality but are rather poles at either end of a continuum.

One-to-one teaching ←------------------------------→ Academic coaching

The tutor, consciously or otherwise, situates their teaching approach somewhere on the continuum between one-to-one teaching and academic coaching. How this works in practice will be explored in the rest of the paper.

Five Factors and the One-to-one Continuum

1. Participant roles

Teacher/Student   ⬅--------------------------------------➡ Coach/Client

Much attention has been given in general education over the past thirty years to the notion of andragogy which distinguishes between the needs of children in an educational setting (the strict understanding of the term pedagogy) and the needs of adults (andragogy). One-to-one teaching is typically embedded in a pedagogical paradigm. The resulting hierarchical structure means that even when the student happens to be a member of staff, the interaction between teacher and staff member defaults to a teacher-student one. In this authoritarian hierarchy, the tutee typically defers to the expertise and insight of the tutor (Thonus 2004:235–6). The nature of this hierarchy is evidenced by studies of the types of discourse used in tutoring sessions. Thonus, in a review of the literature on the discourse of tutoring sessions points out that these sessions

> share certain features with other institutional discourse types such as medical consultations [...] health-visitor interactions [...] and psychotherapy sessions [...] Tutorials also resemble certain academic discourse genres such as advising interviews [and ...] counseling sessions. (2002:111)

The fact that similarities are drawn between the discourse style of tutoring sessions and consulting or counselling sessions further serves to emphasise the hierarchical divisions. Academic coaching stands in contrast to the other two approaches because the relationship between the participants is typically more egalitarian and modeled on a peer-professional relationship rather than a teacher-student or indeed a tutor-tutee one. This means that even when the client is a student, the teacher can identify the relationship as a peer-professional one (fellow-writer, fellow-researcher, fellow-presenter) and this paradigm can be integrated into the discourse of the sessions, for example, 'In my own writing ... '. Because the distance between coach and client is narrower than between teacher and student, coaching can lead to closer identification between client and coach. Though this can have a positive influence on affective factors and greatly enhance motivation, there may be a danger of creating a culture of dependency. This suggests the need for frequent monitoring of the coach-client relationship based on an intuitive awareness of interactional dynamics.

2. Objectives

Skills/Knowledge ←--------------------------------→ Affective concerns

In one-to-one teaching, objectives are typically the product of a student's own stated needs and/or the result of a formal needs analysis. While this is also largely the case in coaching, one key difference lies in the fact that stated objectives in one-to-one teaching tend to have more of a purely skills-based or knowledge-based emphasis. This can be seen in Straker's (2004) article on what makes a good EAP tutorial; he lists the objectives in the form of items for feedback of one-to-one tutoring for a written assignment. The fifteen items in Straker's list (ranging from checking bibliographies and referencing to saying if arguments are adequately supported) underscore what can only be termed a tick-box approach to the sessions. Thonus (2004) also points to a fundamental dilemma for tutors in one-to-one writing consultations citing the fact that while tutor training manuals promote the concept of the tutee setting session objectives, in real-life consultations it is frequently the tutor who sets the agenda.

All of this is in contrast to academic coaching which tends to adopt a more holistic approach giving equal validity to the wider needs of the client. For example, if the client is noticeably discouraged by reviewers' comments on a recent paper, time can be given in the coaching session to analysing the feedback in order to help restore the client's confidence. Though in one-to-one teaching such intervention may possibly still be seen as a side-track or diversion and difficult to justify in terms of the stated instructional objectives, in academic coaching this is much less an issue as the affective domain is incorporated into the session objectives. One further difference is that a coach tends to closely identify with the client's objectives to the extent that the client's successes and failures become the coach's own. Coaching is less about working one's way through an instructional programme; it is a much more organic, fluid response to the client's needs.

3. Materials

Published/Off the shelf ←--------------------------------→ Derived

The past few years have seen increasing debate on the role of materials in the ELT classroom. Thornbury and Meddings' (2001) advocacy of what Thornbury has termed the dogme or materials-free approach to classroom teaching seems to be making the ELT community reconsider the central role played by instructional materials. In a one-to-one teaching context, while a teacher might use off-the-shelf materials or even a pre-prepared syllabus for the teaching sessions, the more overtly individualised nature of academic coaching means that the coach is more likely to create session materials based on the client's own output. For example, in a one-to-one session with the objective of preparing a series of articles for publication in a professional journal, input required on presenting data in a visual format would be developed from the client's own output rather than simply reaching for published materials or other sample data. This gives the coaching a more tailored feel and also helps overcome the teacher-student hierarchical model implicit in so many coursebooks. Creation of content can, of course, be time-consuming for the coach, but time spent working with the client's output fosters a very useful familiarity with the knowledge, ideas and arguments that matter most to the client. This is not to suggest, however, that there is no place for published materials in coaching. Published materials can be a valuable adjunct to the content of the sessions if carefully targeted. As with all these factors, what is needed is to consciously situate the approach to materials on the continuum.

4. Session dynamics

Programmed/Lock step ←-------------------------------→ Flexible/Individual

A straw-poll of ELT professionals would no doubt show a significant preference for group teaching over one-to-one. One of the reasons for this is classroom dynamics. In group teaching, it is generally easier to foster a classroom dynamic which creates more interesting interaction than the linearity of the one-to-one classroom. However, in coaching the dialogue between coach and client is not perceived in deficit terms of compensating for poor dynamics. Though the dynamic cannot of course be anything other than linear, it can be multi-level, working as it does equally on the instructional and the relational levels. Thonus' (2002) study provides evidence of the need for multi-level, interactional dynamics. Among the seven features of interaction she identifies as leading to sessions being evaluated as successful, a significant number of these operate on what may be seen as the relational level:

- The tutor speaks from their own experience as a writer
- The tutor actively distances themselves from the supervisor role
- The authority and expertise of the tutor is not debated
- The tutor and tutee assessments of the writing agree
- Turn-taking is closer to social discourse than the question and answer discourse style of a service encounter
- There is a high incidence of social discourse features such as volubility, overlaps, backchannels and laughter
- There is evidence of intersubjectivity with the tutor and tutee understanding one another's intent.

(Thonus 2002)

5. Course length

Pre-determined ←------------------------------→ Determined by client needs

The length of a one-to-one teaching programme is typically determined in one of two ways. In many contexts the length and number of sessions is decided from the outset based on a balance between an expert estimate of the time taken to reach the agreed objectives and the budget of the client's sponsor. In other contexts such as drop-in EAP tutorial sessions the allocation of time is limited by the standard policy on provision. With academic coaching, in spite of the setting of financial constraints by sponsors and other stakeholders the commitment fostered in coaching tends to generate more extensions to the initial allocation. In one academic coaching session described below, what was originally supposed to be a one semester, 1.5 hours a week coaching session was extended three times taking it into two years of continuous input. Though it is probably unlikely that in academic coaching sessions the client is a financial decision-maker, there is clearly a great advantage for the client to have some sort of influence over the finances, as might be the case if they are a member of academic staff.

The One-to-one Continuum in Practice

This second part of the paper will focus on two case studies of one-to-one teaching taken from sessions with members of staff at the University of Dundee.

Subjects

The profile of the subjects is outlined in the table below. As can be seen there are numerous contrasts between the two clients.

	Client A	Client B
Status	Staff (research, non-teaching)	Staff (research, teaching)
Gender	Male	Female
Ethnicity	European	Asian
English language status	NNS	NNS
Departmental profile	Medicine/Health care	Law/Business
Session hours at point of survey	58	15
Session focus	Presentation skills, Thesis writing	Research writing, Preparing an academic book for publication

Figure 2. Client profile

Methods

Visual analogue scales, a 'measurement instrument used to measure a characteristic or attitude that is believed to range across a continuum' (Crichton 2001:706) were created based on the first four of the five factors. The scales were given to the clients at the end of one of the later sessions and they were asked to mark two points on each scale:

[O] = Their own view of the *optimum* point on the continuum where they think the sessions would be most effective.

[A] = Their own view of the *actual* place on the continuum based on their experiences of the sessions.

The clients were given as much time as they required to place their marks and they were free to seek clarification. When the clients had finished, they were asked to comment on the rationale for their answers and the resulting prompted monologue was audio recorded. The descriptive data from the scales were then matched against the one-to-one continuum and the recordings were examined with key sections transcribed for more detailed analysis.

Results/Discussion

An analysis of the recordings revealed both similarities of opinion between the two clients and contrasting ones.

1. Roles

Client A referred in a positive way to clear differences between pedagogical and andragogical approaches:

> We successfully combined both the roles as teacher to learner and as fellow-academic to fellow-academic... in terms of the discussion and in terms of my feelings... I felt like another academic with his experiences, with his problems and with his difficulties.

Client B commented on her preconceptions about roles prior to the start of the sessions and how her thoughts changed once the sessions had begun:

> When we started... I regarded you as a teacher and I was going to learn some language stuff from you but I knew on the other hand that we couldn't be real teacher and student in that way so I was expecting the way maybe we have this.

2. Objectives

A similar contrast between prior expectation and eventual experience emerged in Client A's responses to the question of objectives. The client assumed that the session would simply be grammar-focused but then as early as the first session recognised the importance of affective factors:

> Before starting... I had in my mind that it would be another grammar class... a boring activity. ... I remember from the very first session... what encouraged me... was your answer to my question, 'Is there any hope?'... At the beginning I thought okay he is being encouraging because first it is his job and second, you know, the money is there... But then I realised there is a hope.

In contrast, Client B seemed to downplay the significance of the affective aspects of the sessions choosing instead to focus on the instructive agenda:

> The objective for me was to say I improved my language skills a lot but I knew that was hard to reach… Psychologically I got support but I did learn a lot from the tuition.

Though these differences might also be viewed as being culturally-influenced, individual differences are probably also a factor.

3. Materials

Client A stated a clear preference for materials created from his own writing. He presented the reason for this preference in the following way:

> I prefer to go back to my materials to see okay I write this in 1999 now how can I write this again in 2004 and what is the difference because the difference is so huge and I'm so happy.

Client B confessed to being confused before the start of the sessions why copies of her own writing were being requested:

> At the first place when you asked me for my chapters I thought you just try to find my problems.

She goes on to give her reaction when she realised how her writing was eventually used:

> But later I found you almost entirely base [the sessions] on my writings and you raise different problems really much broader than I expected.

4. Session dynamics

Both clients classified the sessions as relaxed and seem to associate it with enjoyment:

> I feel relaxed and I really enjoyed the whole session like you told me where the problems are but it's like you are relaxed which made me feel comfortable.

What Client B seems to be suggesting is that the teacher is setting the tone of the sessions which in turn impacts on the overall atmosphere in the sessions. Client A suggested that the measure of success in sessions is less to do with meeting task objectives and more connected with personal interaction:

> The personal interaction... is tremendously important. I have been with so many teachers, professors, academic staff... and very few have impacted my knowledge just because the vast majority of them had *a different task from my task* [my italics]. Their task was not to see the improvement in my knowledge but to tell some things then go to another class. This made the learning process, you know, a manufacturing event.

Client A seemed to see the session dynamics more as being the product of a collaborative approach (note the use of 'we') rather than a tone being set and suggests that the dynamics arose out of a shared value (learning as a personalised activity).

Conclusion

There is a need for further research into one-to-one EAP teaching and it is hoped that this paper will foster this. Above all, though, it is hoped that teachers who like the author lacked a frame of reference for one-to-one instruction, will find the notion of a continuum helpful and, in particular, that they will be more able to consciously adapt their teaching approach to fully meet the needs and expectations of the client.

Bibliography

Crichton, N. (2001) 'Visual analogue scale (VAS)'. *Journal of Clinical Nursing*, 10/5, 706.

Hewings, M. and Dudley-Evans, T. (eds) (1996) *Evaluation and course design in EAP*. Hemel Hemstead: Phoenix ELT.

Shaw, P. (1996) 'One-to-one work on dissertations: effectiveness of correction and efficiency of pedagogy' in Hewings, M. and Dudley-Evans, T (eds), 86–95.

Straker, J. (ed.) (2004) 'What makes a good EAP tutorial?' in Sheldon, L.E. (ed.) (2004) *Directions for the Future: Issues in English for Academic Purposes,* 127–36. Bern: Peter Lang AG.

Strategic Leadership and Decision Making. n.d. [http://www.au.af.mil/au/awc/awcgate/ndu/stratldrdm/pt3ch11.html] Retrieved 31/3/2005.

Thonus, T. (2002) 'Tutor and student assessments of academic writing tutorials: what is "success"?' *Assessing Writing*, 8, 110–34.

—— (2004) 'What are the differences? Tutor interactions with first- and second-language writers'. *Journal of Second Language Writing*, 13, 227–42.

Thornbury, S. and L. Meddings. (2001) 'Using the raw materials: a 'dogme' approach to teaching language'. *Modern English Teacher,* 10/4, 40–3.

Wilberg, P. (2002) *One to one: a teacher's handbook.* London: Heinle.

ANN SMITH

11 Developing Critical Awareness through Case-based Teaching

Case-based teaching prepares students for seminar discussions by engaging them in a reflective, interactive approach, which develops critical awareness, discussion skills and cooperative team work. Case materials introduce issues within an authentic socio-cultural context, which encourages learners to contribute their own knowledge and experience to the discussion.

Cases focus students' attention on simulations of real life situations, which are less predictable than most textbook examples. 'A typical case is a written narrative of some real life event, situation, or experience centred in a problem or issue faced by a person, group of persons, organisation, community, or even an entire society.' (Hachen, n.d.)

Case-based teaching is now popular in many disciplines, from business to law and medicine. However, it is not always familiar to students, especially international students. For example, most Asian students are used to a traditional, teacher-led classroom with large numbers of students following a textbook. They are often unfamiliar with group discussion and not used to giving and supporting their own opinions.

It is time for EAP practitioners to consider a number of questions relating to case-based teaching. Firstly, why use case-based teaching in EAP courses and EAP teacher development? Secondly, what characterises good cases and how can they be used effectively in EAP classrooms? Finally, how can Asian students make the transition to this cooperative, participatory learning style?

Why use Case-based Teaching in EAP?

Case-based teaching has been used extensively in many disciplines to make connections between practice and underlying theory and to encourage reflection and analysis of real life dilemmas in professional development. During the case analysis, students cooperate and communicate in order to reflect, analyse or problem-solve. For Boehrer (1994) 'The result is students' increased capacity, for example to sort information, analyse it, see alternatives, make a choice.'

Developing critical awareness and using problem-solving approaches fits well with learner-centred, task-based approaches to EAP in which the teacher does not present, but engages the learners in a deeper analysis rather than surface overview. 'A critical perspective then, is not taking for granted, or accepting facts as given, but rather maintaining a questioning stance' (Keily 2004:214). In fact a range of terms relating to critical analysis frequently occur throughout the literature on case based teaching. Students are expected to question, explore, analyse, interpret context, synthesise sources, make connections, share ideas and opinions, restructure and rethink. When solving a problem they are expected to speculate, question, evaluate alternatives, assess advantages and disadvantages, reflect and come to consensus.

Because a case is situated in a real context, it encourages learners to draw on their experience and their own context/cultural background knowledge to interpret the situation. Then they share their opinions, elaborate on their ideas and state their preferences. Kumaravadivelu (2001:537) agrees that 'a post method pedagogy must […] tap into the socio political consciousness that participants bring with them in order to aid their quest for identity formation and social transformation.' In addition, students can learn to respect and build on the diverse opinions of others and may rethink and even restructure their own point of view.

Cases are also particularly relevant for developing face-to-face interpersonal discussion, as participants have to interact responsibly, listen actively, voice opinions, support opinions, question others and build on the ideas of others. These discussions will help students gain confidence, extend sociolinguistic competence and strategic competence and overcome the typical difficulties faced by international students identified by Kennedy and Bolitho (1984 in Jordan 1990). These include understanding English spoken rapidly, trying to quickly phrase an idea or contribution and overcoming shyness or frustration.

> Students recognise the importance of such things as: listening, clarifying statements and providing feedback; keeping discussions on task; probing assumptions and evidence; eliciting viewpoints and perspectives; mediating conflicts and summarising and presenting findings. (Cooperative learning 1999)

In the final presentation, students aim to communicate their ideas coherently to an audience both orally and in writing.

Group cooperation and teamwork is essential for successful case analysis. The genuine situation requires students to work together to identify the key issues, share perspectives and generate alternatives. According to Ehrman and Dornyei (1998:253) this cooperation promotes language learning and 'not only enhances peer interaction and the emergence of cohesive groups but also directly increases individual student motivation to learn.' This in turn brings an increase in commitment and responsibility to the group, which develops positive interdependence and thus more willingness to share personal and professional experience. This commitment should also increase the learner's sense of group belonging and learning responsibility en route to learning autonomy.

What Characterises Good Cases and How can they be Used Effectively in EAP Classrooms?

Although there are criteria for writing good case studies, there appears to be no perfect case study formula, because every group of students has different needs and a different context. Case studies may vary in a number of ways: source, length (mini cases to 40 pages), complexity, format (print/multi-media), authenticity (real/fictitious), and style (narrative/dialogue/facts and figures). Generally cases should follow a relevant, recent significant or controversial topic which is interesting, engaging, and universal 'At the heart of case-based learning is the exploration and analysis of a real-life, problem-based event, or case' (Jackson and Smith 1992).

There are many types of cases, but three types are considered here. Perhaps the most familiar is the problem solving case, which presents a dilemma; the students identify the problem, analyse the causes and possible solutions and decide on an appropriate solution. The second type of case encourages reflection through consideration of real experiences and is now frequently used in teacher education. The third type provides an example of best practice or effective teaching, which can be analysed. In fact there are many more variations but there appears to be no best case study, as most teachers need to adapt or create their own cases tailored to meet the specific content and language needs of the group involved.

Although most cases follow the twists and turns of an authentic socio-cultural context, some case writers prepare composite cases. These combine components from various typical situations with characters that appear realistic and feasible. In such a vignette or fictitious case, the challenge is that 'the characters, situations and dilemmas must ring true' in order to engage the students (Christudason 2003:1).

So when writing an EAP case where should the teacher begin? Guceri and Akin (1998) suggest you should consider the time frame, level of difficulty, cultural framework, topic, tasks and the course objectives. Firstly think about your objectives: what you want the students to learn and what they know already. Then select an interesting controversial topic or ethical question relevant to your course or student interests. This will involve background research, as it should be plausible. Next, decide which type of case to write and introduce the main characters (who), the context (where), the timeline (when) and the events (what). It should have a clear purpose, raise issues open to various interpretations and offer some uncertainty or some difficult choices with enough detail for a full picture.

Once written, pilot the case, so you introduce sufficient detail and some ambiguity. Owenby (1992 in Reichelt 2000:350) advises cases be 'both compete and mysterious, offering enough information for readers to be able to respond to the case study, but also leaving the case open enough to arouse interest.' The final vital component is to create a few, rather than too many, well focused open-ended questions to direct students' attention to particular features or broaden the discussion. Finish by developing a consistent format for student handouts and teaching notes. According to Wrage (1994:22) the best cases are 'brief, well written, well focused, full of conflict, exciting to students, susceptible to analysis from more than one direction and sufficiently complete in themselves to require little extra factual elaboration'.

In the EAP classroom, cases fit well into a task-based framework following a pre case phase, case analysis and post case summary and feedback. Initially the pre-case phase involves introducing the case study, providing a rationale and exploring the students' prior knowledge and experience of the topic. This can be done through activities such as brainstorming for ideas and developing key topic vocabulary. Students also need various elements of language necessary for seminar discussions and for case analysis. In the case phase, the teacher groups the students, introduces the procedures, the case reading and the discussion questions. Students need clear instructions for the activity. Finally, close by summarising the key points raised, reviewing features from the discussion phase in conjunction with consolidation activities and offering comments on the group dynamics. Boehrer (1994:6) recommends teachers avoid giving an authoritative answer to the case as 'good group discussions spill over into the halls and the dorms'.

It is essential to ensure students have the language they need for participation in a case discussion. This goes well beyond basic classroom language, as students need specific language functions to give opinions, support points, agree or disagree, praise or follow up good ideas, persuade and much more. In addition, it requires language to identify causes of problems, speculate about possible effects and evaluate solutions. Moreover, communication skills such as turn taking skills and interrupting appropriately need some practise, which takes time and involvement.

It is also important to outline the expectations of the group discussion and set group ground rules. Factors such as friendships, status, approval and power relations will all influence group dynamics during the group process. Jackson (1998:62) agrees that

> there must be a climate of trust and respect; students must feel secure enough to express ideas that differ from those of their colleagues and explore new ways of thinking about an issue. Heterogeneous groups, rather than random or homogeneous groups, are frequently promoted for effective cooperative group or project work and produce more effective case discussion, providing all are expected to participate.

The role of the teacher or facilitator changes as the lessons progress and the teacher actually plays a variety of roles. During the case phase, the teacher becomes a cooperative facilitator and developer of critical awareness. She or he needs to play an active role as a catalyst, supporter, guide and prompter to explore avenues and create links in the discussion that might otherwise be overlooked. Students can be encouraged to engage with the cultural implications embedded in the case material and explore culture bound beliefs and assumptions within a safe classroom environment. In addition, the teacher needs to be patient and tolerant and accept the students' opinions as valid. She or he can request further context, reasons or support for the view rather than simply reacting to the language being used.

How can Practitioners Help Asian Students Make the Transition to this Cooperative, Participatory Learning Style?

Most Asian learners are used to large classes and a traditional lecture based system that follows the textbook (Brick 2004). So it is important to introduce case-based learning as part of an approach to education used in seminar discussions and professional training. Teachers should explain the rationale carefully and develop students' awareness of the connection between theory and applied practice created during case analysis and critical thinking. In addition, they should encourage student involvement, independent study and responsibility in the group. This will assist in building English language skills and the confidence needed to communicate and problem solve more effectively.

Many Asian learners may be unused to working in groups in the classroom and prefer to work alone. It is important to group learners into heterogeneous, multicultural groups whenever possible in order to develop group cohesiveness, friendship and support as well as cross-cultural understanding. In addition, teachers should stress the import-ance of group interdependence, and give a group mark and shared feedback, otherwise learners will divide up the task and work indivi-dually. Group ground rules should be agreed, stressing the need to be supportive rather than competitive and excluding phrases such as 'You're wrong!'

The role of the teacher in Asia is generally hierarchical. As Scollan and Scollan point out (1994 in Ho and Crookall 1995) the authority of the Asian teacher tends to be more caring and benevolent, whereas Western teachers tend to be more restricting. Asian students will seldom challenge the teacher's authority and frequently look to the teacher for the right answer. As cases offer a range of possible options, but no right answers, students may feel frustrated. Therefore the teacher should withhold an opinion on the case, otherwise Asian students will generally follow the teacher's point of view.

Asian learners seldom speak in English classes in their own countries so many students are not used to giving and supporting their own opinions. Although in seminars all participants are expected to express opinions, Asian students often express frustration at having to listen to various opinions or preferences presented by classmates. They may be reluctant to disagree with or challenge classmates' opinions, as direct confrontation is generally unacceptable (Ho and Crookall 1995). So teachers need to encourage classmates to listen carefully and teach the language to question, express constructive comment, tentative agreement and reservations.

Finally, encourage Asian learners to self-monitor their own language learning during the discussions, as they tend to rely on the teacher to provide feedback and correction (Brick 2004). They often also say that speaking to other students means they pick up their errors. It is essential to point out that this is seldom the case and group discussion is important for developing communication strategies and sharing views in seminar discussions (Flowerdew 1998). If typical errors are highlighted before the discussion, learners can be encouraged to listen for these errors and work on practice and correction.

Conclusion

Case-based teaching can help students develop seminar discussion skills and critical awareness, as cases can be used with students at all levels providing they are carefully introduced. Students can engage in a process of case analysis and communication which allows them to share their opinions and life experiences. Although few prepared cases are really appropriate for students' interests or needs, being too long or too culturally specific, most teachers will find the time invested in adapting or creating their own cases pays dividends in terms of student engagement, interaction and critical awareness.

Bibliography

Boehrer, J. (1994) 'On teaching a good case'. *International Studies Notes*, 19/2, 13–19.

Brick, J. (2004) *China: a handbook of intercultural communication.* 2nd ed. Sydney, Australia: Macquarie University.

Christudason, A. (2003) *A case for case-based learning. Ideas on teaching, 1.* [http://www.cdtl.nus.edu.sg/ideas/iot24.htm] Retrieved 7/03/6.

Cooperative learning: students working in small groups. *Speaking of Teaching*, 10/2, Winter 1999, 1–4. [http://ctl.stanford.edu/teach/speak/stwin99.pdf] Retrieved 7/03/6.

Ehrman, M.E. and Dornyei, Z. (1998) *Interpersonal dynamics in second language education.* London: Sage Publications.

Flowerdew, L. (1998) 'A cultural perspective on group work'. *English Language Teaching Journal,* 52/4, 323–9.

Guceri, M. and Akin, A.R. (1998) 'Case studies in education'. *Forum,* 36/4, 18–24. [http://exchanges.state.gov/forum/vols/vol36/no4/p18.htm] Retrieved 07/03/06.

Hachen, D. 'What is a Case? Sociology Cases Database Project'. [http//www.nd.edu/~dhachen/cases/define.html] Retrieved 07/03/06.

Ho, J. and Crookall, D. (1995) 'Breaking with Chinese cultural traditions: learner autonomy in English language teaching'. *System,* 23/2, 235–43.

Jackson, J. (1998) *Cross-cultural teaching cases: vehicles for teacher development.* Proceedings of the 1998 Korea TESOL Conference, March 1999, 59–66.

—— and Smith, A.F.V. (1996) *The art of case-based teaching in Asia: from ESP business to tourism.* Thai TESOL Conference Proceedings, 9, Bangkok, Thailand.

Jordan, R.R. (1990) 'Pyramid discussions'. *English Language Teaching Journal,* 44/1, 46–54.

Keily, R. (2004) 'Learning to critique in EAP'. *Journal of English for Academic Purposes,* 3, 211–27.

Kumaravadivelu, B. (2001) 'Towards a postmethod pedagogy'. *TESOL Quarterly,* 35/4, 537–60.

Reichelt, M. (2000) 'Case studies in L2 teacher education'. *English Language Teaching Journal,* 54/4, 346–53.

Wrage, S.D. (1994) 'Best case analysis: what makes a good case and where to find the one you need'. *International Studies Notes,* 19/2, 21–7.

ALISON STEWART

12 Using Communities of Practice in Academic Writing Instruction in Japan

The concept of 'community' has been enormously influential in the fields of sociolinguistics, following Dell Hymes' (1972) 'speech communities', an influence which has made itself felt also in English for Academic Purposes. Given that formal education brings together large groups of people with common interests and purposes, it would appear that an understanding and deployment of this concept should be helpful in enabling us to devise ways of optimising student learning of academic practices, such as writing.

However, whereas Hymes' speech communities have been widely accepted, applying the concept of community to academic writing has proven to be quite problematic. Some have noted that the academic discourse community to which students are supposed to claim membership in their writing is not a real community at all, but rather is rhetorical (Bizzell 1992) or imagined (Spack 1998). Others have sought to make the academic discourse community more concrete. For example, John Swales' (1990) concept of discourse community justifies an analysis of genres in actual texts as an instructional method (Swales and Feak 1994). More pragmatically still, Ann Johns (1997) argues that the discourse community should be narrowed down to very specific contexts, such as a single classroom or professor, since it is only in such concrete settings that the practices that students are expected to adopt can be made explicit. Johnson (2000) also takes issue with the tendency for much academic practice to be implicit and intuitive. Arguing that the structure of the academic setting limits the extent to which academics (including students) are able to share and develop a culture of practice, he proposes a reorganisation of the setting to create a functioning community of practice.

This paper describes an academic writing course for English majors at a Japanese university, which was designed with the aim of creating just such a community, and examines, through the comments of the students who took the course, the benefits and limitations of using such a model in the Japanese higher educational context.

Communities of Practice

The term, community of practice, was coined and first theorised by Jean Lave and Etienne Wenger (1991) in their examination of how learners outside of formal educational institutions become inducted into particular practices or discourses through a process of apprenticeship and then go on to become expert practitioners themselves. Some of the examples they gave were true apprenticeships, that is, novices working and learning under the tutelage of an expert practitioner, for example, an apprentice tailor in West Africa, or midwives in Mexico. Others were novices in highly technical working practices, such as naval navigators, or in discourses of recovery and life-enhancement, such as Alcoholics Anonymous. What all of these have in common is the engagement of the most junior members in real practice and the transformative power of the community on the individual.

In a subsequent work, Wenger (1998) used his observations of daily working life inside the medical claims processing unit of a large insurance company to elaborate further on the concept of community of practice. The key characteristics of such communities are that they are groups of people who are mutually engaged in a common purpose and who share a common repertoire of knowledge, discourses and practices. Contrary to discourse or rhetorical communities, communities of practice depend on physical proximity. Although the primary reason for social interaction is the joint enterprise in which the members of a community of practice are engaged, members also interact in ways that enhance the sense of community, but have little to do with that enterprise directly.

It may be argued that any classroom could be termed a community of practice to the extent that the teacher and students are mutually engaged in the common purpose of negotiating a syllabus. However, the task of writing in academic contexts is one that is generally assigned to individuals alone. Moreover, despite the practices of peer editing and shared repertoires of knowledge, associated with process writing, – discourses and practices that have been explicitly taught or have developed through pre-writing discussion – there is little real sense of mutual accountability or investment in what is produced by individual students. The question here is does a different and better kind of learning occur where there is mutual accountability for and investment in the writing assignment?

The Joint Writing Assignment

The academic writing class described in this paper is an elective two-semester course meeting once a week for ninety minutes. The first semester of the course consisted of a review of basic features of academic writing, which covered form (sentences, paragraphs, format), style (formal versus informal register) and voice (quotation, summary and paraphrase, the separation of self from source). One aspect of writing was covered each week and students discussed and completed short tasks in class and more extensive written tasks for homework. Students were evaluated in two written tests taken during class, one reviewing the basic features of academic writing, the other a response to a text.

In the second semester, students were given two major assignments. The first was the joint writing assignment, the second was a research paper, which students wrote individually. Students divided themselves into groups of four or five and were given six weeks to co-write an essay of around 3,000 words on a subject of their choice. I provided them with samples of the best essays produced the previous year and feedback from that year's students about this task. The students were asked to submit a proposal, consisting of an introductory paragraph and a working bibliography by the second week. After completion, the essays were graded and returned.

During the six weeks devoted to the joint writing assignment, about twenty minutes of each ninety-minute class was given over to the groups to work on their essays, but most work was done outside of the class. The rest of the class time was devoted to sessions on various aspects of academic writing, in particular the research process, getting a focus and making a claim, library and Internet research, and compiling and presenting bibliographies. Some of these sessions were requested by the students to assist them in their assignment.

In the interests of creating an open and mutually supportive atmosphere in the class, I encouraged students to talk as much as possible in English and most did, but I did not penalise groups who preferred to speak Japanese. To this end also, I endeavored to learn the names of all the students as quickly as possible and to call on each student to report their group's discussion or to give their opinion on a question. Although some students were more active than others, I tried to give all students the chance to be heard in the course of a lesson. In addition to the sense of community that I attempted to foster within the classroom, I also invited students to come to my office for lunch after the class. The students themselves organised two lunches out at a local restaurant.

After completing this assignment, the students filled in an anonymous questionnaire on what they felt they had learned, what they found particularly difficult, and what they had found helpful. I also asked what advice they would give to students in the following year. This was the same questionnaire that the previous year's class had completed, which the students had read prior to commencing the assignment. In addition to the questionnaire, three students agreed to a taped discussion about the course, and their comments are included in the discussion below.

Benefits of Joint Writing

The assignment of 3,000 words was significantly larger than anything that the students had undertaken before, and many of them commented that it was exceptionally difficult, both because of the size, and the effort to reach a common consensus among group members. Nevertheless, this was not a criticism of the assignment. The following are identified as the main areas in which students felt that the assignment was of benefit:

1. Focus on thesis, structure and argumentation

The process of researching and writing a single paper in a group entailed extensive discussion and negotiation. As one student commented: 'It was hard to make one common idea among four people.' The most successful papers were those where the authors had devoted time to this, and who realised that such negotiation could continue after a first drafting of the paper, as is clear in the following comment:

> It was the hardest to exchange opinions and have a collective view because after we reached an agreement sometimes it became clear that some of member misunderstood it. So it was hard to make our paper coherent.

2. Mutual investment in and ownership of assignment

2.1 Cooperation

Working in groups meant that students were accountable to the group, not just to themselves. There is a note perhaps of guilt in the following student's remark: 'I strongly feel I should be more responsible because once I'm late everyone in my group will be troubled and cannot go on working on the paper.' In a comment by another student, the expectation of mutual investment and accountability emerges in the form of a veiled complaint against those who did not pull their weight in the assignment: 'The hardest part of this assignment is that we have to put together our ideas even if some of the members are not cooperative.' Overall, comments from the students implied that co-operation among group members was in itself an enjoyable and motivating aspect of the assignment.

However, co-authorship also involved an element of trust, an aspect that had its advantages: 'If you are working in a group, someone will, other persons will do their part, so you don't have to worry that part, if you trust the group member.' But there were also disadvantages: 'Working in groups was hard. I found it hard to trust other people in the groups and I don't know whether we worked together well.'

2.2 Management

In the group interview, one of the authors of the highest marked paper reported that one member of her group had taken on the role of manager, organising meetings and deadlines so that this group had perhaps twice as much contact time as any of the others. Other students commented that one of the main things they had learned in carrying out this assignment was time management: 'Construct the most efficient schedule and stick to it!' While another student summed up the benefits of the assignment as 'the importance of cooperation, participation and time management'.

3. More critical attitude towards own and others' ideas

The questionnaires indicated that mutual investment in the project resulted in students taking a far more critical stance on each other's work than is usually encountered, for example, in peer editing. One student writes that the greatest difficulty in writing the paper was '[agreeing] on a subject we are going to write about. If it does not work for everyone in a group, many changes are made, and sometimes what we have done goes down the drain'.

This more rigorously critical attitude is also apparent in the comments made by one of the students in the group interview.

Not this paper, but I was asked to check another classes' paper before, and I also asked somebody to check my paper, but it was a little bit difficult to point out someone's bad points... because it was a completely different person's paper, you know. But in group paper, I think we can point out another person's... not bad point, but something weak in the group, because we are working on the same big project. So even if it was another person's part, it wasn't included into our paper.

4. Active learning

4.1 Sharing information

One of the most challenging aspects of the assignment was discovering and assessing information relating to their topic in a relatively short period of time. All of the groups benefited from sharing information, and a few students commented specifically that this for them was one of the major benefits:

By working in a group we were able to use many kinds of resources such as books, the Internet, or newspapers, which might be difficult by oneself in such a short time. Thanks to that, I believe our paper became more convincing.

4.2 Sharing expertise

Other students found that they benefited from collaborating with students whose English was more proficient. As one student remarks:

I could read friends' writing and could learn more sophisticated English. I was stimulated and enjoyed the eagerness of trying to write 'better' sentences. And I could see how they searched for the resources they needed.

4.3 More active approach to seeking new resources

As mentioned, various issues in academic writing had been addressed in the semester prior to conducting this assignment. A number of students commented that they actively drew on this knowledge, in particular on model texts, in their own writing. For one student, this was a sample paper of an essay written in MLA format: 'We referred to it whenever we didn't know how to do the citations.' Another student mentioned more general advice: 'The notice about the form in citing sources helped me to realise the importance of making a broad research, not only to avoid plagiarism, but also that if I study more, I will find more interesting materials.'

Japanese students often hesitate to express opinions about what they want or need in English language classes. In this instance, the students were clear on the specific issues or techniques that they believed, on the basis of their experience, would be helpful to them, for example, 'we want more samples on citation, especially on web pages of books written in Japanese.'

Limitations to the Concept of Community of Practice

Despite the benefits that the students felt that they derived from the exercise, a number of comments on the feedback questionnaires, and in particular in the taped discussion, problematised the claim and original intention that the joint writing project, or the class as a whole, could be described as a community of practice at all. These comments can be grouped into three categories:

1. Student evaluation

Grading is one of the most immediate difficulties concerning group work. As the teacher, I was influenced in my planning by my knowledge of university expectations to grade my students individually, and this was how I evaluated the students in all other assignments for the course. For the joint writing project, however, the paper was graded, regardless of the contribution of individual students. Limiting the implementation of the community of practice approach to this extent, however, undoubtedly undermines its effectiveness. At the same time, the feedback showed that some students were uncomfortable with the fact that they would not be judged individually, as can be heard in the comment that 'some of the members are not cooperative' and in the admission of another that she 'found it hard to trust other people in the group'.

Wenger (1998) does factor the pressures and constraints of institutional factors into his theory of community of practice. However, the issue of evaluation is more than a pressure or constraint; evaluation is the primary purpose of the educational institution. For this university, what is of chief concern is the ranking of students, and only secondarily, if at all, what they have produced or learned (see also Cutts 1997). Reorganising a class to create a community of practice may more realistically approximate real-life tasks, but this conflicts fundamentally with the principles of hierarchy and individual competition which are enshrined in higher education in Japan.

2. Conflicting student priorities

Although time management was highlighted as a benefit in some of the comments, constraints of time pointed to a further limitation to the notion of a community of practice. Although all of the groups contrived to meet and discuss their projects outside of class time, making time in busy schedules was difficult. Moreover, however stimulated and engaged students were in this particular class and project, other commitments claimed higher priority in their schedules. The six-week period in which the joint writing assignment was conducted coincided with the International Festival, the largest social and cultural event in the university calendar. Many of the students were also involved in this as well as taking several other classes in the semester.

A more important priority for these third-year students was their seminar, that is, a specialist class led by a professor, who guides students in their choice and writing of a graduation thesis. Unlike other classes, the seminar stays together for two years, and in many cases (depending on individual professors) meets more often and more extensively. For some students, the seminar does indeed adhere to Wenger's description of communities of practice:

our seminar is a community because our professor doesn't say anything and she just let us do the research what we want to do. We divide into four groups and we work together. I don't know how we are graded in the seminar class, but I don't think we are worried about the grades, we just want to know what we want to know, so that's why we do the research. And we really cooperate with each other.

Conclusion

The experience of teaching an academic writing class and assigning a project incorporating the main features of a community of practice, namely mutual engagement in a joint enterprise and a shared repertoire of knowledge and practices, was felt by the students to have been stimulating and beneficial. Nevertheless, creating a community of practice was extremely limited due to the university's demand for individual ranking of students, and more importantly, due to the lack of time students could spend together and relatively low level of priority accorded to the course by them.

As an epilogue, the course is now in its third year, and enrolment for it has risen by 30%. The academic writing class gives students the opportunity to undertake writing tasks that are significantly more challenging than anything demanded of them previously. Creating communities of practice, however limited, offers them the stimulation, motivation and support to do this successfully.

Bibliography

Bartholomae, D. (1985) 'Inventing the university' in Rose, M. (ed.) *When a writer can't write*, 134–6. New York: Guildford.
Bhatia, V. (1993) *Analysing genre: language use in professional settings*. London: Longman.

Bizzell, P. (1992) *Academic discourse and critical consciousness.* Pittsburgh: University of Pittsburgh Press.

Cutts, R. (1997) *An empire of schools: Japan's universities and the molding of a national power elite.* Armonk, NY: M.E. Sharp.

Hymes, D. (1972) 'Models of the interaction of language and social life: directions in sociolinguistics' in Gumperz, J. and Hymes, D. (eds) *The ethnography of communication*, 35–71. New York: Reinhart and Winston.

Johns, A. (1997) *Text, role, and context: developing academic literacies.* Cambridge: Cambridge University Press.

Johnson, D. (2000) 'Intuition, culture and the development of academic literacy' in Atkinson, T. and Claxton, G. (eds) *The intuitive practitioner*, 239–53. Maidenhead: Open University.

Lave, J. (1991) 'Situated learning in communities of practice' in Resnick, R., Levine, J. and Teasley, S. (eds) *Perspectives on socially shared cognition.* Washington, DC: APA.

—— and Wenger, E. (1991) *Situated learning: legitimate peripheral participation.* Cambridge: Cambridge University Press.

Spack, R. (1998) 'Initiating students into the academic discourse community: how far should we go?' in Zamel, V. and Spack, R. (eds) *Negotiating academic literacies: teaching and learning across languages and cultures.* Mahwah, NJ: Lawrence Erlbaum.

Swales, J. (1990) *Genre analysis: English in academic settings.* Cambridge: Cambridge University Press.

—— and Feak, C. (1994) *Academic writing for graduate students.* Ann Arbor: University of Michigan Press.

Wenger, E. (1998) *Communities of practice: learning, meaning and identity.* Cambridge: Cambridge University Press.

FRED TARTTELIN

13 Reading Out of Class and the Integration of Other Key Skills

Introduction

For international students on pre-sessional courses it is essential that extensive reading is an integral part of their EAP programmes. Day and Bamford (1998) would argue that it should be part of any fully comprehensive L2 reading syllabus. Unfortunately, extensive reading is often neglected in class because of time restrictions and equally neglected out of class due to lack of motivation on the part of the student. One way, however, to encourage students to read longer, more extensive texts in their own time is to link the reading they do with their assessment.

This paper describes how a group of pre-sessional, intermediate EAP students at the International Centre for English Language Studies (ICELS), Oxford Brookes University, were encouraged to choose a literary text to read in their own time and how the experience provided the groundwork for in-class discussion, presentations in the form of a review of the chosen book, listening and note-taking activities, summary writing and constructive peer feedback.

Using Literary Texts in EAP: a brief look at the literature

The case for using original or simplified literary texts in the teaching of EFL has been challenged and discussed at length over the years. But incorporating such texts in EAP reading programmes would seem to be particularly unusual and even controversial (Horowitz 1990). In response to this writer's recent enquiry to ten UK university departments[1] offering similar EAP courses to those at ICELS, all said they did not use literary texts as part of their EAP reading programmes. This is presumably because they choose Media texts or texts that are more closely related to students' future academic subjects. For the lower level student, however, and even for many upper intermediate students, such texts often prove to be far too difficult, especially as extensive reading material, although these texts may be adapted or specially written if time and budgets allow for this. In contrast, the ICELS English for University Studies Programmes in their EAP reading modules currently use academic, Media and literary texts. The latter have proved to be particularly helpful for out-of-class extensive reading practice.

There is currently an abundance of reading texts available that are specially prepared for the L2 reader at appropriate levels. The texts range from rewrites of classics and modern prose fiction to non-fiction and stories written specially for the series. Most come in attractive, relatively cheap editions with a variety of optional supplementary material. They are indeed a potentially rich teaching resource to draw on. Yet Horowitz (1990) entering the fiction/non-fiction debate suggests that reading and writing about literature does not prepare students for the specific needs of HE courses and that such activities are irrelevant to the needs of most students. But surely, this must depend in the first place on what sort of literary text is being used and how its exploitation serves the aims of the course and contributes to improvement in the students' level of academic literacy.

In her research on reading instruction in an ESP context, Kasper (1995a, 1995b, 1995/96, 1997) found that students on content-based instructional programmes not only showed a preference for reading academic texts but these students also out-performed students who had been using literary texts. In sharp contrast, however, Krashen (1993), Day and Bamford (1998), Hirvela (1988, 1990, 2001a, 2001b) and Hedge (2000) would agree that regular reading of literary texts

---

1   The universities in question included Luton, Southbank, Bristol, Nottingham
     Trent, Southampton, Portsmouth, Reading, Lancaster, Bath and East Anglia.

can not only significantly improve language skills in general, particularly reading and writing proficiency, but also enhance both passive and active vocabulary, develop critical awareness and provide opportunities for practising transferable skills.

For a number of years, both original literary texts for higher levels and readers for lower levels have been included in English for University Studies (EUS) reading modules at ICELS as a means to promote and practise extensive reading. It was found, however, that a few students managed to avoid reading any of these set texts. Although the students were not necessarily failing modules as a result, it did seem they were missing out on an experience that was supposed to support autonomous learning and practise a skill that is crucial to academic success. It was clear that a new set of aims and procedures had to be devised. Before considering these in detail, I will look briefly at attitudes to reading amongst a group of recent international students at ICELS.

EUS Students' Attitudes to Reading

The tables below show the results from questionnaires completed by EUS 3 and 4 students who were asked how they felt about reading in L1 and reading in English. The aim of this exploratory exercise was to investigate current international students' attitudes to reading, prior to setting up a research project to consider how effective and useful literary texts might be in an EAP reading programme (Tarttelin 2003). The sample interviewed consisted of sixty-two students who were mainly Asian.

The most striking aspect of the responses was the relatively high percentage of students who said they liked reading in both L1 and English. Students in general tend to give the impression that they do not like reading *per se*, and that, especially in English, it is too slow or too difficult to be enjoyable. Later, the outcomes of the main research project greatly influenced decisions in the development of the current

EUS reading programmes, particularly regarding the sort of texts students would find interesting, who should choose the texts and to what extent literary texts might be exploited in an EAP context.

Language	No. of students who like reading	No. of students who dislike reading
L1	54 (87%)	8 (13%)
English	40 (65%)	22 (35%)

Table 1. Attitudes to reading in L1 and in English

Most students preferred reading prose fiction, newspapers or magazines, either in their L1 or in English, rather than reading academic texts on their future subject.

Type of reading	Reading in first language		Reading in English	
	Number of students	Percentage	Number of students	Percentage
stories/novels	47	76	34	55
newspapers	35	56	28	45
magazines	37	60	23	37
texts related to future academic subject	19	31	11	18
other (e.g. comics, computer literature, website news, poetry, essays)	7	11	1	2

Table 2. What students enjoy reading in L1 and in English

These figures suggest that literary texts are popular among most of the students interviewed and might be very motivating for extensive reading practice, especially for lower level students who still cannot cope with many academic texts. The attitude of materials developers and teachers towards literary texts must also be part of the equation. Materials that are the fruit of close collaboration between teachers, writers and students are more likely to be engaging in a way that stimulates more effective teaching and learning. As far as ICELS is concerned, staff are largely in favour of incorporating literature into the centre's EAP reading modules.

Integrating Extensive Reading into the English for University Studies (EUS) Level 2 Programme

The aims of the programme are to encourage students to
- read more out of class
- be motivated to read (the reading should be an integral part of the programme and contribute to students' overall assessment)
- feel more confident when reading in English
- take more responsibility for their own learning.

Out of this systematic focus on extensive reading has emerged
- critical reading
- language awareness
- vocabulary extension
- cognitive learning
- autonomous learning.

The students are required to read two novels, which, though simplified and abridged, are nevertheless sufficiently challenging for students at this level. The first novel is a set text, *Great Expectations* (Oxford Bookworms Library, Level 5, re-told by Clare West), which the students read during the first three weeks of the course. After an introductory in-class session, the class are allocated chapters to read each week at home and asked to make notes. Individual students are given the additional task of preparing an oral summary of a chapter or chapters for the coming class, leading into class discussion of characters and events. The pre-reading/post-reading optional activities in the book might be exploited in class or set as extra homework. A cassette recording of the text and scenes from the David Lean film version of the novel are also used in both the reading class, and the listening and speaking class. As regards assessment, the end-of-term reading test includes a section containing a series of tasks that require written answers.

The second novel is chosen by the students themselves, following guidelines set down by the tutor. This text is read entirely in the students' own time. As well as completing an extended writing question in their final reading test, the students have to prepare a short individual oral presentation in the form of a book review. This is assessed as part of their listening and speaking module.

While the work the students have to do on their chosen text is intended to be as self-directed as possible, a certain amount of supervision is included at various stages. The students are encouraged to make notes on each chapter as they read before preparing a brief review of their chosen book for the assessed presentation. The instructions given to the students for this task are shown in Figure 1 below. During each presentation, the rest of the class take notes using the worksheet in Figure 2, which requires an evaluation of each presentation. Finally, the students choose three presentations, and using their notes, write three short summaries for homework. This is not part of their assessment but consolidates the skills taught and practised in their academic reading programme. Thus the practice of a number of key academic skills such as note taking, summary writing and giving a presentation is entirely dependent on the students reading this second text. What is more, because some of the post-reading activities form part of their course assessment, students are motivated to complete these tasks.

Now is the time to choose and read your own choice of book.

1. Either borrow one from the library (section 428) or buy one from Blackwell's Bookshop in Broad St. Oxford (in both places there are multiple copies of the OUP Bookworm Series).
2. Before making your choice, read the information on the cover, read the introduction, and read the first chapter to make sure it's a book you might enjoy.
3. Repeat this process with several books.
   (You should do this immediately, otherwise you won't have enough time to carry out the task properly. Try not to choose the same book that another student has chosen.)
4. Choose a text similar in length and difficulty to *Great Expectations*, which is Level 5 in the OUP Bookworms Series. Level 4 is a bit easier and Level 6 is a bit more difficult than *Great Expectations*.
5. Read the book at least once.
6. Make brief notes on each chapter, about the main characters and what happens.
7. Prepare a short presentation (about 4 minutes) for your listening and speaking class in Week 7. In this presentation you should talk about the main characters, the plot and whether or not you liked the book and why.

In next week's class your tutor will make a note of the title of your chosen book.

Figure 1. Instructions to students before choosing their own choice text

Speaker's name: ....

Topic of presentation (title) ....

Main points:

1

2

3

Other information

Speaker's conclusion/views/feelings or recommendations

Question for the speaker:

Evaluation:

Was the presentation

clear?	yes	No (Why not?)
easy to follow?	yes	No (Why not?)
well organised?	yes	No (Why not?)
interesting?	yes	No (Why not?)

Figure 2. Worksheet for note-taking during peer presentations

Conclusion

The idea of setting up an extensive reading programme is not new. David Hill's inspirational work, for instance, for The Edinburgh Project on Extensive Reading (EPER) has been on-going for almost thirty years now. Indeed, much of his advice (Hill 1997) has served the ICELS English for University Studies reading programmes well. However, where the reading programme described in this paper might claim some originality lies in the fact that its extensive reading component is closely linked to other areas of an EAP, as opposed to an EFL, course. A key element in the programme is that the students are allowed freedom of choice in text selection. Instead of being limited to a class library, they can choose from the range of titles available in either the university library or one of the larger local bookstores. It should also be said that great emphasis has been put on motivating students to carry out and enjoy the tasks they are set and that the hard work they might invest in the process is appropriately acknowledged and rewarded in terms of feedback and assessment.

The programme was piloted over the three terms of the academic year 2004/2005 and has been revised and consolidated since then. The response from tutors and students has been mostly very positive. Students, almost without exception, have proved themselves capable of taking responsibility for their own learning and clearly appreciate being given an opportunity to select and evaluate a text of their own choice.

The success of the project owed much to the excellent Bookworm Series from Oxford University Press. The series, originally edited by Tricia Hedge in the 1980s, has done much to transform the reputation of the class reader. These attractive, well written books, graded from low intermediate to advanced level, also come with a good deal of useful and imaginative support materials. Not all the titles are rewrites of prose fiction and other publishers are bringing out an increasing variety of readers and other specially written graded fiction. The wide choice available in current catalogues would seem to cater for all tastes.

Finally, Sandra Cardew, in her talk at the BALEAP/SATEFL Conference 2005, recommended tutors to share 'their own intellectual life' with their students. Tutors who love reading would have an endless supply of ideas and inspiration to incorporate into their teaching. In his plenary talk at the same conference, Brian Tomlinson, focusing on 'localising global themes', said materials must be 'affectively and cognitively engaging for true learning to take place' and that this may be achieved by using 'stories, humour and the bizarre'. This would suggest that literature, in all its many guises, is a potentially rich store of inspiration for both teaching and learning. The debate as to whether this is appropriate for EAP studies or not will doubtless continue for some time to come.

Bibliography

Day, R. and Bamford, J. (1998) *Extensive reading in the second language classroom*. Cambridge: Cambridge University Press.

Cardew, S. (2005) 'He can play the piano therefore he can speak Chinese'. *BALEAP-SATEFL Joint Conference* Edinburgh, April 2005.

Hedge, T. (2000) *Teaching and learning in the language classroom*. Oxford: Oxford University Press.

Hill, D.R. (1992) *The EPER guide to organising programme of extensive reading*. Edinburgh: The Institute of Applied Language Studies, University of Edinburgh.

Hirvela, A. and Boyle, J. (1988) 'Literature courses and student attitudes'. *ELT Journal* 42/3, 179–84.

—— (1990) 'ESP and literature: a reassessment'. *English for Specific Purposes,* 9, 237–52.

—— (2001a) 'Connecting reading and writing through literature' in Belcher, D. and Hirvela, A. (eds) *Linking literacies*, 109–34. Ann Arbor: University of Michigan Press.

—— (2001b) 'Incorporating reading into EAP writing courses' in Flowerdew, J. and Peacock, M. (eds) *Research perspectives on English for academic purposes*, 330–46. Cambridge: Cambridge University Press.

Horowitz, D. (1990) 'Fiction and non-fiction in the ESL/EFL classroom: does the difference make a difference?' *English for Specific Purposes* 9, 161–8.

Kasper, L.F. (1995a) 'Theory and practice in content based ESL reading instruction'. *English for Specific Purposes*, 14, 223–30.

—— (1995b) 'Discipline-oriented ESL reading instruction'. *Teaching English in the Two-Year College* 22, 45–53.

—— (1995/96) 'Using discipline-based texts to boost college ESL reading instruction'. *Journal of Adolescent and Adult Literacy* 39, 298–306.

—— (1997) 'The impact of content-based instructional programmes on the academic progress of ESL students'. *English for Specific Purposes* 16, 309–20.

Krashen, S. (1993) *The power of reading: insights from research*. Englewood, USA: Libraries Unlimited, INC.

Tarttelin, F. (2003) 'Reading in English for academic purposes: how prose fiction as a resource for extended reading might contribute to the target needs of higher level international students on an English for university studies course'. Oxford Brookes University, Unpublished MA Thesis.

Tomlinson, B. (2005) 'Localising the global: matching materials to the context of learning'. *BALEAP-SATEFL Joint Conference* Edinburgh, April 2005.

Section IV

Using Sources in Writing

MARTIN MILLAR

14 Sources for Courses: Past and Present Practice, Future Possibilities

This paper addresses the issue of sourcing and selecting suitable materials for EAP by reflecting on past and present practice, and looking ahead to how changing uses of materials may lead to the transformation of EAP. Materials and methods have to be considered together (McDonough and Shaw 2003). Methods in EAP include text-based and task-based learning (Knight 2001:162–3) content-based instruction (Dueñas 2003 for an overview) and project work (Stoller 1997, Beckett and Slater 2005). A decision also has to be taken to develop materials rather than adopt a professionally published course book (McGrath 2003:103–6).

Texts and Sources: definition and discussion

The word 'text' is used here to denote a linguistic manifestation of some sort – a verbal message of variable size and complexity, which is encoded within a particular linguistic system (in this case English) and displays certain stylistic and possibly genre-specific features (e.g. exposition), transmitted in a particular mode i.e. speech or writing Halliday 1978:133–42, Widdowson 1996:132). By text in the EAP context, I mean verbal material from a printed source that may or may not contain visual support in the form of pictures and diagrams, or spoken material, which has been recorded and can be accessed mechanically. Examples include newspaper cuttings, excerpts from books and articles and off-air recordings of radio and TV broadcasts.

Willis (2000) provides a set of course design principles which she uses to contextualise the practical activity of materials collection and selection. She suggests that the assembly of a pedagogical corpus, which she characterises only in terms of linguistic data, is done at the first stage of the design process:

Assemble >   sequence > analyse >   identify useful >   check coverage
language   texts and
data   language features

This model emphasises the fact that course designers work from texts which are printed or recorded. In developing materials for courses, we select texts that we can exploit for teaching and learning purposes. We then specify suitable tasks designed around the text, and it is in both of these professional activities that our productivity and creativity as EAP teachers come to the fore. It is satisfying to find good materials to work with. Whether they are responsible for the overall design of whole courses, or just individual course units or lessons, language teachers are always on the look-out for what I shall refer to as pedagogically-exploitable texts (PETs).

PET Selection Criteria

A number of criteria connected with positive learning experiences and outcomes help to identify PETs (Dudley-Evans and St John 1998:173, Jordan 1997:138 and McGrath 2003:107).

1)   Availability – the text is available in a useable format
2)   Facility – the range of vocabulary, the syntactic and stylistic repertoire employed, the discourse structure, the communicative aims of the writer or speaker(s) and the informational content of the text are within the linguistic and cognitive competence of the student

3) Utility – the text contains information that the student can make use of either now or in the future for life in general or for study purposes (see also relevance below)
4) Interest – the text addresses topics or themes that the student will find intellectually, emotionally, culturally, socially or personally compelling (see the discussion below)
5) Relevance – the content is relevant to the student's field of study
6) Adaptability – the text contains a linguistic sample that the teacher can adapt to achieve learning outcomes and/or assessment modalities
7) Flexibility – the format of the text is such that it can be exploited in a number of ways, in whole or in part, in several courses
8) Currency – the text addresses topics or themes of current interest
9) Durability – the text addresses non-ephemeral topics or themes whose interest value is likely to endure beyond the life of one course.

The interest value of a text can sometimes stem from its novelty, either in terms of its content or of the expressive quality of the language used. Another factor could be the seriousness of the topic, which can be called the gravity factor, when the text addresses an issue construed as politically or culturally significant, and is therefore educationally worthy of exploration and thus exploitation. In addition the course designer will always have at the back of his/her mind the need for variety.

New Ways of Sourcing

PET–spotting and PET–stocking have long been a feature of ELT and certainly pre-date EAP as a sub-branch of ESP (see Flowerdew and Peacock 2001 for an overview of EAP/ESP history). Teachers regularly spent time collecting materials from newspapers, TV and radio-broadcast and would hoard cuttings and audio and video cassettes for years.

Now print-based sources such as newspapers and magazines provide electronically archived material which can often be searched online. Search engines such as Google have an advanced search option which will lead to myriads of PETs containing thematic key words. Instead of having to look out for useful texts as they appear in the public domain, teachers can use the web to search much more pro-actively than in the past.

Collecting off-air recordings may still be a spontaneous and serendipitous enterprise, but what is of interest now is that related support materials – articles, commentary and even tapescripts – can often be tracked down using the Web. An example is a lecture in the BBC Learning Zone series given by the late Roy Porter on the subject of the life and work of the medical scientist Edward Jenner (BBC 1996)[1] for licensing details of BBC materials visit era.org.uk) To prepare students for the subject of the lecture, they can read websites such as http://www.sc.edu/library/spcoll/nathist/jenner.html . Another example is the 2002 Dimbleby lecture by Rowan Williams 'Nation, Markets, Morals' (BBC 2002)[2] together with references to Philip Bobbit, who is mentioned twice in the lecture, and to letters published in the Guardian, including one by Bobbit, giving a variety of re-sponses to the lecture. This accumulation of related texts provides an instant raft of materials – a flotilla might be a better analogy – upon which to float course units and lessons. Perhaps more important than this instant availability of a PET, the new technology affords the opportunity to teachers to include an autonomous dimension in the design process.

The traditional stance towards text selection and exploitation is that teachers choose texts which they think students will find inter-esting and useful. Dubain and Olshtain (1986:153) mention the place of course designers' intuitions about the interest value of texts in particular design scenarios, and their reliance on hunches in choosing

---

1   For licensing details for copying BBC materials off-air visit [www.era.org.uk].
2   For which a full transcript was available at [http://www.anglicancommunion. org/acns/articles/32/25/acns3236.html].

a particular text for a reading lesson. However, teachers also want to give students the opportunity to choose their own texts, which they can explore and indeed exploit for their own learning. Again, past practice – the show-and-tell activity in which students would be asked to produce hard copies of texts that they had come across in relation to a particular theme or event – can be contrasted with the same activity today, in which students search for relevant texts using the Web. At its simplest and most basic, the technology allows students to find texts that they themselves judge to be useful and interesting in the context of the particular course, unit or lesson. But this is still in the world of the classroom and in the domain of the teacher.

Project Work and Student PET Selection

In preparing for a new module in our Foundation course, to be named Preparation for University Studies, I wondered how much autonomous learning was taking place outside of class and formal study contexts within the institution (e.g. the computer room or library). I became interested in the question of what students were learning about life in Britain, whether in Oxford in particular or more locally in the suburb of Headington, home to Oxford Brookes and their new home. I designed a task which would invite students to investigate a specific aspect of the local environment using a local website as a portal to a range of topics. Figure 1 shows an excerpt of the task rubric from the student handbook.

Group Surveys
Your first assignment for this module is to give a group presentation in week 4. First you need to carry out some research, using both *primary* and *secondary* sources of information. In this first session you will be asked to choose one of the following topics for your investigation, to form yourselves into working groups, and to plan your survey. As mentioned earlier in this Handbook, one of the chief sources you will be using for your research is www.headington.org.uk: all of the themes below are connected to this website – but of course you need to add lots of other information yourselves.
The topics you can choose from for the group presentation are:
    Education: a survey of educational provision in Headington
    Law and Planning: the case of 'The Shark House'

Academic field(s)	Education
Topic	A survey of educational provision in Headington
Research Question(s)	What is the scope of educational provision in Headington? How many schools are there, how do they relate to the education system? Are there any links between the schools and Oxford Brookes?
Action Points (steps)	Explore website and check relevant links. Establish visits, conduct interviews. Collect, review, analyse information. Organise notes for presentation. Acknowledge website.
Academic field(s)	Law/Planning Permission/Tourism
Topic	The Shark House
Research Question(s)	What were the initial objections of Oxford City Council to the placing of the shark inside the roof of a house in Headington? How were these objections overcome? How do local people and visitors feel about the statue today?
Action Points (steps)	Explore website and check the relevant links. Visit real site, conduct interviews (possibly using a video camera). Design questionnaire. Collect, review, analyse information. Prepare notes for presentation. Acknowledge website

Figure 1. Extract from U70501 Preparation for University Studies:
Oxford Brookes University 2004

Readers are referred to articles by Beckett and Slater (2005) and Stoller (1997) for an evaluation of project work as an issue in course design. The salient point of the project work illustrated above is that it highlights the practical opportunities afforded by IT and provides an example of how EAP course designers can turn the job of text assessment and selection over to the users. The real exploitation can then be done by the learners themselves.

The Continuing Transformation of EAP Practice

In the range of teaching assignments that I am involved in, which includes contributions to content subjects both on the Foundation course as well as on two undergraduate fields, I have come to see the web as a gold-mine. I have been inspired by students, whose presentations draw upon an impressive array of web-based material including images and segments of spoken discourse. In the very near future, teachers may go to class without photocopied handouts and whiteboard pens. Indeed many teachers already prepare lessons in Power Point but the increasing use of Interactive Whiteboards will enable presentation and discussion to take place around images and texts – written and spoken – downloaded as required.

This implies a change in emphasis from skills development and the dominance of methodology over materials, to an emphasis on the quality of the sources themselves. There are still some basic resource and technological issues to be resolved (e.g. wireless web linked classrooms, built-in data projectors that actually work) before the BBC and other websites can be employed as portals to learning experiences and skills i.e. listening, reading, speaking, grammar and vocabulary work, which are not overtly identified as such in the Content-based Instruction syllabus. The days of PET-spotting and stocking are coming to an end. The new methods involve PET-searching, finding, and keeping EAP materials at the click of a mouse. Once stored in the computer, texts can be assembled and transformed at will, offering great potential to the enhancement of the educational process in which we and our students are engaged.

Bibliography

BBC (1996) 'Defeating Disease: the history of vaccination in Britain' by Roy Porter. Transmitted and recorded 3/9/1996.
—— (2002) 'The Richard Dimbleby Lecture: Nations, Markets, Morals' by Rowan Williamson. Transmitted and recorded on 19/12/2002.
Beckett, G.H. and Slater, T. (2005) 'The Project Framework: a tool for language, content and skills integration'. *ELT Journal* 59/2 108–16.
Dubin, F. and Olshtain, E. (1986) *Course Design: Developing Programs and Materials for Language Learning* Cambridge: Cambridge University Press.
Dudley-Evans, A. and St John, M.J. (1998) *Developments in English for Specific Purposes: a multi-disciplinary approach.* Cambridge: Cambridge University Press.
Dueñas, M. (2003) 'A description of prototype models for content-based instruction in higher education'. Available online at [http://www.publicacions.ub.es/revistes/bells12/PDF/art04.pdf]. Retrieved on 21/3/05.
Flowerdew, J. and Peacock, M. (2001) 'Issues in EAP: a preliminary perspective' in Flowerdew, J. and Peacock, M. (eds) *Research Perspectives on English for Academic Purposes* Cambridge: Cambridge University Press, 8–13.
Halliday, M.A.K. (1978) *Language as social semiotic: the social interpretation of language and meaning.* London: Edward Arnold.
Knight, P. (2001) 'The development of EFL methodology' in Candlin, C. and Mercer, N. (eds) *English language teaching in its social context: a reader.* London: Routledge.

Jordan, R.R. (1997) *English for Academic Purposes: a guide and resource book for teachers.* Cambridge: Cambridge University Press.

McDonough, J. and Shaw, C. (2003) *Materials and methods in ELT: a guide for teachers* (2nd ed.) Oxford: Blackwells

McGrath, I. (2003) *Materials Evaluation and Design for Language Teaching* Edinburgh: Edinburgh University Press

Stoller, L.F. (1997) 'Project Work: a means to promote language content'. *Forum (English Teaching) Online* 35/4. Available online at [http://exchanges.state.gov/forum/vols/vol35/no4/index. htm]. Retrieved on 21/3/05.

Widdowson, H.G. (1996) *Linguistics.* Oxford: Oxford University Press.

Willis, J. (2000) 'A holistic approach to task-based course design'. *The Language Teacher*, available online at [http://www.jalt-pub lications.org/tlt/articles/2000/02/willis]. Retrieved on 21/3/05.

JOAN MCCORMACK

15 An Integrated Approach to Teaching Extended Writing and Research Skills

Introduction

There has been a growing awareness in recent years of the need to provide a more integrated approach to the teaching of extended writing in the academic context, in order to more accurately reflect the conditions of writing in that context. This paper describes materials developed to equip students to participate in post-graduate study and research.[1] The materials are taught as one component of a pre-sessional course – the extended writing class. This component emphasises the integration of skills being taught in the written and spoken language components of the course, where students work on developing individual skills. The materials have been trialled over a period of three years, during which time feedback from both teachers and students has informed their modification and development. This process highlighted a number of apparently key issues, for example plagiarism and the degree of scaffolding required during the course.

Aims of the course

The purpose of the materials is to equip students with the skills necessary to carry out research, take part in seminars, give oral presentations, and contribute effectively in online discussion tasks. The approach is an integrated one with a particular focus on producing a piece of extended writing (referred to here as a project) in the

---

1   The materials have been written and developed with co-author John Slaght.

students' subject specific area. The materials are designed to encourage critical thinking and get students to be evaluative in their approach to writing. There is also a strong oral component through discussion of their work in class, in tutorials and at a final conference at the end of the course when students present their work. Students are required to write two projects. During the first of these they receive considerable support in the form of scaffolded tasks, while during the second they work with increasingly greater autonomy. Online materials are used both in the classroom and by students working independently.

Students are asked to consider the structure of introductions and conclusions and they will receive language feedback on their work. However, these materials do not explicitly teach reading, writing and presentation skills or grammar, which are assumed to be taught in other components of the pre-sessional course.

Student needs

The following areas have been taken into consideration in the design of the materials, based on an analysis of what students need to do on future courses.

- the ability to produce an extended piece of writing in their own subject area within the academic conventions of UK higher education
- the development of discursive skills – to communicate effectively both orally and in writing
- the development of critical thinking skills
- the development of learner autonomy
- an understanding of the conventions of the academic community they will be joining
- the development and consolidation of study competences.

Principles on which the Materials are Based

The learning process as a cycle

Mayes (1997) examines how different learning activities enhance students' understanding of new concepts and resolve misunderstandings. He refers to three stages, which are known as the conceptualisation cycle. In this cycle, at the conceptualisation stage, students are exposed to the ideas or concepts of others through lectures, reading and seminar discussion. During the construction stage students apply these new concepts in the performance of meaningful tasks. It is during the dialogue stage, however, that learning takes place through the performance of tasks when these new concepts are tested during written communication and conversation with tutors and peers. Feedback enables students' misconceptions to be resolved. A similar approach is adopted with the present materials.

Also, the integration of skills from other components of a typical pre-sessional course is an essential aspect of these materials. Students bring with them awareness of the micro-skill of writing and an awareness of how to use appropriate reading strategies to deal with texts. These are aspects which are recycled as they work on their projects. In this context, writing is learned rather than taught because learning how to write occurs through the understanding and manipulation of content.

Reading for the Purpose of Writing:
writing from multiple texts

The approach taken in these materials is that students are reading to learn, rather than learning to read. As Hirvela (2001:109) points out, reading in the academic context is the basis of writing 'it is through reading that the required writing material is appropriated'. To encourage this, students are given a reading purpose which is to complete two extended writing assignments (projects). This purpose should generate a selective reading approach which will help students to deal with the literally hundreds of pages they may be confronted with weekly during their future academic courses. It is also generally accepted that teaching students to write from sources is essential preparation for academic success. Grabe (2003:225) points out the complexity involved in deciding how much and what should be used; how it can be used in relation to the task; how accurately it should be represented and finally the formal mechanisms which need to be used.

The process and problem-solving components of writing development can make intense demands on students, particularly when students are reading difficult texts in order to collect new information for their writing. In many reading-writing tasks, students are forced to make a number of complex decisions (Grabe 2001:245). It is with this in mind that students are given a range of sources to consider when working on their first project. The rationale behind this approach is that the teacher has an element of control and can identify ineffective strategies such as plagiarism as a way of coping with multiple, fairly dense academic texts. With the second project students will be working with texts in their own subject area and with a much greater degree of autonomy. By this stage, it is hoped that they will have begun to develop the ability to make the 'complex decisions' that Grabe identifies.

A Process and Product Approach

A process approach to writing is advocated, based on research that shows that the process of doing helps the development of organisation as well as meaning. Writing development occurs through the process of drafting and re-drafting the work. At each stage students are encouraged to generate ideas, organise them, evaluate what they are writing and identify clearly what their writing purpose is. Revision is essential, not just to edit the language but also to re-organise, modify the text and clarify ideas through expansion or re-phrasing as necessary. At every stage of the process, students are encouraged to critically assess what they have written and to develop this criticality through discussion with their academic colleagues, both fellow students and teachers.

These materials also strongly emphasise the importance of the end product. This is in line with the needs of the students on their future academic courses, where they will have to produce a finished piece of work incorporating the aspects of academic writing and academic study skills advocated in these materials. Appendix 1 is an example of how completed projects may be evaluated, taking into account not only the content, the use of source materials, the organisation and the language of the final draft, but also the actual written presentation of the text and the degree of learner independence exercised by students in producing the final product.

Students Finding their own Voice

In the complexity of the reading and writing process, students often find it challenging to formulate their own ideas. A strong element in these materials involves getting students to voice their ideas before writing them, a process which helps to clarify their own ideas. It is important to emphasise to students that even though they are writing in their own subject area, they should be writing with the educated reader in mind and should be able to explain their topic to non-specialists in their field.

Verbalising their ideas before writing also helps combat plagiarism to some extent, as one of the reasons that students plagiarise is that they want to use information they may not have fully understood to support a point. Resources are provided in the first project to allow the issue of plagiarism to be dealt with very directly, as all texts are familiar to teachers. From the beginning they are asked to be critical but this may not come easily if they come from a culture where they are not accustomed to question authoritative sources. A certain level of language competence, as well as confidence in their understanding of content, is necessary in order for the student to find their own voice.

Learner Autonomy

Students are expected to be independent learners in higher education. They need to work on study skill techniques, such as note-taking and compiling a bibliography, but also on acquiring study competences which involve the development of critical questioning. Control over one's learning is the basis of learner autonomy; not only attempting to exercise this control, but also actually managing it successfully. However, student attitudes to working autonomously vary in terms of their personality and cultural background. The stage of learner autonomy of any student is at a certain point along a continuum. These materials contain scaffolded tasks which provide support that is gradually withdrawn to encourage autonomy, especially during the writing of the second project. In their article on issues in the EAP curriculum, Flowerdew and Peacock (2001:82) emphasise the importance of this. By asking learners to research and investigate resources available to them inside and outside the academy, as well as encouraging them to take responsibility for their own learning, teachers will set their students on the path to full autonomy.

The Content and Delivery of the Materials

The materials comprise eight units in total, plus appendices. Each unit focuses on one aspect of extended writing. From Unit 2 onwards students look at how reading can be used to support their writing, and in Unit 3 they begin writing the first project. Each of the units contains a number of tasks, many of which students complete for homework. Parallel to this, students are working on their projects, and they get feedback on each stage of the process e.g. on their initial plan, or whether the introduction contains a clear focus.

The first project is 1,500–1,800 words long and is written while students are working through the early units, requiring them to apply the skills they are developing beyond the level of simply applying them to individual tasks. Students are asked to select material from the five source texts and two websites which are provided. Some work is done in class on these texts.

For the second project, which is 2,500–3,000 words long, students need to find their own resources in their own subject area. They negotiate their own title and specific aim through discussion with their tutor. Students work independently without scaffolding at this stage. Class time is mainly concentrated on individual tutorials. Students are encouraged to take responsibility for what happens in the tutorial, and guidance on this is given in Unit 4.

Feedback and Assessment

Assessment includes continuous assessment and assessment of the two projects and the presentation, given at the end-of-course Conference (sample evaluation criteria for the project are shown in the appendix).

Although students may be familiar with the process of peer evaluation in the writing component of their course, the extent to which it is a part of the continuous assessment of the project class varies according to the individual group. If a group is struggling with both the content and the structure of the project, it may be too demanding to expect students to also give effective peer feedback. However, a great deal can be gained from using colleagues as sounding boards in order to try out ideas and to explain the content as clearly and effectively as possible.

Students should receive both formative and summative feedback on their written drafts of the project from the tutor, and have the opportunity to discuss their work in an individual tutorial. Certain aspects of feedback sessions are particularly significant: for example, written comments on the final project as well as the drafts. Students also need feedback on their oral performance in preparation for their conference presentation. On longer courses, it is often possible to organise mock tutorials as part of the students' spoken language assessment. In order to make this a more authentic experience, the students' projects can be used as the focus for discussion. Students can be asked to introduce their project, outline the key details and then discuss issues relating to their project with the assessor.

Issues Related to Teaching the Course

There are certain issues relating to these materials and how they are introduced and used on a pre-sessional course. One issue concerns the previous academic experience and cultural background of the stu-dents. In addition, their level of intellectual maturity has to be considered. Both of these issues will impact on the amount of scaffolding which should be given and possibly the extent to which the first project should form part of the overall assessment. The third issue is that of plagiarism; this has been described as a 'sticky issue – not seen as black and white by academics' (Sutherland Smith 2005). For example, there is the need to 'imitate in the early stages of learning a new discourse' (Angelil-Carter 2000). On the other hand, as expressed by Sherman (1992:194), the students 'find it hard to believe that I really want what I say I want: their own half-formed ideas expressed in their own limited English.' Some students feel that they are representing writers more fairly by using their words.

The materials aim to raise awareness and develop the skills to help overcome plagiarism. There is a strong emphasis on being evaluative and on students commenting on what they have read. There is also an attempt to help students develop the skills to be able to express ideas effectively. It is recognised that helping students avoid plagiarism may be part of the whole process of students' finding their own voice, and this takes time.

Conclusion

These materials for teaching Extended Writing and Research Skills attempt to equip students with the skills they need for their future academic courses. These skills are of necessity generic and do not allow for the variations within departments according to the norms of a particular field. Students should be encouraged to bridge this gap, especially in relation to the second project, by making contact with their departments and getting suggestions for relevant project titles, as well as some of the key reading texts. The writers of these materials are currently engaged in this in order to establish a pool of subject specific material to develop further resources, thus enabling us to meet the needs of students in a more specific way.

Appendix: Written Project Evaluation

Name:		Overall Grade
Title:		

Grades for individual aspects of the Project (detail overleaf)	
Content	
Use of Source material	
Organisation	
Language	

Presentation of material		Tick as appropriate
Well-presented	Contains all appropriate sections e.g title page, abstract, headings in main body, appropriate font, bibliography	
Presentation needs development	For example, not enough headings, inappropriate font, missing bibliography/list of references at end.	

Learner Autonomy		Tick as appropriate
Appropriate	Asks for help/advice when necessary or appropriate, but otherwise is capable of working on their own	
Needs to develop	At times independent, but tendency to be too dependent on teacher	
Inadequate	Does not show the ability to work on his/her own but fails to ask for help or can only complete project under pressure by teacher.	

Comment

Teacher:
Grades for individual aspects of the Project

Content

Clearly focused content, relevant to title. Length, scope and level of detail are appropriate/relevant. Arguments are well presented and developed, with supporting evidence from a variety of sources. Shows awareness of complexities of the topic.	A
Generally well-focused content. May be lacking in level of detail or development of ideas and/or limited in scope (which may affect length). Much of the content may be descriptive (when a critical approach is required). Some understanding of complexities of topic evident. Argument may be inconsistent or insufficiently developed.	B
Focus at times waivers; some content may be irrelevant. Clearly limited in level of detail, superficial treatment of subject, with no development of ideas. Shows lack of awareness of complexities of topic. May be very short.(Little or no evidence of evaluation of ideas, staying mostly at the descriptive level. No clear line of argument	C
No obvious focus; clearly content inadequately researched; unable to deal with topic (probably very short) *or* wholesale plagiarism has made it impossible to assess true level. Too much personal/ anecdotal material.	D

Use of source material

Effective use of a range of sources, appropriate incorporation through paraphrase/quotations/summary. Shows ability to synthesise well from several sources to support ideas. Bibliography and referencing follow academic convention, and a range of sources are used. No obvious/ conscious plagiarism.	A
Effective use of sources, mostly when summarising/paraphrasing ideas clearly. Shows some evidence of synthesis of information. Bibliography and use of sources show an understanding of the concept of referencing, though this is not always followed e.g bibliography missing publisher/not in alphabetical order; references in text include first name/title. No obvious/conscious plagiarism.	B

Limited sources used, and summary/paraphrase of ideas not always clear. Some attempt at synthesis of ideas. Clearly has problems compiling bibliography and incorporating sources in an appropriate way, although there is some attempt to do this. Poor language control may be a factor. Suspicion of plagiarism in some sections.	C
Inadequate attempt in terms of using source material e.g may only use one source or none. Content based mainly on students view with no evidence to support it. Shows little understanding of the importance of referencing and academic conventions. No bibliography, or where this exists, totally lacking in following appropriate academic convention. No reflection of course content.	D

Organisation
* Refer to the *Language* section for some aspects of *Organisation*

Overall structure and main ideas are clearly organised, and easy to follow. Introduction outlines structure of project, and has clear thesis. Conclusion is clear, with evidence of evaluation of the work. Ideas are effectively linked together and 'flow' coherently and cohesively, making it easy for the reader to follow. Appropriate headings in text make it easy for reader to follow.	A
Overall structure and main ideas are generally obvious. Introduction and/or conclusion may not be appropriately linked to main body. Lack of headings in some sections hinder reader. At times a tendency to move from one idea to another with no attempt to link them.	B
Difficult for reader to establish overall structure/identifying main ideas. May be due to poor language control, which may also affect cohesion. Introduction/conclusion may be inadequate. Frequent move from one idea to anther, with no attempt to link them.	C
Ineffective attempt to organise the work. Very difficult for reader to follow the text. The introduction fails to give the reader an overview/clear idea of what will follow (or wholesale plagiarism has made it impossible to assess true level).	D

Language

Complex ideas clearly expressed, with wide, accurate usage of vocabulary and grammar; any errors are non-impeding. Appropriate academic style, with good grasp of hedging etc. Use of a wide range of connectors to link ideas at paragraph and sentence level.	A
Ideas on the whole clearly expressed. Linking of ideas within paragraphs generally appropriate, but at times lacking between sections. Some vocabulary and/or grammar problems, but generally non-impeding. Spelling and/or punctuation may lack control, although this generally does not interfere with comprehension.	B
Some ideas are simply expressed, but other ideas are not clearly expressed. No evidence of ability to express complex ideas. Linking between and within sentences may be inconsistent. Fairly serious vocabulary and/or grammar problems; can be impeding. Spelling and/or punctuation may be fairly seriously flawed. May be too much use of lists rather than continuous prose	C
The level of vocabulary & grammar is so consistently weak and the spelling/punctuation may be so poor that the end product fails to achieve its purpose due to ineffective communication. (or wholesale plagiarism has made it impossible to assess true level).	D

Bibliography

Flowerdew, J. and Peacock, M. (eds) (2001) *Research perspectives on English for academic purposes.* Cambridge: Cambridge University Press.

—— (2001) 'The EAP curriculum: issues, methods, and challenges' in Flowerdew, J. and Peacock, M. (eds) 179–94.

Grabe, N. (2003) 'Reading and writing relations: second language perspectives on research and practice' in Kroll, B. (ed.) 242–6.

Hirvela, A. (2001) 'Connecting reading and writing through literature' in Belcher, D. and Hirvela, A. (eds) 109–34.

Kroll, B. (ed.) (2003) *Exploring the dynamics of second language writing.* Cambridge: Cambridge University Press.

Lynch, T. (2001) 'Promoting EAP learner autonomy in a second language university context' in Flowerdew, J. and Peacock, M. (eds,) 390–403.

Mayes, J.T. (2001) *The conceptualisation cycle*. Available online at [http://led.gcal.ac.uk/clti/papers/Groundhog.html].   Retrieved 4/04/04.

—— and Fowler C.F.H. (1999) 'Learning technology and usability: a framework for understanding courseware'. *Interacting with computers* 11/185–497.

Robinson, P., Strong, G., Whittle, J. and Nobe, S. (2001) 'The development of EAP oral discussion ability' in Flowerdew, J. and Peacock, M. (eds,) 347–59.

Waters, A. and Waters, M. (2003) 'Designing tasks for the development of study competences' in Kroll, B. (ed.) 375–89.

LYNN ERREY

16 What is it About Other People's Words?

HE Literacy Practices and the Issue of Plagiarism

The literacy practices of university students are often problematised around the frequency of plagiarism in their writing. Plagiarism may be defined as deliberate 'literary theft' (Park 2003:472), or as 'passing off someone's work, whether intentionally or unintentionally, as your own for your own benefit' (Carroll 2002:9). Research on plagiarism issues has focused mainly on causes and forms of plagiarism in student writing (Norton et al. 2001, Robinson and Kuin 1999, Pecorari 2003, Bennett 2005) and institutional attitudes to plagiarism (Carroll 2002, Larkham and Manns 2002, Sutherland-Smith 2005). Although HE institutions try to address plagiarism by means of post-hoc detection, solutions for tackling the problem pedagogically lag far behind.

In practice, citation mechanics are most commonly taught through the use of study guideline handouts, including formal warnings against plagiarism. However, decontextualised blanket edicts on good citation practice do not necessarily help students assimilate the deeper rationale for such practices, rooted in the culture of academic integrity (Hendricks and Quinn 2000, Currie and Clay 2004:3). Positive reasons for referencing – other than to avoid punishment – may not be 'universally apparent' to students (Bannister and Ashworth 1998).

Specific EAP Challenges

EAP students have specific sociopragmatic challenges in citation: firstly to identify and accommodate differences in practice between previous and current writing cultures; secondly to develop the linguistic skills for using others' words correctly and meaningfully when taking notes, paraphrasing or summarising. Even if students readily understand plagiarism as a concept (Errey 2002), good practice entails a conscious shift into a new area of 'situated literacies' (Barton et al. 2000, Hyland 2001, Pennycook 1996) and a certain amount of language mastery.

Language difficulties do seem to be one cause, since non-native students are over-represented in plagiarism statistics (Bull et al. 2001). Many non-natives, new to academic discourses and practices, may understand the concept of citation long before they master the language to do it well. Trying out various interlanguage strategies in expressing themselves may lead to incoherence and frustration, so that they may fall back on the equally dangerous practice of patchworking, i.e. stringing together paraphrased chunks from various sources, rather than framing a personally expressed idea based on those sources. Pecorari (2003) suggests that patchworking may be an essential experimental process that allows students to shift between their own voice and those of others.

Pedagogic Dilemmas

It is essential to teach students to produce accurate references (Lynch and McGrath 1993). But limiting citation teaching to the mechanics does not help students pragmatically to notice their own literacy practices nor to develop language for highlighting their own voice in writing, the deeper purpose for citation (Lillis and Turner 2001). We need materials and processes that allow students to explore and critique their own citation knowledge and practice, and to address the following questions:

How do we clarify differences between common and authored ownership of knowledge?

Students new to a subject may be unsure whether certain knowledge is individually owned or held in common. Even for academics, what constitutes commonly-owned knowledge seems to be a grey and subjective area (Errey 2002). Angelil-Carter's study (2000:158) highlights how inconsistent individual tutor judgment can be, reacting differently to different students' use of others' ideas.

How do we teach the grammar of citation?

Interweaving one's own voice with those of others can involve complex language decisions: firstly how to incorporate quotations grammatically into the text; secondly how to synthesise different views and 'voices' into a single coherent style; thirdly how to foreground one idea over another, situating each in relation to one's own position. All these citation practices involve complex linguistic choices and processes, linked to task purpose and intention. And yet the grammar of citation in EAP textbooks is often taught as a decontextualised product, restricted to sentence level practice of reporting verbs, or the use of hedges. Leki and Carson (1997) observe that students recognise the need for grammar teaching to be closely linked to task functions, e.g. learning to manipulate forms for specific writing purposes rather than just learning grammar for its own sake. Angelil-Carter (2000) and Pecorari (2003) also argue that students must learn through 'trying on the discourse' of others, in developing an authentic personal voice.

How do we clarify the difference between good and bad para-phrasing?

Bad paraphrasing is a common cause of plagiarism. But although extensively taught as a major citation skill, good paraphrasing, without distortion of the original textual meaning, is very difficult for linguistically unsure learners. In fact over-teaching paraphrasing as the best citation strategy may compound rather than solve problems, as it is both linguistically risky and time-consuming. Little in the literature seems critical of how it is taught. Yet most EAP textbooks teaching paraphrasing offer abbreviating and substitution exercises decontextualised from any authentic purpose for citation. Instead of paraphrasing for its own sake, students might be better learning a metastrategy for citation i.e. to consider the most appropriate repre-sentation of a source for the purpose of writing, whether quotation, paraphrase, brief summary or single reference. Textbook exercises on paraphrasing tend to ignore this kind of strategy.

If bad paraphrasing involves reproducing too much of an original text, just how much is acceptable is unclear. Errey (2002) found that academics varied on how much of an original text was acceptable to use, and what kind of punishment was appropriate in cases of excess. Comments ranged from 'no more than a few key words' to 'this is what academic writers *do*, weave the discourse of the discipline into their writing'.

How do we avoid disempowering students afraid of accidental plagiarism?

Misunderstanding of official edicts can create an inhibitory 'climate of fear' of citation. (Pennycook 1996). Students may understand the con-sequences of plagiarism, but not yet be linguistically confident to adapt their reading sources for their own purposes. Fear of inadvertent plagiarism may lead to working too slowly, or losing any sense of individual voice (Errey 2002). And even where students have been taught good strategies for using others' words, they may still feel insecure about inadvertent plagiarism of others' ideas (Angelil-Carter 2000). EAP instruction needs to address understanding of both.

Pedagogic Approaches for Teaching Citation

Writing pedagogy may have developed in the decade since Pennycook (1996:227) condemned some EAP teaching of citation as 'pedagogically unsound'. Process-oriented and genre-oriented approaches encourage students to think about their own goals and the context goals in writing. However, it may be that teaching citation remains a poor cousin behind other factors, needing a 'discourse of transparency' (Lillis and Turner 2001:58) and systematic tasks which will lead to understanding of how citation works in text.

But this is not so simple. Limited success is achieved if one-off citation workshops remain theoretical without connecting to practice (Hendricks and Quinn 2000). Even process writing approaches, learning by doing, do not seem enough to impact sufficiently on certain students' performance in citation (Hinchcliffe 1998)

In many EAP teachers' experience, classroom-based teaching alone does not go far enough: even at final draft stage of writing, many students will be found plagiarising either through negligent referencing, crude paraphrase, or even deliberate cheating. Raising student awareness of the multifarious considerations and practices related to using others' words critically and correctly for one's own purposes may need consistent, sustained and reflective practice over time to build student confidence and understanding of these processes.

Methodologies that include such sustained reflection are student logbooks or interactive discussion groups, in and out of class (possibly on-line) to focus students on the issues. This paper discusses a study which aimed to raise student awareness of personal citation practices gradually over time, using weekly guided web discussions within a process-oriented writing project. In this study the topics for web-discussion were informed by the pedagogic questions discussed above. The aim was to determine whether such a reflective approach would improve students' understanding and practice of citation in their academic writing.

The Study

This one-semester study was conducted within an Extended Writing Project EAP module which integrated a number of reading and writing skills. The students had experienced writing WebCT-based logbooks, but had not written on specific issues such as citation. Thirty-eight graduate students, from Japan, China, Thailand, Korea and Russia, with an English language level of between IELTS 5.0 and 5.5 on entry, followed the module as part of a masters preparation pre-sessional course.

The teaching approach

The process for raising student awareness of citation and plagiarism issues was embedded in a 3 stage cycle:

> Stage 1: A set 11-week in-class syllabus of staged writing activities to support the writing of a research paper, framed around a self-chosen research topic using primary and/or secondary sources. Teaching included process writing with feedback and editing. Classroom input covered research reading, note-taking, paraphrase and summary for citation, argumentation, language for report writing, and bibliographic skills.

> Stage 2: A weekly syllabus of themed web-based discussion tasks required students in small groups, to reflect and write to each other on aspects of their reading and use of sources. Each group of three or four students read and discussed others' logbooks and together produced a weekly group report for the tutor, outlining shared needs and questions related to their general reading and citation practices. Peer collaboration was intended to promote reflection, discovery, and confidence.

Weekly themes covered reader/writer responsibility, strategies used and problems perceived in reading. Students discussed different uses and practices of citation, good and bad practices in note-taking, quotation and paraphrasing. They considered plagiarism in their own cultures and in the UK, causes of plagiarism, and personal fears. Difficulties and solutions for paraphrasing were considered: how to fit others' words with one's own voice; to use others' words to distance or support an argument; and the rationale for accurate referencing. Uses and dangers of the Internet were also considered. Each group's weekly summary of discussions was used by their tutor for ongoing needs analysis and feedback into subsequent class sessions.

Stage 3: Tutors used the group discussion for further input into the syllabus, firstly by producing a weekly WebCT commentary highlighting student identified problems, questions and useful strategies (see Appendix). Secondly, the tutor used student reports adaptively to remediate gaps in learning, reinforce weak learning, promote problem-solving interactions and explore student-offered solutions. Problems identified were addressed also through remedial mini-lectures and reinforcement tasks. Thus a dynamic and negotiated reflective element was introduced into the pre-planned component of the syllabus.

Data analysis

Analysis of the WebCt discussions revealed strengths and weaknesses in students' knowledge of citation practice and its use. Analysis of the tutor WebCT letters highlighted which issues were addressed or recycled in class. Post programme interviews with tutors and students' end of term self evaluations were also analysed. Data was collected from submitted writing assignments to determine how far students had plagiarised in the final draft.

Findings

Knowledge and understanding of use of sources

Students were found to have quite a sophisticated conceptual understanding of citation. However, this contrasted with low performative confidence in four main areas:

- close reading of sources with unfamiliar language; students easily lost their own line of reasoning
- uncertainty about whose ideas to foreground when integrating their own ideas with another's
- uncertainty about whether ideas arrived at independently might be plagiarism if found in another source
- uncertainty about whether an idea was valid if unsupported by sources.

Citation strategies

Students were generally clear about the concepts and mechanics of citation. However, although they understood knowledge held in common need not be cited, they were uncertain about what was common. They acknowledged the consequences of too little citation (leading to poor argument support) and too much (leading to loss of personal voice), but were unclear exactly how much might constitute over-citation or under-citation. Paraphrasing was seen as the biggest problem. To avoid plagiarism, students were painstaking in thesaurus use but this led to anxiety about time and loss of focus.

Student perceptions about plagiarism as a punishable offence

All understood the concept of plagiarism but little previous experience of writing (exams only), and poor enforcement of good citation practice, meant regular feedback and reflection (in the discussion groups) was reassuring. Compared to UK students, they felt disadvantaged by the time required to process reading. Knowing the dangers of cutting and pasting from the Internet, they nevertheless discussed using it if it saved them time. The tension between time and technique was very clear: although appreciative of the uses of safe and thorough citation practices, they still felt tension between slowing down for this, and cutting corners which led to slips. Many wanted the same extra time as dyslexic home students.

Discussion

Student feedback indicated that they had valued developing a collective metalinguistic voice for identifying weaknesses, sharing problems and devising strategies for citation in an online small group environment. They agreed that the discussions raised their awareness of citation issues, and raised confidence in use of sources.

Tutors reported finding the blended reflective methodology useful: feedback from online discussions had led to efficient ongoing needs analysis. Rich data on the state of students' knowledge and understanding of issues meant tutors could prioritise student needs before the final writing draft. Having access to a wide variety of student interpretations of various questions allowed tutors to manage coherent and collective views on practice.

Tutors reported that this method produced some surprises for teaching, mainly in relation to language needs. Echoing Leki and Carson's (1997) observations, students wanted strong links between task-specific elements of writing and the functional language to produce them. For example, if students could not find any literature to support an idea, they wanted to explore specific language to put forward their own claim and hedge it whilst acknowledging the limited supporting evidence. Occasionally tutors had to review their assumptions about what students had learned, negative feedback leading them to take care recycling information on difficult points.

Whether this teaching approach generated an improved product is arguable, as plagiarism was not entirely eliminated in the students' work. Around 1 in 5 students produced some *patchworking* or unsuccessful paraphrasing in first drafts although most had reported benefiting from the online citation reflection and classroom training. However, the teachers' summation was that there was a marked relative shift from previous typical cohort learning curves, in that good students tended to produce better texts, whilst poor students who might previously have tried to lift whole essays or chunks from other sources, were found to be more circumspect, plagiarising less frequently, even though they still had to be monitored for plagiarism.

As Pecorari (2003) notes, avoidance of plagiarism is a complex and sometimes confusing challenge for student writers, and it is not altogether surprising that the shift in students' perceptions and performance was only one of degree. Nevertheless, tutors agreed that promoting a problem-solving and reflective methodology led to a better quality of classroom discussion, and better awareness of citation practices and plagiarism through the necessity of discussing these.

Recommendations

The methodology of this study was perceived by students as useful in focusing on a number of issues in citation. It is recommended that students in EAP classes be given opportunities firstly to see citation as embedded in academic writing culture and be offered opportunities to evaluate different cultural takes on plagiarism, including the target context rationale. It would also help for tutors to identify potential grey areas in the disciplines.

Secondly, in reading for information, students should be encouraged to have clear pre-reading questions in relation to their purposes and separate these from the writer's purposes, which may be quite different. Where students do cite, they need to keep in mind the interetextual overview that links their own ideas to the citation. They also need to be taught that IT cut and paste note-taking techniques can be dangerous: such notes must be logged for reference, and never worked upon within the essay itself.

Thirdly, in teaching paraphrasing, tutors should present it as only one of many useful strategies. Sometimes a greater distance from the text is more useful with less paraphrase and more summary. Teaching should also go beyond mechanistic translation techniques to link paraphrase with the students' thinking processes around purpose and content of their work.

Fourthly, criticality in citation should be highlighted so that it is accompanied where appropriate with evaluation or personal commentary to reinforce the idea that citation is not just for display but to link critically others' ideas as evidence to support one's own purpose. If an EAP syllabus can build in opportunities over time for gradual reflection of practice, for example in online discussions, this may stand students in good stead for their future studies.

Appendix: extracts from tutor webct letters

Week 3

Hello cohort A!
Firstly, this week's logbook was extremely well done, with lots of viewpoints expressed and very good summaries which grasped the trends expressed by your groupmates very effectively. You all make lots of attempts to define the difference between quotation and citation – some of you give dictionary definitions, others guess, others admit they are really not clear. Your views include the following points: Quotation is something you associate with words (especially words in quotation marks), poetry, literature, lyrics, speech, can be direct or indirect. Citation is the act of extracting reference from a topic, the author's ideas, a way of giving evidence, something for academic use only, only original ideas, something that supports arguments. There is a debate as to where to put citation which could be defined as 'that depends'! Most of you are very clear that there needs to be a balance between your own opinions and those of others, so too much citation would result in your own opinion being lost; too little would mean that your argument lacks support and evidence, and would not convince the reader. Some of you said too much citation is OK – so I think we should also discuss why it is in fact not OK!
Well done on some very thoughtful work M.

Week 5

Dear students,
As usual, I am delighted to read your interesting reflections, especially on a subject as important as this. I am glad to see you all recognise how crucial it is to avoid plagiarism in order to progress in your study in the UK. Most of you acknowledge that it is a more serious issue here than in your own country, although many of you have varying experiences – some of you admit cheating directly in your own

country, while others suggest that your previous tutor was also strict about plagiarism.

You also make an interesting variety of points regarding how it is possible to 'accidentally' plagiarise. Reasons given include – if you don't cite properly, if you use an idea gained from your previous knowledge but you don't know where, if you use a well-known idea and consider it a general point, if you copy an idea without thinking, if you are lazy or forgetful when you are getting information. Others claim it is impossible to plagiarise accidentally – you must always be aware of whether you are plagiarising or not. We will spend some time discussing these points in class.

As most of you also noticed, it is easy for your tutor to spot plagiarism, because it is clear that another author's style of writing is not the same as yours. Unfortunately for you, as non-native speakers, it is even more obvious when you make use of phrases written by a native speaker, 'SO DON'T DO IT!' – as one of you intelligently suggested!

Best wishes, and see you all on Thursday D.

Bibliography

Angelil-Carter, S. (2000) 'Understanding plagiarism differently' in Leibowitz, B. and Mohamed, Y. (eds) *Routes to Writing in South Africa.* Cape Town Silk Road International Publishers, 154–77.

Bull, J., Collins, C., Coughlin, E. and Sharpe, D. (2001) *Technical Review of Plagiarism Detection Software Report*, available on-line at [www.jisc.ac.uk/pub01/luton.pdf] retrieved 31/07/06.

Bannister, P. and Ashworth, P. (1998) 'Four good reasons for cheating and plagiarism' in Rust, C. (ed.) *Improving Student Learning: improving students as learners.* Oxford: OCSLD, 235–40.

Barton, D., Hamilton, M. and Ivanic, R. (2000) *Situated literacies: reading and writing in context.* London: Routledge.

Bennett, R. (2005) 'Factors associated with student plagiarism in a post-1992 university'. *Assessment and Evaluation in Higher Education,* 30/2, 137–62.

Carroll, J. (2002) *A handbook for deterring plagiarism in higher education.* Oxford: Oxford Brookes Centre for Staff and Learning Development.

Curry, P. and Clay, E. (2004) 'ESL literacy: language practice or social practice'. *Journal of Second Language Writing* 13/2, 111–32.

Errey, L. 2002 'Plagiarism: something fishy? ... or just a fish out of water?' Teaching Forum 50 Autumn, 17–20, available online at [http://www.brookes.ac.uk/virtual/NewTF/50/T50errey.pdf] retrieved 31/07/06.

Hendricks, M. and. Quinn, L. (2000) 'Teaching referencing as an introduction to epistemological empowerment'. *Teaching in Higher Education* 5/4, 448–57.

Hinchliffe, L. (1998) 'Cut-and-Paste Plagiarism: preventing, detecting and tracking online plagiarism'. Available online at [http://alexia.lis.uiuc.edu/~janicke/plagiary.htm] retrieved 31/07/06.

Hyland, F. (2001) 'Dealing with plagiarism when giving feedback'. *ELT Journal* 55/4, 375–81.

Larkham, P. and Manns, S. (2002) 'Plagiarism and its treatment in Higher Education'. *Journal of Further and Higher Education* 26/4, 339–49.

Leki, I. and Carson, J. (1994) 'Students' perceptions of EAP writing instructions and writing needs across the disciplines'. *TESOL Quarterly* 28/1, 81–102.

Lillis, T. and Turner, J. (2001) 'Student writing in higher education: contemporary confusion, traditional concerns'. *Teaching in Higher Education* 6/1, 58–68.

Lynch T. and McGrath, I. (1993) 'Teaching bibliographic documentation Skills'. *English for Specific Purposes,* 12, 219–38.

Norton, L., Tilley, S., Newstead, A. and Franklyn-Stokes, A. (2001) 'The pressures of assessment in undergraduate courses and their effect on student behaviour'. In *Assessment and Evaluation in Higher Education* 26/3.

Park, C. (2003) 'In other peoples words: plagiarism by university students – literature and lessons'. *Assessment and Evaluation in Higher Education* 28/5, 471–88.

Pecorari, D. (2003) 'Good and original: plagiarism and patchworking in academic second-language writing'. *Journal of Second Language Writing* 12, 317–45.

Pennycook, A. (1996) 'Borrowing others' words: text, ownership, memory and plagiarism'. *TESOL Quarterly* 30/2, 201–30.

Robinson, V. and Kuin, L.M. (1999) 'The explanation of practice: why Chinese students copy assignments'. *Qualitative Studies in Education* 2/2, 193–210.

Sherman, J. (1992) 'Your own thoughts in your own words'. *ELTJ* 42/6, 190–8

Sutherland-Smith, W. (2005) 'Pandora's box: academic perceptions of student plagiarism in writing'. *Journal of English for Academic Purposes* 4/1, 83–95.

CATHY BENSON, JACQUELINE GOLLIN AND HUGH TRAPPES-LOMAX

17 Reporting Strategies in Academic Writing: From Corpus to Materials

Introduction

Our aims in this project have been to investigate reporting strategies in academic writing, to consider implications for teaching and materials writing, and to gain experience in creating and using a corpus of academic text.[1] In particular, we set out to:

1) investigate citation choices, specifically to explore the relationship between 'integral-ness' (Swales 1990) and 'prominence' (Weissburg and Buker 1990)
2) investigate stance, specifically to evaluate the Swales and Feak (1994) classification of 'objective/evaluative' reporting verbs and to look at other (including non-verb) ways in which stance is realised in the corpus data
3) evaluate a sample of existing teaching materials
4) create EAP materials based on our findings and drawing on the material in the corpus.

---

1 The corpus (of approximately 301,000 words) was created from 50 articles published in *Edinburgh Working Papers in Applied Linguistics*, between 1994 and 2003, including contributions from both NS and NNS.

What do Learners Need to Know?

We begin by summarising the knowledge and skills in this area which proficient academic writers may be expected to possess, and which novice academic writers need to acquire. Learners need to know

- *why* we refer to previous research. Such reference provides the reader with the background information needed to understand the study, establishes the present research as one link in a chain, shows respect to previous scholars, affords evidence that the writer qualifies as a member of the scholarly community, and demonstrates familiarity with the field; in short, 'creates a research space' for the writer (Weissburg and Buker 1990, Swales and Feak 1994).

- *what* kind of thing is reported. Academic writers relate a finding or claim with the person who has found or claimed it (Swales 1990). They attribute previous findings to particular researchers, and adopt a stance (a set of attitudes) towards the findings. They report on authors[2] (research agents), activities (research events/processes), and ideas (hypotheses, research outcomes), referring to single studies, groups of studies, or general level and trends of research.

- *how* writers refer to previous research, in terms of both specification, attribution and stance. Connected particularly with the former are choices affecting prominence (Weissburg and Buker 1990) and integral-ness (Swales 1990), as well as related choices of theme, grammatical subject and voice, and tense or aspect in the reporting verb. Connected particularly with the latter are choice of reporting verb (or noun) and of collocating adjectives and adverbs. Reporting verbs have been categorised into objective and evaluative (Swales and Feak 1994) and into those whose use asserts the writer's commitment to the attendant proposition (*show* etc.) and those whose use does not (*suggest* etc.).

---

2   For reasons of clarity we adopt the convention that 'writers' cite and 'authors' are cited.

Finally, learners need to be aware that translating the process of discovery (research action) into an account of that process (research rhetoric) is not only a technical act of considerable complexity, requiring careful planning, feedback and revision, but also a social act of considerable delicacy, a 'careful balance of factual information and social interaction' involving 'the perilous negotiation of a successful writer-reader relationship' (Hyland 1999). The need to create a research space may be implicitly threatening to the positive face of predecessors in the field. The need to have achieved something, to be original, is at odds with the maxim of modesty. In what follows, we focus on the 'how', with particular reference to the articulation of prominence and stance.

Prominence and Integral-ness

Prominence (Weissberg and Buker 1990) and integral-ness (Swales 1990) are closely related but usefully distinguishable concepts in understanding how research is reported, the former relating to content and the latter to structure. Table 1 represents the relationship between them, with choices in prominence (column 1) anticipating, and largely determining, choices in integral-ness (column 2). Thus, an initial choice to make an author-prominent reference entails selection of an integral mode of citation, with three available grammatical options: author(s) as subject, as agent or in preposition phrase (according to). To Weissberg and Buker's four types (author prominent, information-prominent, weak-author prominent and general statement) we have added author + information, which captures the type of reference illustrated in example g) in the table.

choose as prominent:	Make citation integral?	Simple list?[3]	Examples
specific author-named research item(s)	yes a) as subject b) as agent (by/in) c) according to in accordance with following		a) Ferguson and White (1994) found higher correlations – 0.39 for IELTS/ outcome and b) a critique of Bassnett 1991, Gentzler 1993 and Venuti 1992, and the wider tradition(s) they represent, is offered in Parkinson 1995b. c) According to Halliday and Hasan (1976) there are two broad functional uses for …
information	no	yes bare citations in brackets	d) … speakers of English are reported to have taken the test between 1981–5 (Criper and Davies 1988). e) it has been argued (Bachman 1990) that before we can evaluate a test's validity we must have some insight into the …
		no see e.g./cf (+/- comment)	f) … social and cultural event created and experienced by its participants (see e.g. Breen 1985, Prabhu 1992, Coleman 1996, Sandhu in this paper).
Author + information	yes possessive NP		g) The use of the deontic modal verb, we should not … is a typical example from Simpson (1993)'s 'internal, positive perspective.'
un-named group ('weak author prominence')	no [reference to group (e.g. 'several recent studies') may appear as subject, agent or following 'according to' etc]	yes citations in brackets	h) Other authors (O'Connor 19 91:210; Lock 1977:108) advocate avoidance of 'approximately'.
		no see/e.g./cf (+/- comment)	i) *Some linguists (e.g. Wierzbicka 1986)* have attempted to make fine distinctions between different approximators.
general statement	no	no (?) see/e.g./cf (+/- comment)	j) In the wider perspective of research into second language acquisition (e.g. *Faerch and Kasper 1986; Rost 1990),* listening is regarded as a powerful source of input …
	or do not cite		

Table 1. Prominence and integral-ness

3   Our data provided us with the basis for a simple grammar of non-simple citation lists (those using cf., e.g., etc) which for reasons of space we have not included here.

Stance: does the writer agree with the author?

The other major issue we addressed, when considering how previous research is referred to, was the question of stance: whether and to what extent the writer agrees with the author. In our experience, this is a difficult area for many EAP students. Many learners from Asian countries, for example, have told us they find it strange that authors are cited with whom the writer disagrees. They maintain that in their academic cultures, they would omit such authors, restricting their citations to writers whose ideas they accept. In order to help students to understand and recognise stance in their reading and to express it in their writing, we as teachers need to increase our own awareness of how writers reveal their stance towards the work they cite. To this end we explored various devices for indicating stance in the EWPAL corpus and also examined how this area is dealt with in pedagogical materials.

One example of awareness-raising in teaching materials can be found in Swales and Feak (1994), which includes a table (reproduced below) showing reporting verbs and suggesting how a writer's choice of verb can reveal her or his attitude towards the author or work cited.

	Objective	Evaluative
Describe	X	
Discuss	X	
State	X	
Present	X	
Explain	X	
Maintain	X	
Examine	X	
Affirm	X?	X?
Argue	X?	X?
Reveal	X	
Presume		X

Assume		X
Assert		X
Contend		X
Allege		X
Claim		X
Imply		X

Table 2. Swales and Feak's (1994) analysis of selected reporting verbs

We felt there were various problems with this table. For one thing, it only considers verbs, omitting other means of citation. Moreover, we find their 'objective vs evaluative' classification confusing. The word 'evaluative' usually implies either positive or negative evaluation, but here it is used mainly with a negative meaning; we prefer Thomson and Ye's (1991) 3-way classification of writer stance (neutral, positive and negative), while adding the caveat that the default interpretation of neutral is in fact positive, as we believe that it is logical to infer acceptance where an author is cited without comment.

We also found that we were sceptical of some of their decisions about classification, and turned to our corpus to investigate the occurrence of the verbs in the table. As we suspected, our findings, were not always in accordance with the table.[4] Some verbs did not occur at all, e.g. *allege* (unsurprisingly perhaps, as this verb seems to belong in the realm of journalism rather than in academic writing); others occurred predominantly as text-organising verbs used by the writers to refer to their own texts (e.g. *present, examine, describe*).

We chose to focus on three verbs: *claim, assume,* and *argue.* In several instances, we found the writer's stance could only be deduced by reading some lines (or even paragraphs) ahead in the text; this emphasised for us the importance of the larger context in determining whether the writer agrees with the author.

---

4   In their revised (2002) edition of the same book, Swales and Feak recognise this deficiency, noting that the first edition was based on intuition rather than a corpus.

For example, let us look at the verb *claim*. According to Swales and Feak, this is evaluative; i.e. used when the writer intends to express doubt about the author's assertion. In the first paragraph below, this would appear to be the case, although this can only be ascertained by reading on beyond the single sentence in which the verb occurs. However, in the paragraph following, there appears to be no such intention for the writer to distance him/herself from the author's claim:

> In support of this proposition, Aslin et al. (1981) demonstrated that infants from an English-speaking environment can reliably discriminate an irrelevant VOT contrast, occurring within the same English-adult phonemic categories. Following this pattern of findings, Eimas (1985), in his subsequent study, CLAIMS that human beings are endowed with innate perceptual mechanisms which facilitate the acquisition of a language.
>
> This proposition derives from the view, advanced by Chomsky (1981), that innate knowledge and capacities underlie the use of language, whereby infants are born with innate perceptual capacities/sensitivities which enable them to discriminate between the universal set of phonetic distinctions, according to universal phonetic boundaries; if these perceptual mechanisms do represent an innate biological endowment, they should be universal. The same perceptual patterns should occur in infants of every linguistic background.

Rarely does the reporting verb or noun alone carry any intrinsic evaluative meaning, apart from in the case of factive verbs; rather, the interpretation of stance depends on other elements in the syntax or in the discourse, including the use of

- an adverb in conjunction with a reporting verb, to cite two examples from the data: Romaine and Lange (1991:245) very lucidly point out that ... (where *lucidly* adds positive meaning) ... concludes somewhat lamely... (where *lamely* adds a negative interpretation to a verb classified by Swales and Feak as objective)
- as in conjunction with a reporting verb indicating the writer's acceptance, e.g. As Criper and Davies (1988) point out, even when medical or family reasons for non-completion are cited, it may well be in order to save embarrassment...
- a discourse marker such as *however* (perhaps some sentences or even paragraphs later) as the first explicit indication that

the writer does not accept the ideas or arguments that she/he has been reporting *in xxx's words*, followed by exact quotation, adding positive evaluation e.g. In Underhill's words (1988:241) she 'leaves the statement slightly open', because... [5]

- explicit opinion verbs such as *agree with, share, accept, follow*, with the writer as subject e.g. I agree with Green (1992) in including second person plural personal pronouns...; I follow Ferrara and Bell (1995) who...
- other explicit agreement expressions such as *in accordance with, in line with, following* e.g. Following Schiffrin (1987), such items can be analysed as discourse markers; The results of the present study, in line with Schwarz and Sprouse (1996)...

Other Issues

Reporting nouns

Claim occurs as both a verb and a noun and our corpus contains instances of both argue and argument. Indeed in our corpus, *argument* occurs slightly more frequently than *argue* while *view* as a noun occurs 66 times, as opposed to five times as a verb. Nouns such as these, of course, can serve a dual function of not only reporting but also packaging and labelling the discourse, as discussed by Gill Francis (1986, 1994).

5   We found no contrary instances of e.g. disagree, differ from, or diverge from.

Inanimate subjects

According to Peter Master (1991), the combination of an inanimate subject with an active verb may seem strange to students from certain L1 backgrounds.

> Many students, particularly those whose first language is an Asian one, find it difficult if not impossible to use an active verb with an inanimate subject in writing English because they find it unacceptably anthropomorphic .... A Japanese student once told me that she was able to produce the sentence 'A thermometer measures temperature' in Japanese but that it was a humorous and unlikely one because she had to imagine that the thermometer had little arms and legs. (Master 1991:18)

Two examples from our corpus which might fall in the same category include the following:

> Sweetser's analysis of the English word lie (1987) similarly argues against traditional semantics...
> But the article continues and concludes somewhat lamely...

Teaching Materials

Professional writers have a range of sophisticated means of citation, and the communication of stance is a complex issue which is given a rather cursory treatment in published teaching materials. We evaluated some published materials and some of our own in-house EAP materials, looking at whether they dealt with the following features of reporting language: writer stance, reporting language other than verbs, prominence and integration, range of reporting items, collocation, syntactic environment, and contextualisation in extended stretches of discourse. We found that, in general, existing materials do not provide a sufficiently delicate categorisation of reporting verbs, fail to provide information on collocation and pay little attention to reporting by means of other parts of speech.

We include two examples of our own preliminary attempts at exploiting our corpus for teaching materials in the appendix. Worksheets A and B explore stance and prominence, looking at reporting by means of words other than verbs. Question 4 in Worksheet B explores the different kinds of entities that different reporting nouns may refer to. Question 5 (also Worksheet B) touches on the combination of an inanimate subject with an active verb which many learners, as described above, find unacceptably anthropomorphic.

Though they will benefit from further refinement, these sample worksheets show that a corpus such as ours provides a rich seam to be mined for teaching materials which would give our students a more comprehensive grasp of the multifaceted nature of reporting language.

Appendix: sample materials for helping learners with the language of reporting

Worksheet A: adverbs in reporting

Use one of the adverbs from the box below to complete the sentences. In each case try to decide whether the writer accepts the words/views/ ideas reported.

> interestingly   notably   uncritically   carefully
> insufficiently   especially   reasonably   adequately
> correctly   loudly   strongly   reportedly   memorably
> immediately   lamely   widely (x2)   fully

In the boxes on the right put a ✓ if you think the writer accepts the words/views/ideas reported, a X if not, and a ? if you are not sure.

1. There is a large body of research in this area, of which O'Brien (1985) and Sato (1986) are _____ worthy of mention. We quote from these in the Suggestions section below.

2. But the article continues and concludes somewhat _____: 'Unfortunately, this issue leads us too far at this stage, but further work is needed to find out whether a threshold level like this really exists'

3. It is now _____ recognised that all research which depends upon written responses engages the respondent in a kind of dialogue with the 'implied reader', usually identical with the question setter, involving unspoken questions such as 'What do they mean?' 'What do they want?' 'What will they think of me?'

4. Their argument has been widely (and at times perhaps a little _____) adopted as a rationale for the use of verbal report procedures in a wide range of investigative contexts.

5. In her penultimate paragraph, pessimistically but
    _____, she argues that her data support
    Cummings' (1981) view that: 'there exists a threshold
    level of proficiency in the L2 below which strategy
    acquisition is not possible'

6. As we pointed out in the Introduction, there is no
    universal agreement among SLA researchers that feed-
    back has any direct effect on learners' spoken perform-
    ance; _____, Truscott (1999) has argued that
    oral correction by the teacher has no impact on spoken
    grammatical accuracy - following his similar claim that
    grammar teaching does not improve writing performance
    (Truscott 1996). However, the majority of SLA studies
    have borne out the assumption that some forms of
    feedback are effective in the short term, in the sense of
    leading to modification of the error and/or imitation of
    the correct form.

7. Bokamba quite _____ points out that the sources
    of lexical innovations in African English are mother
    tongue interference, analogical derivation based on Eng-
    lish and the milieu and conditions under which English is
    learned and used in Anglophone Africa. (Bamiro 1994:
    48)

8. A special issue of TESOL Quarterly, number 29, 3
    (1995), is devoted to qualitative research, mostly of a
    loosely ethnographic type, and treats more _____
    the above ideas, especially in articles by Davis (1995)
    and Lazaraton (1995).

9. Although we have not yet had time to analyse the data on
    a full case-study basis, we believe there is enough
    evidence to confirm that the _____ expressed
    faith in tutor feedback does have an empirical basis, at
    least in the particular one-to-one form that the English for
    Medical Congresses course design allows.

10. The feature of Basic trumpeted most _____ by Ogden, the fact that it had done away with verbs, has a direct parallel in Newspeak (Nineteen Eighty-Four, 165).

11. For abstracts, the work most _____ relevant to the current study is by Salager-Meyer (1990a, 1990b).

12. Brindley (1989), for example, has argued quite _____ for the adoption and adaptation of such schemes for the Adult Migrant Education Program (AMEP) in Australia.

13. The adaptor Fred Burke _____ perceived artistically undesirable connotations in some of the original names when transferred into English (anonymous website author 2001).

14. Ogden & Richards, in the British empiricist tradition, _____ considered Saussure's view and rejected it on the grounds that it was self-negating.

15. I will not outline here the history of verbal report procedure as an investigative tool, for this is _____ reviewed in Matsumoto (1993) and Pressley and Afflerbach (1995).

16. The main point is that, after several decades of rejection on the ground that they were _____ empirical, introspective procedures are once again widely accepted as legitimate data-gathering tools.

17. Its treatment of abstracts is therefore less comprehensive, but, _____, the authors take a less prescriptive approach.

18. Described as 'his most influential essay' by his biographer Michael Shelden (1991: 430), it is interesting for the insight it offers into his process as a writer and stylist as well as in how it anticipates the core problem of language he would address so _____ in Nineteen Eighty-Four.

Worksheet B: reporting the research of others

1.   What shortcomings of previous research are indicated by the writer of this extract from an academic journal article?
These criticisms have not really been answered, and it would seem that since 1988 academic work on learner diaries has moved forward very little. In the more prestigious journals, articles on diaries are now mostly about teacher diaries, or 'logs' kept by teacher 'trainees', or occasionally, in the Schumann tradition, teacher as learners (Ahrens 1993). Local journals and working papers do sometimes contain competent but anecdotal reports of small-scale experiments which teachers and learners seem to have enjoyed, but attempts to demonstrate something more substantial have been few and unconvincing.

One example must suffice. Halbach (2000) is among many writers hoping to use diaries as a window on 'strategy' use, and she claims that her better students were more able to respond to learner training and increased the range of strategies used, thus moving even further ahead of weaker classmates. In her penultimate paragraph, pessimistically but reasonably, she argues that her data support Cummings' (1981) view that:

> there exists a threshold level of proficiency in the L2 below which strategy acquisition is not possible. If this, as it seems, is the case with the weaker students, we are facing a vicious circle: weaker students do not have enough strategies to help them with language learning, but at the same time, they are not proficient enough to benefit from strategy training, since they cannot use these strategies in their L2. This, in turn, means that they will not be able to speed up their learning with the help of their strategies. (p. 93)

But the article continues and concludes somewhat lamely:

> Unfortunately, this issue leads us too far at this stage, but further work is needed to find out whether a threshold level like this really exists What does become is the need for [...]

2. Identify the words used for reporting the work of other researchers and list them in the appropriate column in the table.

Nouns	Verbs	Adjectives	Adverbs

3. Which of these words appear to be used for negative comment, which for positive comment and which are used neutrally? Put Neg, Pos or Neu against each word in your lists.

4. Look at the nouns again. Can you find examples which refer to the following?
- a. written end product
- b. research procedure
- c. function of the writing
- d. theory, ideas, school of thought

5. Note the following sentence:

> But the article continues and concludes somewhat lamely [...]

Can you combine a noun like article with a verb like conclude in your language?

Can you find another example of this kind of combination in the passage?

6. Write a short paragraph suitable for a literature review related to your own academic area. Try to use at least five of the words you listed in the table for Question 2.

Bibliography

Francis, G. (1986) *Anaphoric Nouns*. Monograph. English Language Research series. Birmingham: Department of English, University of Birmingham.

—— (1994) 'Labelling discourse: an aspect of nominal-group lexical cohesion' in Coulthard, M. (ed.) *Advances in Written Discourse Analysis*. London and New York: Routledge, 83–101.

Hyland, K. (1999) 'Academic attribution: citation and the construction of disciplinary knowledge'. *Applied Linguistics* 20/3, 341–67.

Master, P. (1991) 'Active verbs with inanimate subjects'. *ESP Journal* 10, 15–33.

Swales, J.M. (1990) *Genre analysis: English in academic and research settings*. Cambridge: Cambridge University Press.

Swales, J. and Feak, C. (1994) *Academic writing for graduate students*. Ann Arbor: The University of Michigan Press.

Thompson, G. and Ye, Y. (1991) 'Evaluation of the reporting verbs used in academic papers'. *Applied Linguistics* 12, 365–82.

Weissberg, R. and Buker, S. (1990) *Writing up Research: experimental research report writing for students of English*. Prentice Hall.

Section V

Assessment

SIÂN ETHERINGTON

18 Teaching and Testing Academic Writing: Exploring Staff and Learner Experiences

Introduction

There has long been a strongly perceived need within EAP for further work on testing instruments and procedures (Clapham and Wall 1990, Blue et al. 2000, Alderson 2000). The research reported here grew out of a wish to address some of the issues concerning testing used on a pre-sessional EAP programme, particularly the validity of the tests in relation to students' future academic needs.

The project focuses on the assessment of academic writing. This particular skill was chosen because of its fundamental importance within the EAP context. Writing is the key Academic English skill, where lack of proficiency leads to serious student demotivation, lack of progress and very often, failure and withdrawal from programmes. For academic staff too, writing is a crucial area as it is through writing that most course assessment is carried out.

It is important then, that the academic writing we focus on in pre-sessional programmes, both in teaching and testing, prepares students adequately for their future needs and this concern has been reflected in recent work within the Academic Writing assessment field (e.g. Cushing Weigle 2002:172ff). In particular, it has been suggested that greater emphasis is needed on the processes of writing and the intertextual nature of academic writing (e.g. Grabe 2003, Cho 2003). In light of these concerns, this research investigated academic tutors' understanding of and priorities within academic writing in order to align pre-sessional testing more closely with authentic writing needs.

The Research: stage one

The setting for this research will be familiar to EAP tutors in UK universities. It is a summer pre-sessional programme consisting of three blocks of teaching. Students work on all four skills throughout each block, but the emphasis on writing becomes stronger as students progress through the blocks. In the final block, in addition to other writing work, students complete an individual extended piece of writing (study project). The student body is mixed, both in terms of English level and future academic plans: destinations include PhD or Masters study, undergraduate degrees, and the International Foundation year. English language proficiency ranges from approximately IELTS 4.0 to 7.0.

There were two phases to the research. The first explored perceptions of academic writing expressed by academic subject staff. These findings were then used as the basis for the development of a revised test of writing within the 2004 pre-sessional EAP programme. The second phase investigated student views of the approaches to writing on the pre-sessional programme and also their perceptions of academic writing in general.

Stage one: academic staff interviews

Data collection targeted academics in the schools which were the most likely destinations for pre-sessional students (Information Systems, Accounting and Finance, Art and Design, and Management).Seven semi-structured interviews were conducted with key personnel. Academic staff were asked to indicate
- the range of written work students were expected to produce
- the value placed on various aspects of language in the marking of student assignments
- particular student writing difficulties.

Interviews typically lasted an hour and were recorded, then transcribed and the content analysed.

Stage one: findings

Findings relating to aspects of writing valued by academic tutors suggested that for these staff the most important aspects of student writing were at the macro-level; the development of logical argument and the clarity of writing were most highly valued. Many of the staff saw these issues as aligned to thinking or understanding of the subject, rather than as writing skills. For example, one tutor commented

> I would say that those that we've marked as important are to do with the actual content of the – of what we want them to do rather than how they are saying it.

Grammatical and lexical accuracy were important for tutors, but particularly when problems made access to content difficult. Some tutors admitted to being fussy about grammar and spelling and specifically used mark schemes to allow for reduction in marks for inadequacies in these areas. More than one interviewee reported that they would not award a first class mark to students with poor grammar. However, there was variation in the weighting attached to grammatical problems: one tutor suggested that students should find out who their marker was and how accurate they needed to be.

Avoidance of plagiarism through the correct use of sources was another important concern for staff. Staff recognised that there was a certain 'vagueness' about the term, that it covers many different cases and different levels of intent. However, it was felt that for international students a lack of understanding of appropriate use of sources was often the cause. One tutor expressed the wish to help students see that

> engaging with the literature was a sort of learning journey that they have to come on, rather than it being a cliff – a cliff of plagiarism.

Less important elements of writing for staff appeared to be grammatical and lexical variety and the use of academic style, particularly at lower levels of study. Tutors felt that these were aspects of writing which could be developed throughout the students' time in the university. One tutor indicated that academic style was an element of writing which could be developed in the final year of a degree, but was not necessary earlier than this.

In relation to marking it was revealed that greater regularisation is taking place through the implementation of marking criteria for written work. Staff felt that such criteria helped to provide students with clearer feedback on their writing. However, one of the main issues remained that students did not have enough practice in writing in English before they reach assessment.

Test Development

Following the results above, a new test of academic writing was developed in order to reflect more closely the aspects of writing which had been highlighted as of importance to academic tutors. In particular, tutors' discussions of student difficulties in engagement with literature and their problems with plagiarism prompted a wish to include the notion of the intertextual nature of academic writing, working to help students to see writing as part of the academic conversation where the use of others' writing and thoughts is an important part of the writing process and product.

This was achieved through the integration of reading and writing within the test, creating a source-based rather than prompt-based test (Cushing-Weigle 2004). Prompt-based tests expect students to use their own knowledge and opinions to create a piece of writing, whereas authentic academic writing typically asks students to summarise, refer to, comment on and argue with the writing of others within their work. Thus, in the new test, students were expected to use information from two extended texts to argue and support a position, with references made to extracts from the texts where appropriate. It was felt that this provided a test which was more in line with subject tutors' understandings of academic writing. EAP writing research also indicates that an integrated test of this kind is more authentic in terms of academic writing (Grabe 2003).

A further development in the test related to the choice of topic. Most academic writing typically is undertaken after students have spent a considerable amount of time thinking about, discussing and reading about a subject. In order to reflect this interactive aspect of academic writing, the essay title chosen for the test was within a topic area (Sport) which students had worked on throughout the block.

It was hoped that these changes would help develop students' understandings of the nature of writing within this context away from a 'language practice' or 'language display' view of writing, as often held by EFL students (Leki and Carson 1994), to a perception of academic writing as concerned with the development and communication of ideas.

The Research: stage two

Stage two: student interviews

The second phase of the research tracked a group of students from the pre-sessional course into their degree programmes, using interviews at the beginning and end of their first semester to evaluate how well the pre-sessional programme had prepared them for the writing tasks they faced. In addition, the interviews investigated if and how student understandings of academic writing had changed over this time. It was felt that this information would provide another indication of how successfully the new testing approach had helped in preparing students for academic subject writing.

Seven students volunteered for this phase of the research. All were Masters students from a range of postgraduate programme (IT Management in Construction, Human Resources Management, Purchasing and Logistics, and TEFL). They were from different levels within the pre-sessional programme. With the exception of one Russian student, all were Chinese or Taiwanese.

In the first interview students were asked to talk about what the term 'academic writing' meant for them and to comment on the most important aspects of academic writing from a list of elements. They were also asked to discuss what made a successful piece of writing, what they felt their subject tutors valued in academic writing and, finally, their impressions of the teaching and learning of writing on the summer EAP programme.

The second interview, which took place at the end of Semester 1 and, importantly, after the first assignments and examinations for these students, revisited several of these questions. Students were also asked how their recent experience of writing differed from writing in the pre-sessional course, and how the pre-sessional could have prepared them better for this writing. Each interview lasted approximately one hour.

Stage two: findings

Analysis of both the quantitative and qualitative data collected through the interviews indicates several changes in perception of academic writing taking place over the semester (Table 1). This change is seen most clearly perhaps in a comparison of the elements of academic writing which students rated as 'very important' at each point in time. In interview 1 responses indicate that students prioritised 'use of quotations and references' and vocabulary accuracy. By the time of the second interview, however, their views have changed so that 'clarity of argument and writing' and 'logical development of argument' along with 'avoidance of plagiarism' had become more important.

	Interview 1	Interview 2
Aspect of academic writing	No. choosing 'very important'	No. choosing 'very important'
Clarity of argument and writing	1	5
Logical development of argument	2	5
Grammatical accuracy	2	1
Grammatical variety	1	1
Vocabulary accuracy	3	1
Vocabulary variety	1	0
Use of suitable style	1	2
Use of graphics	0	0
Use of quotations /references	5	4
Avoidance of plagiarism	3	6

Table 1. Changes in students' perception of what is important in academic writing

The data indicate a move from a view of writing which foregrounds the micro-level to one which reflects the students' engagement with writing about particular content and their encounters with marking criteria which value clarity of content and ideas. This is confirmed by a comparison of the qualitative data in both sets of interviews. In the first interviews students tend to view successful academic writing as grammatically accurate, using the right kinds of academic phrases and a 'good number' of references. For example, comments include

> I try to improve my writing by write down email to my uncle... he will correct my mistakes
> Most of the pieces of work I write is going to be corrected by teachers and it will affect my marks so it would be more important to me to have no grammar mistakes or spelling mistakes
> I know a lot of language about academic writing and can use this to be successful writer
> You should make the teacher think that you are working hard by giving references.

By the end of Semester 1, however, students are turning their attention to other aspects of academic writing. Comments now include

> Accuracy is still important, but just a small point to be successful as a writer needs writing with my mind
> High mark in grammar and language is not our business, because we always have grammar and language problems!
> I can produce better writing by paying more attention to conclusions and adding my own ideas and evaluation
> Success in writing comes because of good point of view, good arguments in assignment.

The change from a concern for using references and quotations to anxiety about plagiarism also suggests a move from a mechanical level (the details of referencing) to an understanding that plagiarism is a bigger issue. By the time of the second interview, referencing was reported as 'easy to resolve', whereas several students indicated that they still did not know how to avoid plagiarism. Indeed, for two students significant problems with plagiarism had affected their marks on Semester 1 assignments. One student voiced her confusion about the use of others' writing as a model for her own; this was something she felt was good practice, but was unsure whether to reference the phrases and words she had borrowed. The issue of what constituted plagiarism had become even more complex with the move into full academic study.

Connected to this point is the indication from several students that it is only after the semester's work that they realise the connections between reading and writing. For example, in the course of the semester one student found that 'research for writing is not just a game – we need to pay attention to research'. Another mentioned that the 'big change' in her writing was that 'when I write now, I *read* first and then plan my assignment'. Others are still struggling: 'I have not quite grasped the selective reading from the text' and 'I feel confused about note-taking and organising my notes for writing'.

Given the motivation for the changes to the pre-sessional test, it is perhaps of concern that it is only after the first semester that these ideas emerged for students. Indeed, several interviewees commented that the length and nature of written work expected on the summer programme had not allowed them to explore this connection fully. Although pre-sessional students complete a study project within their own subject area, it was felt that this was not of sufficient length. Interviewees commented that

> Writing is very short – we cant cover introduction, main body in this size
> Summer programme just prepare us for the test – not for writing long assignments – I thought that I could write 1000 words in one day!
> I need to learn how to narrow down my topic and narrow down the words in my essay
> The study project does not use extensive reading
> Only one project is not enough

These comments also suggest that the projects did not provide sufficient engagement in the process of writing for these students.

Similarly, EAP tutors' lack of subject knowledge makes students feel that their use of sources in their pre-sessional writing could not be judged in the same way as in their degree programme work. Students observe that 'What is important for subject tutors is not important for SESP tutors' and that study projects would be more valuable if marked by teachers 'who were somehow close to that topic'.

Most students also appear to feel that EAP tutors' concerns are mainly with the mechanics of language, rather than with academic writing as a whole. For some this means that specialist subject knowledge is not needed: 'They don't understand the subject but this is not important because they are looking only at grammar and references etc'. For others this means that pre-sessional work does not focus on the important aspects of academic writing: 'the summer programme is pure linguistic pieces of work, not about arguments. Just about describing information from reading. The study project would fail in my course now – it does not give a critical view'.

While students hold the view that EAP writing is purely about language practice, there will be an inevitable gap between writing purpose on the pre-sessional and degree programmes. It is the need to explain and deliver their own meanings within a context where content is primary which provides the impetus for students to improve their academic writing. One student encapsulates this in her comment,

The summer English study is just about language – we not know language. The teachers need to provide idea and information for students because our language is limited. Now our language is also limited but able to find ideas and information more easily – is easy to learn language because have ideas and need to find language to express these.

Conclusion

The findings above illustrate these students' development of more sophisticated, authentic understandings of academic writing during their first semester. Indeed, over this time their priorities within academic writing converged with those reported by academic subject tutors. To find that students can adapt to their new contexts with some success is encouraging. However, it is also disconcerting that these students appear to have left the pre-sessional programme with a great deal of progress in understanding of academic writing still to be made. Despite developments in teaching and testing, it seems that the pre-sessional academic writing did not provide adequate preparation for the students' writing futures. Something more is needed in order to help students to move towards these realisations earlier.

One could ask how important it is for a pre-sessional programme to fulfil these needs. It could be argued that it is the basics of grammar and vocabulary which are the main business of pre-sessional work. Once these are in place then students will be able to learn about other aspects of writing within their own departments. However, the findings here suggest that such an approach will not allow students to move beyond a view of writing for linguistic practice. Without an understanding of the purpose and nature of academic writing they are unlikely to succeed. (It should be noted that the participants in this research were well-motivated Masters level students. Students at lower levels and with less interest in their writing are likely to undergo a longer and more problematic process of change.)

Alternatively, the research can be interpreted as supporting a move towards a Content-Based Instruction syllabus (Brinton, Snow and Wesche 1989). This would allow closer integration of reading and writing in an academic sense and a level of writing for purpose as yet not achieved within the pre-sessional programme. It seems that we need to treat our students as future academic *writers*, not simply as test takers or language learners. Students will not survive within academic life without the ability to write in the ways in which the academy expects. This involves a change in perception, which we need to foster through the academic writing we encourage.

Bibliography

Alderson, J.C. (2000) 'Testing in EAP: Progress? Achievement? Proficiency?' in Blue G.M., Milton, J. and Saville, J. (eds) 21–47.

Blue G.M., Milton, J. and Saville, J. (eds) (2000) *Assessing English for Academic Purposes*. Bern: Peter Lang AG.

—— (2000) 'Introduction: Assessing English for Academic Purposes' in Blue G.M., Milton, J. and Saville, J. (eds) 7–17.

Brinton, D.M., Snow, M.A. and Wesche, M.B. (1989) *Content-based second language instruction*. New York: Newbury House.

Clapham, C. and Wall, D.M. (1990) Report on a BALEAP questionnaire to British universities on the English language testing of overseas students. *Language Testing Update* 7, 2–24.

Cho, Y. (2003) 'Assessing writing: are we bound by only one method?' *Assessing Writing* 8/3, 165–91.

Cushing Weigle, S. (2002) *Assessing Writing*. Cambridge: Cambridge University Press.

—— (2004) 'Integrating reading and writing in a competency test for non-native speakers of English'. *Assessing Writing* 9, 27–55.

Grabe, W. (2003) 'Reading and writing relations: second language perspectives on research and practice' in Kroll, B. (ed.) *Exploring the Dynamics of Second Language Writing*. Cambridge: Cambridge University Press.

Leki, I. and Carson, J. (1994) 'Students' perceptions of EAP writing
instruction and the writing needs across the disciplines'. *TESOL
Quarterly* 28/1, 81–101.

JOHN SLAGHT AND BRUCE HOWELL

19 TEEP: A Course-driven Assessment Measure

Introduction

The Test of English for Education Purposes (TEEP) forms part of the assessment process implemented on pre-sessional courses at the Centre for Applied Language Studies (CALS) at the University of Reading. TEEP has been reviewed and revised several times over the past sixteen years. Revisions to the test carried out specifically since 2001 have been based on the principle that assessment measures are designed to complement the course rather than drive it. Part of the motivation for this ongoing project is to counter the (understandable) attitude students often have that passing the test is the main objective of attending a pre-sessional course. It is apparent to us that if pre-sessional courses use large-scale public EAP tests as the main focus for assessment, they may become test driven.

In this paper a brief overview is given of the pre-sessional course design at Reading which attempts to replicate the activities which students will encounter in their future academic studies. For example, the texts and tasks used in the reading component provide linguistic support and conceptual content for both the macro- and micro-tasks carried out in the writing component. In turn, assessment measures attempt to replicate such activities as far as is practicable. An outline of the assessment measures, an overview of the content of the TEEP test and its development is included. Examples of how the test design has evolved to fit in with the pre-sessional course design principles are then addressed. Because of the basic premise that course content should drive test design, TEEP forms only part of the overall assessment process. The complementary roles of formal continuous assessment measures and impressionistic classroom assessment are also addressed and analysed in this paper.

Overview of TEEP

Originally named TEAP (the Test of English for Academic Purposes), this test was developed for Professor Cyril Weir's PhD thesis (Weir 1983) in response to the increasing needs of assessing pre-sessional students' level of English. The test was ground-breaking at the time for a number of reasons: the underlying concept of communicative testing, the very specific nature of the test construct and the large scale of the needs analyses undertaken. Though periodically under-used since inception, for the last five years TEEP has been used on a regular basis with significant numbers of pre-sessional students in the UK.[1]

The main function of TEEP is as an exit test of the pre-sessional courses at the Centre for Applied Language Studies (CALS), University of Reading, and therefore the majority of test-takers are students who both complete a pre-sessional course and intend to go on to further their academic studies at the University of Reading. In such cases, CALS produces reports which incorporate TEEP scores alongside continuous assessment scores. However, TEEP can also be administered as a stand-alone EAP test for entry to the University of Reading when students do not attend a pre-sessional course. Although this secondary function as a stand-alone test is not actively encouraged, TEEP may be used in this way when a CALS student goes on to study at a different UK university. In some such cases, the admissions office concerned prefers to see a test result rather than a report score, even if the latter is available.

Final reports from CALS pre-sessional courses give as balanced a view as possible of a student's potential in using English for academic study. This claim can be made from two perspectives –

1   Appendix 1 shows a breakdown of the current structure of the test.

thoroughness and fairness. The reports are thorough because they include not only exit test results, but also grades given for continuous assessment (which in itself consists of periodic formal tests as well and informal classroom observation), grades for final written projects and project presentations, and comments from the Course Director. Reports are fair because they include grades from performances over time as well as those under examination conditions. Students may perform better or worse under either condition for a number of reasons other than actual ability, and it is felt that this system allows for unfortunate episodes such as a student under-performing under test conditions.

CALS Pre-sessional Course Content and Assessment

The underlying aim for pre-sessional courses at CALS is to enable students to function effectively in an academic environment. This is achieved by integrating skills in order to complete purpose-driven activities.[2] Examples of this integration can be seen in
- the combining of Reading and Writing into a Written Language course – the Reading and Writing textbooks relate directly to one another in terms of topic and progression, while focusing on different skills (Pallant and Slaght 2003)
- the Lecture Cycle classes, which consist of a genuine lecture – usually given by academic members of staff from different departments within the University of Reading – preceded by both pre-reading and pre-discussion, and followed by a post-discussion

---

2   The full rationale behind CALS's pre-sessional courses can be found in the course books in the English for Academic Study series published by Garnet: *Reading* (Slaght and Harben 2004), *Writing* (Pallant 2004), *Extended Writing and Research Skills* (McCormack and Slaght 2005) and the forthcoming *Listening and Speaking* (Campbell and Smith).

- the Extended Writing and Research Skills course, which puts into practice skills learnt in other classes and expands on them – students have to read extensively, write extensively, discuss and finally present, all on a related chosen subject

Continuous assessment takes various forms during the pre-sessional courses. Formal mid-course listening, reading and writing tests are given, projects (i.e. extended essays and related oral presentations) are graded based on both progression and the standard of the final product and speaking is assessed via interview, presentations and observed seminars. In addition, an impressionistic view from teachers who have spent many hours observing students is taken into consideration. The Course Director's final report is based on the above data combined with the TEEP test grade.

Although assessment is rigorous, it is from the course design that the assessment system evolves. Being aware of the danger of over-doing assessment and the fact that students may perceive a course as one continuous test, all the above measures are essentially integrated as part of the syllabus and materials. Thus, for example, although a student is being tested when writing a timed essay mid-term, it is intended that the event is perceived as a culmination of many days' build-up through subject-related reading, relevant discussion, and guidance in essay planning.

Integrating skills within TEEP

As suggested by Murphy (1996) in his text on 'bimodality connections', listening and reading represent closely linked learning experiences in an academic environment. He cites Flowerdew (1994) and Benson (1989 and 1994) for their studies which demonstrate 'pervasive linkage between orality and literacy in academic settings' as evidence that academic lectures are closely connected in various ways to assigned course readings. He further suggests that such analyses 'illustrate that students' abilities to draw connections between their academic listening and reading experiences are essential for university learning.' In conclusion, it is claimed that to prepare EAP students for ties between orality and literacy in academic courses, EAP listening practice needs to challenge learners to integrate what they hear during an EAP lecture with what they have already read, or what they are going to read. Likewise, EAP reading tasks need to be prefaced, guided, and complemented by EAP listening experiences. (Murphy 1996:107)

From such claims it is reasonable to suggest that if the reading and listening classes should interact then the testing of such skills should be organised in similar fashion and, while there is an argument for separating skills in tests due to reliability concerns, integrating skills is a fact of academic life and TEEP attempts to emulate this, much like the pre-sessional course itself. Referring to Appendix 1, it can be seen that other than the first section, the various components of the test are topic-related. The candidate is allowed 10 minutes to brainstorm ideas about the essay question before attempting the Reading and Listening sections. Schemata are raised, so that the texts presented do not come as a shock, and indeed when the essay is to be written in the final section, ideas and even quotes from the texts may and should be used. In other words, *reading and listening into writing* occurs.

This encouragement for the candidate to refer to both the relevant reading source and the relevant listening source should be seen as highly appropriate in an EAP context. The skills involved in synthesising information and ideas from various sources is one of the main driving forces of EAP syllabus development, and therefore an attempt has been made here to replicate this in the test. Although a timescale of a few hours from introduction of topic to final product is extremely compact when compared to the reality of many weeks, practicality issues are obviously the reason for this. Evidence shows that TEEP can discriminate EAP students' abilities to incorporate ideas effectively from two perspectives: the literal (has the student written about something they learnt from one of the texts?) and the mechanical (has the student correctly referenced the source?). Appendix 2 shows that the criteria for marking writing scripts include descriptions of both factors.

The Writing section is seen as vital, and therefore it is essential that we ensure the task set is relevant for future study. As Moore and Moreton (2004) show, this is not always the case with EAP examinations. Salient features of the TEEP Writing section, other than the integration of ideas mentioned above, are that it follows the principles of the CALS pre-sessional Writing component, for example, the inclusion of a focus task (Pallant 2004: Teacher's Book p. 5). Secondly, the descriptors concentrate on bands 5–7, which is the expected level of achievement for the majority of candidates. Although the bands 0 and 9 exist, they are hardly ever used and therefore require little description. In fact, not only is there little point in having descriptors at bands such as 0–3, but the presence of detailed descriptions of these levels would only serve to distract markers, who essentially need to recognise the difference between 5.5, 6.0 and 6.5.[3]

Assessment of speaking

Ideally, an all-round speaking performance grade should be reported for an EAP test, including not only routine skills and micro-linguistic elements, but also improvisational skills, which are very illusive in speaking tests (Weir 1993:34). In this regard, for an EAP test to properly rate relevant speaking skills, an interview with an interlocutor should be complemented with assessments of presentation skills and discussion skills, the latter involving no interlocutor. A TEEP speaking test including all the above has in fact been developed (O'Sullivan 2001), though it has never been implemented for practical reasons. The numbers of candidates taking the test has recently grown to around 250 at the largest annual administration in September, when results are also demanded in a very short timescale. Thus a test which would involve at least 2 hours per candidate is simply impossible to carry out within restricted time limits.

However, developments in the courses at CALS have led to the introduction of the above methods of speaking assessment integrated

3   Note that TEEP uses a 0–9 band scale, allowing half-bands for each paper as well as for the Overall score. The University of Reading's various undergraduate and postgraduate departments usually require a minimum 6.5 or 7.0 Overall for entry, while the Foundation Programme requires a minimum 5.5 Overall.

into class-time. These presentation, interview and seminar tasks are concentrated towards the end of the course, but not too close to the end to cause overload. Following CALS principles, the Speaking assessments are also topic-linked to other aspects of the courses, so that, for instance, the interview questions are based on the students' projects, which are usually at the stage of a second draft at the time of the interview. Thus once again the assessment of speaking fits into the course content rather than the course being concluded by a major test.

Reliability issues

Thematic linking of test sections may cause problems with reliability; for this reason the IELTS test was changed in 1995. Another possible problem is the open format of the expected responses. However, these issues are dealt with in the following ways:

- original tasks, reading texts and listening scripts are available for reference by all markers
- reading and listening 'short answer question' (SAQ) answer sheets are checked by EAP teaching staff. Grading by these teachers is standardised just before marking, a process which involves taking the test themselves and discussing in depth which alternative responses to allow or disallow. In addition, a moderator is present during marking for any unsure cases
- all writing scripts are double-marked by experienced markers. Again, there is standardisation just before the live scripts are marked, and a moderator is present for third-marking if necessary.

The multiple-choice format of the language knowledge component is by its nature highly reliable.

Conclusion

The TEEP test functions as part of a testing system which is integrated into the CALS pre-sessional course syllabus design. As such it is used to complement the principles underlying the course rationale rather than direct them. The test does have a summative role but it accounts for only part of the final assessment package. Measures are in place to ensure that the pre-sessional does not evolve into a TEEP preparation course. Continuous assessment measures undertaken formally through scheduled continuous assessment tests, extended essay writing and informal classroom assessment all contribute to the overall assessment profile. It is recognised that the major stakeholders, students, and faculty staff, need a final score to ascertain whether the individuals have reached their conditional language level prior to final acceptance on their academic courses. TEEP results contribute to the final assessment profile but the test alone does not necessarily accurately measure the individual student's ability to operate successfully in English on an academic course. The pre-sessional as a whole aims to provide the appropriate development and the final report aims to summarise all relevant ability levels.

Appendix 1

TEEP structure

Section	Format	Features	Section link
Language Knowledge (25 min)	50 4-option multiple choice questions	scores affect borderline cases only format ensures reliability effective as warmer	
Focus task (10 min)	essay title space for notes	schemata-raising for following sections encourages planning and brainstorming	Introduce topic for Reading Listening Writing
Reading (30 min)	1 text 1,000 words approximately 21 SAQ questions	directed selective reading tests global and analytical skills requires inferencing	Topic feeds ideas into Writing
Listening (c. 30 min)	1 aural text 10 min approximately 21 SAQ questions listen once only	lecture style or academic discussion time to both read questions before listening and check answers after listening	Topic feeds ideas into Writing
Writing (60 min)	essay title planning guidance 4 sides of lined A4 paper provided	requires synthesis of previous input marking criteria: Content Organisation and argument Vocabulary and grammar Overall impression	Candidates should use schemata ideas quotes from Focus Reading Listening

Appendix 2

TEEP Writing marking criteria (condensed)

Content:	relevance; development of ideas; critical awareness; synthesis; plagiarism; source acknowledgement
Organisation & argument:	coherence; cohesion; stance; clarity & appropriacy
Vocabulary & grammar:	range; level of accuracy; impact of impeding errors
Overall impression:	effectiveness of communication

Bibliography

Benson, M. (1989) 'The academic listening task: a case study'. *TESOL Quarterly* 23/3, 421–45.

—— (1994) 'Lecture listening in an ethnographic perspective' in Flowerdew, J. (ed.) 181–98.

Flowerdew, J. (1994) 'Research of relevance to second language lecture comprehension: an overview' in Flowerdew, J. (ed.) 2–29.

—— (ed.) (1994) *Academic listening: research perspectives*. New York: Cambridge University Press.

Howell, B. and O'Sullivan, B. (2004) *TEEP examination report 2004.* Reading: University of Reading.

McCormack, J. and Slaght. J. (2005) *English for academic study: extended writing and research skills.* Reading: Garnet Publishing.

Moore, T. and Morton, J. (2005) 'Dimensions of difference: a comparison of university writing and IELTS writing'. *Journal of English for Academic Purposes* 4/1, 43–66.

Murphy, J.M. (1996) 'Integrating listening and reading instruction in EAP programs' *English for Specific Purposes* 15/2, 105–20.

O'Sullivan, B. (2000) 'Progress report on TEEP speaking project'. Reading: University of Reading unpublished report.

———. (2001) *TEEP Extended Handbook.* Reading: University of Reading.

——— (2003) *TEEP Examiner's Report 2003.* Reading: University of Reading.

Pallant, A. (2004) *English for academic study: writing.* Reading: Garnet Publishing.

——— and Slaght, J. (2003) *Integrating reading and writing: materials design.* BALEAP Conference Presentation, University of Southampton 11 April 2003.

Slaght, J. and Harben, P. (2004) *English for academic study: reading.* Reading: Garnet Publishing.

Weir, Cyril J. (1983) 'Identifying the language needs of overseas students in tertiary education in the United Kingdom'. Unpublished PhD Thesis: University of London, Institute of Education.

ANDY BLACKHURST[1]

20 Computer-based and Paper-based Versions of IELTS

Introduction

The three IELTS partners[2] have always understood that the IELTS examination has to remain innovative, both taking onboard new understandings from the field of applied linguistics, and responding to the changing needs of candidates. The introduction in May 2005 of a version of the IELTS test battery delivered by, and taken on, computer continues this tradition of innovation.

CB IELTS is a linear computer-based test, designed to provide as similar experience as possible to the paper-based (PB) IELTS examination, using source texts and questions, drawn from the same pool of previously-trialled material. It is vital that results obtained on the two forms of the test may be regarded as equivalent and inter-changeable, hence the trials which this paper describes. This is not to say that individual candidates might not decide that one test form or the other suits them better. Indeed, that is an argument for the new test. When Bunderson et al. (1989) offered an overview of previous studies of computer and paper-based test equivalence, their concern was that scores on the computer based test were usually lower, prompting speculation that lack of familiarity with computers might adversely affect some candidates. With the great expansion in the use

---

1   I should like to thank my colleagues, Sharon Jordan, CB IELTS Subject Officer, who co-presented at the BALEAP/SATEFL conference, and Louise Maycock and Tony Green, for all their work on the CB IELTS trials 2003/4.

2   IELTS is jointly managed by University of Cambridge ESOL Examinations (Cambridge ESOL), British Council and IDP Education Australia: IELTS Australia.

of computers since 1989, it is increasingly plausible that potential IELTS candidates will be familiar with using computers in their offices, schools, and homes. Many will have experienced computer mediated learning and will have previously encountered tests delivered on computer.

A majority of candidates taking the IELTS test do so in order to pursue higher education, in institutions where the use of computer-based resources will be ubiquitous and where their assignments will usually be completed on computer. It is interesting to note, therefore, that when Russell and Haney (1997) looked at the test performance of school students in Massachusetts, their concern was that test scores appeared low. The researchers' speculated that since most student assignments were completed using computers, but the tests were in paper-and-pencil mode, this change in format was adversely affecting student scores. Making a CB version of IELTS available would allow candidates to choose the form which they believed suited them best, reducing the risk of interference by a less familiar test form. Nevertheless, it had to be demonstrated that the two forms measured to the same scale.

Background

Cambridge ESOL began a series of studies into the comparability of IELTS tests delivered on paper and by computer in 2001. These initial trials were encouraging, finding that test format had little effect on the order of item difficulty, and finding strong correlations between scores on the paper-based and computer-based versions of the listening and reading tests. However, one perceived limitation of the original trial design was that the candidates knew that the computer test would not contribute to their actual assessment. Consequently, further trials were undertaken to address this response validity issue in 2003 and 2004, in which the candidates took both versions of the exam, without knowing which (or indeed whether both) would generate their actual results.

Each candidate took the computer-based test within a week of taking a live IELTS test, half taking the conventional test first and half the CB version. Candidates were allowed to choose whether to answer the written test by hand or on computer, and were also asked to complete a questionnaire covering their ability, confidence and experience in using computers. In the first of these trials, trial A, a total of 423 candidates provided a complete data set, including questionnaire responses, and in the second, trial B, 622 candidates provided a complete dataset, including questionnaire responses.

Results

If the average scores in each skill for all the candidates included in the analyses of the two trials are calculated, it can be seen that the PB and CB tests produce very similar results. This suggests that both are measuring on the same scale.

	Reading	Listening	Writing	Overall
PB	5.95	6.05	5.75	6.03
CB	6.21	6.08	5.66	5.98

Table 1. Mean band scores for trial candidates (combined)

However, it is also important to consider the extent of agreement between the scores which individual candidates obtained on the two versions of the test, so cross tabulations of the paper-based and computer-based scores were constructed and the rates of agreement were calculated for each component. It should be noted that scores for writing tests are awarded in whole band increments, and that overall scores for the two tests (PB and CB) include a common speaking element. The half band scores used in reporting performance on the reading and listening components of IELTS typically represent two or three raw score points out of the 40 available for each test. The table below shows the results for trial A, as reported by Green and Maycock (2004).

	Reading	Listening	Writing*	Overall
% agreement	26%	22%	53%	49%
% agreement to within half a band	72%	62%	–	95%
% agreement to within a whole band	91%	85%	92%	100%

Table 2. Agreement rates in trial A
* Writing scores are reported in whole bands only

Some degree of variation between candidates' results on two different occasions and on two versions of a test is only to be expected. Candidate performance will vary and each test is subject to measurement error. The issue is whether the extent of agreement between CB and PB versions of the test was meaningfully different to the extent of agreement which would pertain if the candidates were to sit two different PB versions a week apart. The following agreement rates, for live and preparatory candidates taking paper-based IELTS reading and listening test versions a week apart, were reported by Thighe et al. (2001).

	Live candidates		Preparatory candidates	
	Reading	Listening	Reading	Listening
% agreement	30%	27%	27%	25%
% agreement to within half a band	68%	62%	61%	68%
% agreement to within a whole band	89%	89%	85%	91%

Table 3. Agreement rates of live and preparatory candidates given in Thighe (2001)

The rates of agreement between the band scores awarded on the CB versions and those awarded on the PB versions in trial A are therefore similar to, albeit slightly lower than, those obtained in the earlier trials, while agreement to within half a band is slightly higher. In terms of the overall band score, almost half the trial A candidates obtained an identical score on both occasions, and a further 45% obtained a score that differed by just half a band on the nine band IELTS scale.

A very similar picture emerged from the analysis of trial B. In this analysis, the sample of 622 was tailored to limit the number of candidates of any L1 to no more than 30% of the sample. This gave a final sample of 487 candidates. The table below shows the percentage agreement as reported in Blackhurst (2005).

	Reading	Listening	Writing	Overall
% agreement	26%	25%	45%	50%
% agreement to within half a band	68%	66%	45%	96%
% agreement to within a whole band	91%	88%	84%	100%

Table 4. Agreement rates in trial B

The kappa coefficient (*K*) measures agreement among pairs of ratings, correcting for expected chance agreement (kappa is always less than or equal to 1, with a value of 1 implying perfect agreement and values less than 1 implying less than perfect agreement). In trial B the kappa coefficient for reading was calculated as 0.1290, for listening 0.1596, for writing, and for the test overall 0.4006. The reliability of the CB versions of the test used in trial B is indicated by Cronbach's alpha, which for Listening version 50001 was 0.893 and for academic Reading version was 0.816. Both of these values are within the range we would expect for ordinary live versions (for which the historical range is 0.710–0.897). The pattern of the distribution of band scores for the computer-based components is broadly in line with those for the paper-based components.

The analyses conducted into writing performance on the CB and PB versions of IELTS indicated, in common with Whitehead (2003), that there are no meaningful differences between scores obtained on the CB and PB versions of the academic writing test. Although there was some evidence that reflected Brown's (2000) concern that legibility may influence rating, the impact on scores appeared minimal.

Are different groups of candidates affected differently by the format of the test?

It is, of course, crucial that different groups of candidates should not be affected differently by the format of the test. Comparison of the performance of male and female candidates produced no evidence to suggest the existence of any gender bias.

Gender		Reading	Listening	Writing	Overall
Female	PB	5.92	6.17	5.81	6.09
	CB	6.26	5.85	5.81	5.95
Male	PB	6.03	6.18	5.73	6.08
	CB	6.35	5.86	5.66	5.94

Table 5. Trial B Band scores by gender

The largest single L1 group in the trial consisted of Chinese speakers. For reading and listening, the average shift in score for Chinese candidates was not meaningfully different to the average shift in score for non-Chinese candidates. It is worth noting that, in trial B, both groups secured on average a lower score in the CB listening test. In trial A, both Chinese and non-Chinese speaking candidates obtained, on average, a higher score in both skills. This indicates that there is no systematic tendency for candidates to perform better on one mode than the other. The scores for Chinese and non-Chinese speaking candidates in trial B are compared below.

Chinese		Reading	Listening	Writing	Overall
N=140	PB	5.81	5.99	5.66	5.87
	CB	6.20	5.59	5.49	5.70
	Difference	-0.38	0.39	0.17	0.18
	Correlation	0.68	0.68	0.56	0.87

Table 6. Band scores for candidates whose first language was Chinese

Non-Chinese		Reading	Listening	Writing	Overall
N=327	PB	6.03	6.26	5.82	6.18
	CB	6.35	5.96	5.86	6.05
	Difference	-0.31	0.29	-0.03	0.13
	Correlation	0.72	0.79	0.69	0.91

Table 7. Band scores for candidates whose first language was not Chinese

Results on the writing test were further investigated using repeated measures analyses of covariance (ANCOVA), with PB writing test scores as dependent variable, to explore differences between groups in the relationship between paper and computer-based scores. Groups were defined by gender (male or female), age (five different age groups) and first language (Chinese or Non-Chinese L1). Handwritten responses to the CB test were separated from word-processed responses for the purpose of the analysis.

Analysis of covariance (ANCOVA) is a method for testing the main and interaction effects of categorical variables on a continuous dependent variable, controlling for the effects of selected other continuous variables which covary with the dependent. In this case, the categorical variables to be considered were gender, age and first language. ANCOVA revealed no significant ($p>0.01$) inter-group differences by gender, age or first language either where CB scripts had been typed or hand written. This suggests that the relationship between CB and PB scores is not meaningfully affected by these differences between candidates.

Differences between scores on the CB and PB tests, when responding on paper or on screen were not indicated to be significant in statistical terms ($p > 0.01$) either for the Chinese L1 or non-Chinese L1 groups when t-tests for repeated measures were performed. These results suggest that the CB and PB versions of the IELTS writing test yielded comparable scores across groups.

Conclusion

The evidence gathered since 1999 provides support for using CB IELTS interchangeably with PB IELTS and indicates that candidates, given adequate computer familiarity, will perform equally well on either version of the test. Accordingly, a limited number of IELTS centres began offering CB IELTS as a live test in 2005. In reporting results, no distinction will be made between candidates who have taken the test in one mode or the other. From the point of view of receiving institutions the results may be considered equally valid, whichever form was taken.

Since the live trials were concluded, revised writing assessment criteria and scales have been introduced. Further studies will be undertaken to assess the impact of these changes on the marking of typewritten scripts and we will also be seeking feedback from examiners involved in marking typewritten scripts from the live test. We will also be studying the reading and listening performance data generated in this initial phase of CB IELTS as there is expected to be a different profile of first languages among the live candidates compared to that obtained in the trials. A further project, commissioned by Cambridge ESOL, exploring candidates' reading test-taking processes will consider the processes in which candidates engage and the nature of the language elicited when taking tests with different formats.

There are important considerations involved in providing an established test in different formats. Not all candidates will have adequate computer familiarity and some candidates may experience fatigue when reading extended passages on computer. Accordingly, Wolfe and Manalo (2004:61) recommended that test designers 'think seriously about providing examinees with a choice of composition medium [...] particularly when high-stakes decisions will be made based upon the test results'. The IELTS partners have always recognised that it is important that candidates should be able to take the test in the form with which they feel comfortable. The pen and paper test will continue to be available so only those candidates who feel confident in their ability to use a computer need do so. In the live test as in the trial, candidates taking the CB test will have the option of responding to the writing test by hand. In this way, as the new form of the test becomes more widely available, IELTS will be able to ensure that candidates will have the option of taking the test that suits them best.

Bibliography

Blackhurst, A. (2005) 'Listening, Reading and Writing on computer-based and paper-based versions of IELTS'. *Cambridge ESOL Research Notes 21.*

Brown, A. (2000) 'Legibility and the rating of second language writing: an investigation of the rating of handwritten and word-processed IELTS Task Two essays'. *IELTS Research Projects* 1999/2000.

Bunderson, C.V., Inouye, D.K. and Olsen, J.B. (1989) 'The four generations of computerised educational measurement' in R.L. Lin (ed.) *Educational Measurement* (3rd ed.) 367–407. American Council on Education. New York: Macmillan.

Green, A. and Maycock, L. (2004) 'Computer based IELTS and paper-based versions of IELTS'. *Cambridge ESOL Research Notes 18.*

—— (2005) 'The effects on performance of computer familiarity and attitudes towards CB IELTS'. *Cambridge ESOL Research Notes 20.*

Russell, M. and Haney, W. (1997) 'Testing writing on computers: an experiment comparing student performance on tests conducted via computers and via paper-and-pencil'. *Educational Policy Analysis Archives*, 5 /3. Available online at: ['http://olam.ed.asu. edu/epaa/v5n3.html] retrieved 25/08/06.

Thighe, D. et al. (2001) 'IELTS PB and CB Equivalence: a comparison of equated versions of the reading and listening components of PB IELTS in relation to CB IELTS'. *Cambridge ESOL Internal Validation Report 288.*

Wolfe, E. and Manila, J. (2004) 'Composition medium comparability in a direct writing assessment of non-native English speakers'. *Language Learning and Technology*, 8/1, 53–65.

Section VI

Online and Blended Learning

PAUL WICKENS

21 IT Skills in EAP Provision: Making it More Relevant

The introduction of a range of targets for the integration of e-learning into teaching and learning in UK higher education (HE) assumes an increasing degree of computer literacy amongst students (Martin 2002). Besides specialist computing needs, students in UK HE can be expected to search online databases and access online journals, use virtual learning environments (VLE) such as WebCT, participate in online discussions, as well as present work in programmes such as Word, Excel, and PowerPoint in an accomplished manner. There has been for some time a clear need to ensure that students on EAP courses have such skills and can use them appropriately in their studies.

Jarvis (1997:44) in a survey of IT skills provision on pre-sessional courses at BALEAP associated institutions wrote that

> Information technology, despite its widespread prevalence and clear relevance at universities world-wide, has not yet established itself as a major EAP component, and this is reflected in a regrettable lack of literature on the subject. Providers of EAP courses wishing to include IT as a course component will need to look elsewhere [...]

In EAP, with the exception of studies on Web skills (Studman-Badillo and Nesi 2000, Jarvis 2001, Slaouti 2002), this is still true. Jones (1999) describes an IT skills course for modern languages under-graduates and there is a relatively substantial literature on such courses for initial teacher training (Owen 2004, Dore and Wickens 2004).

IT skills training is often provided by central computer services and whilst these departments have much expertise, the service courses they run do not always meet EAP students' needs. Firstly, such courses make the software the focus of pedagogic attention with an emphasis on the 'how to' skills rather than a contextualising approach foregrounding the 'why' of academic literacy practices. Secondly, the main materials are often self-study step-by-step manuals which can leave students missing the relevance of what they learn and sometimes feeling de-motivated.

This paper argues that computer literacy needs to be brought fully into the academic literacy objectives of EAP. I will illustrate some of the ways in which these issues can be addressed with examples from a course on the International Foundation Diploma at Oxford Brookes University. The course attempts to integrate tradition-al IT self-study training materials into a situated task based framework which emphasises outcomes that are useful and relevant to students in the context of their present and future studies at UK universities.

Communication and Information Technology in Education

Much has been written over the last decade about the increasing importance of computers in education and in society as a whole and particularly the transformations across a range of literacy practices. Whilst there has been much hype, the context in which EAP operates has seen changing expectations in two main areas. Firstly, changing institutional expectations: the Dearing Report (1997:section 13.2) laid out a key role for IT in HE – whilst providing a blunt rationale.

> C and IT will have a central role in maintaining the quality of higher education in an era when there are likely to be continuing pressures on costs and a need to respond to an increasing demand for places in institutions.

There is now acceptance in UK HE that the sector needs to engage in pedagogic change to embrace e-learning and the theoretical and practical elements of this have been widely written about (Laurillard 2002, Salmon 2004). Individual institutions are interpreting this in various ways. In the case of Oxford Brookes it involves the introduction of a virtual learning environment (WebCT) with the specification that all modules must have a web presence by September 2004. Secondly, student expectations are changing. Schools in the UK regularly use IT in the classroom and students take a range of qualifications (CLAIT, ECDL, GCSE, AS). Wider social changes in the way in which digital media are communicated and consumed have recently perhaps reached a critical mass and become mainstream with the uptake of broadband (and consequent Internet use), digital cameras and music downloads.

There are ongoing shifts in literacy practices and it is possible to outline a range of changes in terms of the modes of communication, the genres used, the processes involved, and the relationships engendered. In university academic life there has been a consolidation of a range of changing literacy practices such as online discussions, online databases and electronic journals and PowerPoint presentations. The latter represent the emergence of a distinct genre (Myers 2000) with implications for structuring, argumentation and stylistic choices. Students in UK HE are expected to engage successfully with a range of computer based literacy practices that are continually evolving.

Situating Computer Literacy within a Course

The International Foundation Diploma at Oxford Brookes is a one-year modular course (8 modules) with EAP study skills modules, foundation level content modules plus one first-year undergraduate module. Students enter at IELTS 5.0 or above. Previous provision of IT skills training was through an undergraduate service module run by the computing department. It was decided to bring this into the foundation course for a number of reasons. Firstly, choosing this module as their sole undergraduate module may give a distorted view of what undergraduate study involves. Secondly, such service modules tend, rightly perhaps, to take an IT skills approach as opposed to a computer literacy approach (Owen 2004). So the ability to create a well formatted table in Word becomes an end in itself as opposed to an understanding of the role that well presented data can play in the support of an argument.

As Dore and Wickens (2004) argue in relation to teacher training, it is not just a case of providing generic computer skills training but of situating the use of those skills in a relevant context. The 'how to' is necessary but not sufficient; we wished to frame IT skills within the 'why' of academic literacy. The underlying rationale of the course is to turn the university generic IT skills programme on its head, focusing on the activities that students need to use the computer for rather than on the software. Even if it were useful to separate the skills for using software from its application in a given context it would not always be possible. For example, there is no sense in separating the mechanics of searching a database from understanding why you are searching it, choosing key words and evaluating the relevance of the articles that are found.

Within this overall approach there were a number of other pedagogic concerns that we wished to address. Firstly, the course is organised around a situated task based approach to learning related to students' academic life at Oxford Brookes. Secondly, assessment is seen as a crucial element and we have tried to base assignments around authentic, meaningful tasks directly related to the study needs on their present Foundation course and future undergraduate needs. Given the range of students' IT skills, we have also tried to create a variety of learning opportunities by integrating a range of modes, interactions and task types. Language is important in EAP and we provide materials which support the acquisition of new concepts and associated lexicogrammar. We have also tried to ensure a focus on capabilities rather than separate specific skills by integrating a learn to learn focus into many of the activities requiring students to access institutional support and engaging in group based work where they can learn from peers.

The course has ten 3-hour sessions each of which has a 1-hour plenary and a 2-hour workshop. The most broad based and important skills students need in the academic context are the sourcing of information and the presentation of assignments and the outline of the course in Table 1 reflects this basic premise. The software we cover is similar to that covered in generic IT skills courses (Word, Excel, Internet etc) and it is important that this is so as they are the most commonly used. The use of online interaction is growing and though not explicitly part of the course, it is dealt with to some degree through the use of WebCT as the main way students access the course materials.

Topic	IT skills
The Brookes environment	Windows and WebCT
Presenting your written work	Word
Finding and Evaluating Resources	The Internet
The Electronic library	Keyword searching
Assignment 1	Annotated bibliographies
Recording, calculating and presenting data	Excel
Assignment 2	Data Commentaries
Presenting your ideas	Web pages/PowerPoint
Assignment 3	In-Class Test

Table 1. Outline of the IT skills training module

The course starts with a broad view of the computing environment as new students need to access and become acquainted with the basic computing environment of any given institution whatever their IT skills. The other important aspect of the first lesson is to assess the IT skills of the students and explore ways in which they can access support both within the course, from computer services support and from printed and online sources.

The most obvious sequencing of these elements that emerges from the rationale is to follow the task process of sourcing and presenting information. This would start with finding and evaluating sources on the internet and comparing them to the sources that can be found through the online databases and electronic journals in the library. Collecting and adding numerical data in Excel, performing simple calculations and presenting the data in graphs. This informa-tion could then form the basis a written piece of work (Word) or presentation (PowerPoint). Building a series of tasks around a process approach would be possible but we have considered other sequencing options such as task difficulty, in terms of moving from more instrumental to more evaluative tasks, and the perceived difficulty of the software. Based on student experience and on the internal logic of the software, Excel tends to be seen as less intuitive than Word.

We have found it useful to modularise the course to some degree so that we can adjust the sequencing to respond to the differing range of skills and needs we find in a given cohort. Table 2 shows an outline of one such two week module based around data commentaries using Excel. It shows the range of modes and task types used over the two three-hour sessions. The initial plenary has two main purposes: firstly to orientate the students to the overall academic literacy goals and secondly to provide them with a visual overview of the way that the software can support these goals together with an example of a possible outcome. In the subsequent workshops, held in computer rooms, we have tried to move away from the step-by-step self study approach used in the generic skills courses. Such self-study materials are important given the range of IT skills students have but we try to vary the learning opportunities with group work, self-paced learning and whole class discussion. We build up a series of task cycles with an initial focus on the overall academic literacy aims, moving through the instrumental learning with the software and onto evaluative and reflective tasks, which build on these acquired skills. One way we have found of dealing with the range of IT skills is to group students according to ability and encourage peer tutoring. These groups usually start the workshops with a deep-end task and at the end individual students and the tutor can assess where the specific difficulties are and deal with them, either in plenary session or through individual self-study. Such peer support is effective on an IT skills course as it mirrors a common mode of learning across the university from the pooled computers to halls of residence.

Plenary (1 hour) Lecture theatre	Overview of literacy practice/ Program/Task	• Preview session outcome (data commentary) • Unite report: read and discuss selection. • Demonstration of Excel based on students own responses to Unite report questions. • Previous students' work – brief critique of presentation and data commentary
Workshop (2 hour) Computers	Tasks	• Group task (often a deep end collaborative task) • Self-paced learning • Whole class discussion of issues.
Plenary (1 hour) Lecture theatre	Review Preview assignment task	• Review/reflect on issues arising. Q + A session • Preview workshop – software: creation of graphs and transfer to Word • Data commentary – more detailed look at the genre: purpose, structure, language and presentation.
Workshop (2 hour) Computers	Tasks	• Group tasks – students collate data and discuss results • Self-paced learning – data handling, graphs
Assignment – students write individual data commentaries comparing international student responses (own data) and data for UK students from the Unite report.		

Table 2. Outline of a two-session module: data commentary utilising Excel

For this part of the course on presenting data we use an annual survey of students in UK HE called the Unite Student Living Report.[1] In the first plenary, students discuss three questions from the report in groups. As a whole, we discuss their views of the UK student data and look at the report as an example of a data commentary. Groups of students then give their own responses to the questions. There is a real time demonstration of their Excel task. Similar student data commentaries are critiqued for the data its interpretation and presentation. The workshops deal with the instrumental software skills needed to input data, perform calculations and format a graph. Between the two sessions, students use the same three questions from the Unite report to survey other international students and in groups they collate the

---

1   [http://www.unite-group.co.uk/data/Research/default.aspx] accessed 24/08/2005.

data in session 2, perform the calculations and discuss their interpretations of the results. This forms the basis for their individual
assignments. We have found that having the tasks build towards an
assessment provides students with a valuable focus and is motivating.

Conclusion

Both Jarvis (1997) and Jones (1999) argue that the integration of IT
skills into the specific academic context where they are utilised is
important for any academic study as it provides opportunities to create
authentic, meaningful and relevant tasks. In our course we have related the tasks and assignments directly to other modules on the Foundation Diploma showing students how the skills they learn directly
support their other coursework. This situating of IT skills into the
specific teaching and learning context is our understanding of situated
task based learning (Errey and Schollaert 2003). The other benefit of a
situated approach is that it forces EAP teachers to look outside the
classroom and the confines of the computer itself to the institutional
context. For example, where we need to teach students to format a
bibliography we set a task which sends them to the Oxford Brookes
library web pages to download a guide to the Harvard system which
they have to read carefully to complete the task.

This use of existing materials is a key recommendation. It not
only supports future autonomy for students to learn to access institutional and online support but in terms of materials writing, it also uses
existing expertise and saves time. The warning is to be aware of program upgrades which require screen shots to be redone. We now use
training documentation from computer services and have found it
useful to link to websites such as the RDN virtual training suite.[2]

This paper illustrates our attempt to integrate IT skills into the
EAP context and to bring to bear elements of good pedagogic practice.
Helping students to master the key academic literacy practices in HE

2   [http://www.vts.rdn.ac.uk/] last accessed 22/08/05.

requires us to understand the role of IT in HE in order to provide students with the precise skills they need. I have argued that this is best done through a situated task-based approach which covers a cycle from instrumental knowledge through evaluative and reflective stages so that students can gain an understanding of the literacy practices involved.

> Learners can be empowered to create electronic documents and communication as never before; however, they need to have a critical understanding of the power of that communication. (Owen 2004:37)

Bibliography

Dearing, R. (1997) *Higher Education in the Learning Society*. Norwich: HMSO.

Dore, B. and Wickens, C. (2004) 'ICT Capability and Initial Teacher Training' in Monteith, M. (ed.) *ICT for Curriculum Enhancement*, 113–26. Bristol: Intellect Books.

Errey, L. and Schollaert, R. (eds) (2003) *Whose learning is it anyway? Developing learner autonomy through task based learning*. Antwerp: Garant.

Jarvis, H. (1997) 'The Role of IT in English for Academic Purposes: a survey'. *ReCALL*, 9/1, 43–52.

—— (2001) 'Internet usage on English for Academic Purposes courses'. *ReCALL*, 13/2, 206–12.

—— (2004) 'Investigating the classroom applications of computers on EFL courses at Higher Education Institutions in UK'. *JEAP* 3/2, 111–37.

Jones, C. (1999) 'Laying the foundations: designing a computing course for languages'. *ReCALL*, 11/1, 58–64.

Laurillard, D. (2002) *Rethinking University Teaching: a conversational framework for the effective use of educational technology*. London: RoutledgeFalmer.

Martin, M. (2002) *Concepts of ICT literacy in Higher Education*, available online at [http://www.citscapes.ac.uk/products/back groundreports/files/concepts_ict_HE.pdf] retrieved 24/08/2005.

Myers, G. (2000) 'Powerpoints: Technology, Lectures, and Changing Genres' in Trosborg, A. (ed.) *Analysing Professional Genres*, 177–91. Amsterdam: John Benjamins.

Owen, M. (2004) 'Just a Tool? The Computer as Curriculum' in Monteith. M. (ed.) *ICT for Curriculum Enhancement*, 26–40. Bristol: Intellect Books.

Salmon, G. (2004) *E-moderating: the key to teaching and learning online.* London: RoutledgeFalmer.

Slaouti, D. (2002) 'The World Wide Web for academic purposes: old study skills for new'. *ESPJ*, 21, 105–24.

Studman-Badillo, B. and Nesi, H. (2000) 'Internet use: assumptions and expectations in British universities' in Howarth, P. and Herington, R. (eds) *EAP learning technologies,* 1–8. Leeds: Leeds University Press.

ROBERT GILMOUR

22 Creating a Flexible, Learner-driven Online EAP Site for Independent Study and Blended Learning in a Higher Education Institution

Introduction

English Language Materials Online (ELMO) is an online self-study site that is flexible, user-friendly and fully integrated into the campus Information Systems and Services (ISS), including tracking of scores that can be accessed by University staff. With numbers of overseas students at Newcastle University at 2,200 in December 2004 and a projected total of 3,200 for December 2006, there is increasing pressure on the provision of English language support. One of the ways to relieve this is to provide a bank of self-study materials online that can be used in a self-access mode or blended learning approach. In addition, this can play a marketing role for the University.

Between September 2004 and June 2005, the ELMO project consisted of three people given remission from teaching hours to manage and develop the website. During the Summer of 2005, an Innovation Award was used to train four new people. As the project becomes publicised and attracts funding from the faculties, we are perhaps turning the corner away from Hémard and Cushion's (2000) description of CALL being undervalued and under-funded.

The first pilot of the full ELMO site took place in May 2005. Feedback was gathered via questionnaire from a total of 31 students and 6 teachers. This small-scale pilot has given us some interesting descriptive statistics[1] although these cannot claim to be generalisable research findings.

---

1   The statistics were processed with SPSS 11.0.

Considerations

The following issues informed the main criteria which guided the design of the site from the very beginning of the project.

Control and ownership

Due to the significant investment of both time and money involved in creating this type of online site, it is crucial to ensure longevity for the project. This means not being reliant on software or systems that may be withdrawn or replaced in the future. The conclusion was to create a customised database-driven container website that activities (in the form of web pages) could be added to. Thus, a skeleton site, essentially a simple virtual learning environment (vle), was created specifically for the Language Centre by Data Management Services[2] (DMS) according to our specification. The site is a database-driven framework that accepts activities written for publication on the web, preventing over-reliance on one authoring tool. The University web team provided help with style sheets and advice on issues such as accessibility.

Hot Potatoes by Half-Baked Software[3] was selected as a suitable authoring tool for several reasons. It has reasonable license fees for password protected activities and the interface is simple to use for teachers with little experience of CALL development. There are also excellent support facilities such as online tutorials, comprehensive help files and an active user group.[4] Finally, the authors give their full permission to alter the code of the final webpage which allowed DMS to insert a line of script to capture users' scores and enter them into a database.

Unit information is added to the site by developers and saved in a database. Units generally contain between five and seven activities

2   Part of Newcastle University's ISS (Information Systems and Services).
3   [http://web.uvic.ca/hrd/halfbaked/].
4   [http://groups.yahoo.com/group/hotpotatoesusers/].

which are entered separately and then attached to the units. Activities can be attached to any number of units, allowing staff to create generic activities which may appear in more than one unit. Activities and units can be uploaded without the user interface changing or becoming more complex although searches for materials will result in more hits. The creation of the site by DMS also allowed us to tie it into the campus authentication system. On-campus, users are automatically identified by the site while off-campus users must go through a simple login procedure.

Interface: user-friendliness

Lynch (1994) and Rühlmann (1998) suggest that there are two main problems in interface design: how to guide the user through a complex body of material and how to create the visual design aspect of the programme. Lynch (1994) identifies two reasons for problematic interfaces as being an inconsistency or confusion in the relationships between objects on screen and poor quality visual design. In contrast to Kenning and Kenning's (1990:106) claim that 'comprehensive and unambiguous instructions' should be given, there is support for the idea that programmes should be self-exemplifying to avoid presenting the user with a large number of abstract rules (Lynch 1994). One reason for this is to reduce the cognitive load on the user (Peterson 1998) which also reflects good teaching practice whereby the main focus of attention remains on what is being taught and not how it is taught. Lynch (1994) proposes two principal ways of achieving this: making interface behaviour consistent and predictable and using metaphor in screen design, i.e. using graphic symbols to represent functions. Creating the container site allowed us to present an interface that is consistent and clear both graphically and in its functionality. Students in a study at London Guildhall University valued a 'clear, uncluttered, robust and professionally designed interface' (Hémard and Cushion 2000). This apparent simplicity, however, disguises a large and complex body of material that can be called up by user searches. Figure 1 shows how the student search materials page is organised hierarchically, offering four routes into the study

units, each of which leads on to another set of choices. Consistency in
the activities is achieved with a team working to an agreed set of
principles.

Search Materials
O List all   O School   ⊙ skill   O title

Choose the language skill type that you want to study
O Grammar   O listening O reading   O speaking
⊙ vocabulary   O writing

Choose your main aim
O Academic word list   O functions ⊙ style (spoken/written etc)
O Compound nouns   O prefixes and suffixes

Figure 1. Hierarchical search function on student search page

The ELMO site has minimal functionality. For example, there
are no discussion boards, diary entries or multiple windows. As well
as helping to achieve clarity and simplicity, this serves to focus the
users on the main point of the website: the activities. As Shneiderman
(1998) pointed out: 'When an interactive system is well-designed, the
interface almost disappears, enabling users to concentrate on their
work'. Lynch's proposal to use metaphor was viewed as a possible
cause of confusion (Allum 2001). Thus we chose to avoid the use of
such graphic representations and complex interface types as those suggested by Lonfils and Vanparys (2001).

The pilot feedback shown in Table 1 below indicates that both
students and teachers found the site and activities fairly easy to use
even though no training was given except for a simple print out
explanation. The mean was negatively influenced by a login issue
which caused problems for 8 of the 31 students and 3 of the 6
teachers.

Students	N	Min	Max	Mean	Std. Dev
In general, how easy was the website to use?	22	2	5	3.6	0.73
In general, how easy were the activities to use?	22	2	5	3.1	0.71
Teachers	N	Min	Max	Mean	Std. Dev
In general, how easy was the website to use?	5	3	5	4.0	0.71
How easy were the activities to use?	4	3	5	4.0	0.81
Valid N (listwise)	4				

Table 1. Pilot evaluation with students and teachers
(Values: 1 = very difficult, 2 = difficult, 3 = OK, 4 = easy, 5 = very easy)

To encourage teachers who may not be pro-technology, it is crucial that the student scores are easy to access. Feedback from the six teachers involved was encouraging with most teachers agreeing that they would set units for homework at least fortnightly or weekly and all teachers saying they would access student scores online.

Combining constructivist and instructional design

The contrasting concepts of instructional and constructivist design provide another useful context to consider how to present the learner with a complex body of information. Rühlmann (1998) describes instructional design as including a strong element of prescriptive guidance. In contrast, constructivism rejects presenting the user with a sequence of steps. Because the individual learns and gains knowledge of the world through experience and interaction with it, he or she chooses what and how to learn. Thus computer-based materials should be designed to allow the learners to choose their own path through them.

In Hémard and Cushion's project (2000), students 'demanded full navigational facilities and control over their interaction'. However, Davies and Williamson (1998) and Rühlmann (1998) both hold the opinion that if CALL is to fully realise its potential, it should provide the possibility for student-driven learning but with the role of the teacher included within it. Rühlmann (1998) states that purely instructional design can be rigid and teacher-driven but warns that constructivist design can be void of learner orientation and guidance (see also Laurel 1991:101). Overall, the learning experience can be best enhanced through the application of both approaches in a complementary way. The ELMO site provides a bank of materials that are accessed according to simple choices made by the user in the search function (Figure 1). Users are able to select units according to list all, topic, skill or title while all scores are recorded and kept as a record of study. Therefore, the learning path created by the user is a result of learner choices in a constructivist environment.

However, there also exists a considerable instructional aspect to the site. It aims to 'provide guidance and make suggestions and recommendations' which 'reassure learners that the developer is a competent educator' (Kenning and Kenning 1990:108). This type of support is evident in several places. Each unit has a main aim and the activities are designed by an experienced teacher with that focus. The unit page itself (Figure 2) contains detailed information of the type requested by students in Hémard and Cushion's project (2000). Furthermore, the activities follow sound pedagogical principles and are checked, commented on and proof-read. In addition, there are FAQs and a dedicated helpline.

Unit Information

Title:	Systems performance: Total Energy
Skill Type:	Listening
Main Aim:	language for Listening
Secondary Aims:	Vocabulary, Academic Word List
Background:	This unit uses an extract from a Marine Engineering lecture given to students at Newcastle University in March 2003. The lecturer is Hugo Grimmelius from the Delft University of Technology in Holland.
Description:	The unit focuses on identifying the way that lecturers or presenters move from one section of a lecture to another. The unit also includes an activity about listening for the main ideas and two activities which practise identifying academic words in the lecture extract.
Study tips:	Identifying when lecturers move to a new point is very important for you to be able to understand lectures and presentations well. Not only does it help your understanding, it will help you to take notes clearly and logically.
Total duration:	50–75 minutes.

Figure 2. Example of content for the main page of a unit

We elected not to support individual users with an online tutor but to develop a model that would be entirely self-study. Practically, to tutor over 2,000 international students would place too great a strain on the staffing in the Language Centre. Furthermore, there are many unresolved issues with regard to supporting language learning at a distance, for example, how to feedback effectively on submitted written work or voice recordings. Thus, although the instructional element is evident, users can create their own learning pathway. By doing this, we would hope to avoid Kenning and Kenning's (1990: 113–14) description of an instructional 1970s CALL package as a 'recipe for discouragement, boredom and infantilisation'. Instead, the learning responsibility is shared between the developer, the computer and the user.

Individualised and autonomous learning

An individual learning pathway can be driven by the need to practice particular skills and sub-skills or to study units in particular academic subject areas. The pace at which students travel this path is also their choice. ELMO aims to develop learner autonomy by giving descriptions of the structure of the unit and study tips (see Figure 2). These aim to develop learners' awareness of self-study skills and the pedagogical reasoning behind the unit. This development is often cited as an important factor in any self-study environment (e.g. Dickinson 1987, Gremmo and Riley 1995, Esch, Sheerin and Nunan in Benson and Voller 1997).

Students have access to a full record of all the activities they have completed, together with scores. These scores also appear on the unit page itself in the list of activities giving a constant reference point of previous study. In early tests of individual activities in December 2004, there seemed to be no uniform preference for particular activities but instead, a varied response for each individual. This may suggest that different learning styles and preferences of individual users will draw them to particular activity types.

Content

The content of the site clearly has to aim to meet the needs of the target users. Thus, the level is aimed broadly at IELTS 6.0–7.0. The units are usually targeted at the research interests of academic schools and based on Newcastle University sources. For example, videos of lectures and discussions, academic papers and news items involving University lecturers. Thus, the content is highly relevant to Newcastle students. Interestingly, 58% of the students in Hughes et al.'s (2004) study rated 'function and content' as the most important reason for liking a website. The content also aims to cover a defined syllabus in terms of skill types (reading, writing, listening, speaking, grammar and vocabulary), main aims and sub-skills. Each unit focuses on one skill type and main aim (see Figure 2) and each activity within the unit is categorised according to the list of sub-skills. The developers check coverage of the syllabus while cross-checking this against the range of academic topics.

All activities aim to promote active learning by presenting some level of interactivity for the user with no simple presentation of information. In class, a teacher would never give students activities or information without checking comprehension and giving feedback. Online language study needs to be supported in the same way. One of the excellent features of Hot Potatoes is the system of feedback, hints and clues which can all play a part in involving the user in the learning process (Peterson 1998).

Variety

Sheerin (1989), Eastment (1996) and Coniam (1998) emphasise the importance of having a variety of activity types. However, it is also important not to have such variety that it impacts negatively on the clarity and consistency that contributes so importantly to user-friendliness. We sought variety in the media presented to the learners in the form of streamed Realplayer video files, mp3 files and graphics. There is much support for their use in relation, for example, to multimedia input improving memory retention (Anderson 2000: 106–10) and the importance of observing kinesic behaviour while decoding speech (Kellerman 1992, McNeill 1985).

Motivation

The motivation for students to use such a language learning site will come from a variety of sources. The students in Hémard and Cushion's project (2001), wanted 'some means of appreciation [...] such as feedback and scoring, for [...] reassurance of work done and [...] self-satisfaction'. This reflects Kenning and Kenning's (1990: 101) comment that 'targeting the learners' needs for achievement and recognition is likely to be an effective way of maximising learner motivation'. Thus, helpful feedback and hints are built in wherever possible and aim to give the type of support a teacher would provide. Peterson (1998) sees this as a means of reinforcing positive learning outcomes and learner confidence. Also, Higgins (1995) and Dickinson (1987:83) both point out that learners sometimes need information about correct answers, not just wrong ones.

The recording and tracking of scores is another area that aims to motivate students. In ELMO, repetition of the activities is encouraged with the lowest, highest and average scores recorded for each activity. Students are also aware that their study record can be accessed by tutors.

The initial feedback from the pilot study is encouraging suggesting that students would plan to make use of the site in their free time at least on a monthly basis (see Table 2).

	N	Min	Max	Mean	Std. Dev
I will use this site in my free time...	23	1	5	3.0	1.22
I would study activities in my free time that relate directly to my academic subject...	30	2	5	3.1	1.16

Table 2. Student self-study plans
(Values: 1 = never, 2 = occasionally, 3 = every month, 4 = every week, 5 = every day)

In contrast, when asked if they would like to use this type of online study as homework 19 out of 23 students said they would. This response suggests that the blended approach is likely to be the way to ensure the site is used more frequently. It may reflect the fact that anything optional will become less of a priority in a student's busy working week.

Accessibility

From the outset, we set out to ensure that the ELMO site fully complied with SENDA[5] requirements. This is not just a hurdle to be jumped but something which must be fully integrated into the conception and design of educational websites from the outset and not just because educational online provision is no longer exempt from the DDA.[6] There are several websites with excellent information about the issues involved in achieving this.[7] Improving accessibility resulted in a number of changes in approach to the activities. To accommodate users such as those who may be dyslexic or have problems with sight or using a mouse, no timing devices are used. The use of drag and drop is avoided for screen readers and keyboard users. However, one of the problems for language teachers is sometimes the lack of technological know-how to achieve these goals. One example of this is the video player which is not currently operable via the keyboard making it inaccessible to those who cannot use a mouse. Such issues are ones that require ongoing attention and development in order to ensure that the site is fully compliant.

Conclusion

In conclusion, the ELMO project is very much in its infancy. There are a myriad of research questions for e-learning (e.g. Conole 2004) which need to be investigated in order to inform further development. At this stage, it is crucial for developers to start producing hard research facts while continuing to develop and add new materials.

---

5   Special Educational Needs and Disabilities Act, 2001: [http://www.opsi.gov.uk/acts/acts2001/20010010.htm].
6   Disability Discrimination Act 1995: [http://www.opsi.gov.uk/acts/acts1995/1995050.htm].
7   For example: [http://www.skillsforaccess.org.uk/ and http://www.webaim.org/].

With ELMO, we hope at least that we have got off on the right foot
with a model that can be developed and grown well into the future.

Bibliography

Allum, P. (2001) 'Principles applicable to the production of CALL-
ware: learning from the field of Human Computer Interaction
(HCI)'. *ReCALL* 13/2, 146–66.

Anderson, J.R. (2000) *Cognitive Psychology and its Implications* 5th
ed. Worth Publishers: New York.

Benson, P. and Voller, P. (eds) (1997) *Autonomy and Independence in
Language Learning*. New York: Longman.

Coniam, D. (1998) 'Interactive evaluation of listening comprehension:
how the context may help'. *CALL* 11/1, 35–53.

Conole, G. (2004) 'E-Learning: the hype and the reality'. *Journal of
Interactive Media in Education (Designing and Developing for
the Disciplines Special Issue)* 12, available online at [http://www
-jime.open.ac.uk/2004/12/conole-2004-12-t.html].   Retrieved
8/01/2005.

Davies, T. and Williamson, R. (1998) 'The ghost in the machine: are
teacherless CALL programs really possible?' *Canadian Modern
Language Review* 55/1, 7–18.

Dickinson, L. (1987) *Self-instruction in language learning*. Cambridge: Cambridge University Press.

Eastment, D. (1996) 'Survey Review: CD-ROM materials for English
language teaching'. *ELTJ* 50/1, 69–79.

Gremmo, M-J. and Riley, P. (1995) 'Autonomy, self-direction and self
access in language teaching and learning: the history of an idea'.
System 23/2, 151–64.

Hémard, D. and Cushion, S. (2000) 'From access to acceptability:
exploiting the Web to design a new CALL environment'.
Computer Assisted Language Learning 13/2, 103–18.

—— (2001) 'Evaluation of a Web-based language learning environment: the importance of a user-centred design approach for CALL'. *ReCALL* 13/1, 15–31.

Higgins, J. (1995) *Computers and English Language Learning.* Oxford: Intellect

Hughes, J., McAvinia, C. and King, T. (2004) 'What really makes students like a web site? What are the implications for designing web-based language learning sites?' *ReCALL* 16/1, pp 85–102.

Kellerman, S. (1992) '"I see what you mean": the role of kinesic behaviour in listening and implications for foreign and second language learning'. *Applied Linguistics* 13/3, 239–58.

Kenning M-M. and Kenning, M.J. (1990) *Computers and Language Learning: current theory and practice.* London: Ellis Horwood.

Laurel, B. (1991) *Computers as Theatre.* Reading MA: Addison-Wesley.

Lonfils, C. and Vanparys, J. (2001) 'How to Design User-Friendly CALL Interfaces'. *Computer Assisted Language Learning* 14/5, 405–17.

Lynch, P.J. (1994) 'Visual Design for the User Interface, Part I: Design Fundamentals'. *The Journal of Biocommunication* 21/1, 22–30.

McNeill, D. (1985) 'So you think Gestures are Non-Verbal?' *Psychological Review* 92/3, 350–71.

Peterson, M. (1998) 'Creating hypermedia learning environments: guidelines for designers'. *Computer Assisted Language Learning* 11/2, 115–24.

Rühlmann, F. (1998) 'Conceptual systems design: a synthesised approach'. *Computer Assisted Language Learning* 11/2, 229–44.

Sheerin, S. (1989) *Self-Access.* Oxford: Oxford University Press.

Shneiderman, B. (1998) *Designing the User-Interface.* Reading, MA: Addison-Wesley.

ELMO can be viewed at [http://www.ncl.ac.uk/langcen/elmo].

LYNNE HALE AND GILLIAN LAZAR

23 Authoring Online Materials for Academic Writing: Issues and Opportunities[1]

Introduction

This paper describes a materials development project at Middlesex University to support students in writing and other academic skills. The project was devised and designed by ELLS (English Language and Learning Support), a team of EAP specialists which delivers EAP and provision in study skills and academic writing skills to Middlesex students. In this paper, we begin by describing the context in which a highly collaborative authoring model has been established to develop materials on WebCT, the university's virtual learning environment. We then focus on key elements in the development of the materials – authorship, audience and medium. These have interacted in complex and problematic ways which has had an impact on both the process of writing and the final product. We will explore some of the tensions and conflicts arising from this interaction and will provide some concrete examples of how we have tried to resolve them. Finally, we will briefly mention the opportunities that have arisen from the project, both for the team and for individual members of staff.

---

1   This paper is based on a collaborative multimedia presentation which included video clips of English Language and Learning Support (ELLS) team members reflecting informally on their work. Unless otherwise indicated, all quotes are taken from these video clips.

The Context

Middlesex University

Middlesex University is a large multi-campus university in North London. The Statistical Digest for 2003/04 records more than 24,000 students, 25% of whom were international, 63% undergraduate and a minimum of 38% of home students from ethnic minorities. In addition, more than 38% of undergraduates were mature students (over 21). Students come from a very wide diversity of backgrounds, and include those who speak English as a first language, as a foreign language or second or third language, or who are bilinguals.

English Language and Learning Support (ELLS)

ELLS is a university-wide free service run by Middlesex University Learning Resources. It offers a confidential and unassessed environment where students can obtain information about and guidance in a range of academic skills, including writing. Support is offered in the form of voluntary attendance at workshops, one-to-one and small group tutorials. This support is aimed at the whole student body including international and home students, postgraduates and undergraduates, students from different schools studying a variety of disciplines, native and non-native speakers of English, students regularly using non-standard varieties of English, part-timers and full-timers and students with dyslexia.

Each of the University's four major campuses has two or more dedicated ELLS lecturers in English language with an additional subject speciality related to the particular campus. For example, the lecturer at the School of Health and Social Sciences has a background in psychology, in addition to being an English language specialist. Over the years, support has been increasingly delivered within subject areas in collaboration with subject specialists, both as part of the curriculum and in additional customised workshops. However, much of ELLS work is not linked directly to student modules, and is accessed by students on a voluntary basis.

Authorship

While there has been a strong emphasis in the past decade on promoting collaboration in student writing, for example through peer review (Frodesen in Belcher and Braine 1995, Harmer 2004, Hyland 2002), less attention appears to have been paid to collaborative writing of materials by teachers or lecturers. In the literature on materials development, the focus appears to have been largely on principles for developing materials appropriate to a given context (McDonough and Shaw 1993, Renandya 2003, Tomlinson 1998) or how the tools provided by new technology can be used to facilitate appropriate pedagogy (Rogerson-Revell 2005). However, Tomlinson (2003:4) has advocated 'a large team approach to writing materials', while Popovici and Bolitho (in Tomlinson 2003) describe a highly participatory writing project in Romania in which a team of teachers collaborated to produce a series of textbooks for the local context. In addition, anecdotal evidence does seem to suggest that many teachers and lecturers often collaborate informally in developing materials, but it does not always seem to be the case that collaborative materials development is institutionalised as an inherent part of a programme or project. When our team began working on our online project, we aimed to encourage collaborative materials writing and during the first year and a half of the project, a highly collaborative authoring model evolved (Hale et al. 2004). This involved members of the ELLS team in a process of brainstorming, writing, critiquing and piloting of materials.

The team began by collating teaching materials that might form the basis for some on-line materials. At the same time, we researched our chosen topic (e.g. academic style or referencing) in more depth, while simultaneously pursuing our research into on-line learning.

Once an initial draft document was written, it was extensively critiqued by fellow ELLS lecturers before being redrafted, piloted with students and other academic staff where possible, and then uploaded as a web document. This process of extensive critiquing was often initially difficult in that it exposed writers to criticism from their peers, as team member Eileen Davies notes:

> The critiquing process to begin with was quite hairy, I suppose, both in critiquing my colleagues' stuff and in receiving criticism. But that level of discomfort did not last very long and it's actually been quite an inspiring process. It's been very, very stimulating and very exciting.

Another difficulty connected with the critiquing process has been the question of ownership of different materials. Team member Victoria Odeniyi states that:

> I think, for me, one of the main issues has perhaps been identifying a sense of authorship as it's been a collaborative project, and I think, from that, there have been some tensions in terms of who should and for how long remain sole author of an individual tutorial or document, and where the boundaries lie between different authors and their input.

We have tried to allow the final decisions about a document to be made by the authors themselves, but it is also true to say that all documents have been through very extensive redrafting following comments and suggestions from peers. As a result, by the time the materials are uploaded there is often a sense of collective, rather than individual ownership of them. At the same time, team members have experienced an increasing sense of ease in asking for and receiving constructive criticism from each other, and have been able to draw on this support in activities unrelated to the web project.

Audience

As has already been mentioned, the audience for the project is extremely diverse. As the brief for ELLS within the university is to provide support for all students, the online project has also been aimed at the whole student body. This has, at times, caused conflict and confusion for materials writers. As Victoria Odeniyi points out:

> I think initially when I started writing, one or two years ago, one of the issues was that I really didn't know who the online audience was going to be. I had a sense of who the audience was, in terms of campus-based support and face-to-face support, so I suppose that, as I was producing and writing documents, I had those real and imagined students in my mind. However, there was a sense that potentially there may be students, staff and users who would be attracted to the website that, perhaps weren't, or were less interested in, coming for face-to-face support.

One interesting conflict which emerged during the critiquing process was that an individual writer's sense of imagined audience, the internalised audience at whom their materials were aimed, was often based on the types of students for whom he or she was providing face-to-face support at a particular campus. Writers on other campuses often had a very different experience of the needs of typical Middlesex students, and thus sometimes felt that a particular document would not meet the needs of these students. Another difficulty relating to audience is that the site is used by both native and non-native speakers of English. As Paul Fanning puts it:

> In thinking about the audience, the main issue for me without a doubt was the fact that I was writing grammar materials, which are very language specific, and my audience was a mixture of native and non-native English speakers [...] It was only when I really got down to the nitty gritty of designing the materials that I suddenly realised that I couldn't just pick any grammar topic but I had to be careful and, as it happened, with experience and having done similar things in the past, I was able to identify a number of topics that I knew would be equally of interest to native and non-native speakers.

We have tried to cope with the complex question of audience in a number of ways. Firstly, we believe that the critiquing process among the team has provided a kind of failsafe position in that each individual writer's sense of the audience for the project has been extensively interrogated by other team members, who often have a very different perspective on the typical Middlesex student. Secondly, we have tried to gather as much information about our audience and their responses to the materials by piloting the materials with as many different groups of students as possible. A number of writers on materials development have stressed the importance of piloting materials in order to ascertain how users make sense of them, and how they can be adapted to be most appropriate to their users (see, for example, Donovan, Littlejohn and Ellis in Tomlinson 1998). To date, we have formally piloted our materials with undergraduate nursing and computing students and post-graduate international relations, interactive multimedia and computing students. In addition, we have received less formal anecdotal feedback from both students and academic staff in Education, Arts and Social Sciences. Questionnaires for both students and staff can be found on the site.

A significant number of changes have been made to both individual documents and the site as a whole as a result of this piloting. For example, feedback from students during piloting revealed that they could not always locate answers to their questions in our documents, often because of a linguistic difficulty. One group of students wanted to find out about citing secondary sources, but as they were not familiar with the terms primary and secondary sources, they were unable to find the relevant information in the document on referencing. Our solution to this problem was to develop a page of Frequently Asked Questions (FAQs), written in language that is easily accessible to students and which avoids academic jargon (see Appendix). Questions on the FAQs page then provide direct links through to the relevant pages of different documents.

On a practical level, we have tried to make use of the web medium to allow for a wider diversity of users. While the majority of documents already uploaded are generic (e.g. Analysing questions, Academic style, Referencing, Plagiarism and Organising essays) more subject-specific pathways through the site have also been provided.

For example, some documents, such as Analysing questions and Organising essays begin with very generic content, but students then have the choice of working through more subject-specific content, relevant to their own needs, further on in the document.

We have also exploited the web medium to layer the materials in terms of both density and difficulty. For example, key points relating to a particular topic are often listed in documents as bullet points. If students wish to know more about an individual bullet point, they have the choice of clicking on it to access a pop-up window which provides them with more detail. Similarly, students have the choice of accessing other pop-up windows which provide information which is more difficult, e.g. in the Referencing document, post-graduate students can click on a pop-up to access information which is important for post-graduates, but which may be unnecessarily difficult for undergraduates.

Finally, we have tried to respond to the diversity of our audience by choosing topic areas which are appropriate. In the case of grammar materials, this has involved developing a mini-syllabus relevant to both native and non-native speakers of English. We are also currently in the process of developing a series of FAQs for students from particular subject areas such as Music and Computing.

The Medium

How has the on-line medium influenced the project, and what kinds of problems has it presented for us? Initially team members experienced a conflict between the need to mediate the content of the materials for students as we would in the classroom, and the exigencies of the medium. Our research into online learning had alerted us to the difficulties of reading online, due to the effects of screen resolution on the reader (McVay Lynch 2002). Lack of resolution when reading text online has been said to slow down both the reading process and comprehension of the text (Nielsen 2000). In general, writers of web materials are advised that 'if you want someone to read what you write on the web, write less' (Price and Price 2002:87). As Eileen Davies explains:

> once I started to write stuff for the web, it became apparent that I would have to [...] give more explanation and explain my explanations and try and second guess the audience and work out the areas of the stuff I was doing that they would have difficulty with. That led to a problem really at certain points of a great density of text and as we're told over and over again when we're designing things for the web, we've got to keep our pages short and it's all got to be snappy and it mustn't be too overwhelming in terms of the amount of words and ideas and that was quite difficult to adapt to the medium. I suppose in many ways the technology is quite helpful because we can use things like pop-ups [...] and in that way keep what is visible to the students less oppressively heavy.

As well as using the technology to reduce density of text, it was also helpful in making our materials more interactive. This was achieved by developing a number of online activities including quizzes where users can click to get instant answers, exercises which are self-marked by clicking on the mouse, pop-up windows which provide explanations or glosses for activities and drop and drag activities.

Another problem we experienced relating to the medium was a conflict between making the design of the site welcoming and accessible to students while simultaneously transmitting a certain academic gravitas. As Zaria Greenhill puts it:

> In terms of the graphic design, it's quite difficult to find a balance between making it look nice and attractive and sort of compatible with what students in particular would think websites should look like [...] and conveying a certain seriousness and academic rigour.

We have tried to incorporate design features which make the materials appear more accessible, such as using handwritten titles for each document, incorporating some cartoon-like drawings into documents which are humorous but also make a serious point and using individually designed icons which differentiate our site from others on WebCT.

Conclusion

In this paper we have focused on the complex interaction between authorship, audience and medium that has arisen while developing online materials and we have explored some of the conflicts resulting from this interaction and how we have tried to resolve them. Central to the project has been the highly collaborative authoring model which we have developed, and which has provided opportunities to reflect on many of the conflicts that have arisen during the project.

The project has generated a number of additional opportunities for both students and for team members. For students, there is now the opportunity to access ELLS in a more flexible way. With the emphasis on widening participation at Middlesex University, we feel that our online materials are an additional way to provide ongoing support to many different kinds of students. In addition, the project has raised the profile of ELLS within the university so that more students and staff have become aware of the service.

For ELLS staff, the project has engendered a lot of collaboration between team members. This has led to high levels of debate and re-flection about what we do and how we do it, and has had a significant impact on staff development. Team members involved in the project have gained increasing experience of materials development, the publishing process and conference output. We have also applied for and received a number of grants for university funding for the project, and this has provided us with valuable experience in this area.

Appendix I

ELLS on OASIS team

Lynne Hale (Head of ELLS)
Gillian Lazar (Project Co-ordinator, writer and critiquer)
Victoria Odeniyi (Project planner, writer and critiquer)
Zaria Greenhill (Web designer and technician until October 2005)
Eileen Davies, Paul Fanning, Julio Gimenez, Amanda Stewart (Writers/critiquers)
Judith Roads (Writer)
Don Hassett (Web designer and writer/critiquer until 2003)

Appendix II

Some sample questions from the 56 Frequently Asked Questions.

Understanding essay questions

1. My lecturer said that 'my essay doesn't answer the question.' How can I improve this?
2. There are some words in essay questions that I really don't understand, such as 'analyse' or 'evaluate'. What do they mean?

Academic style

1. Is there such a thing as academic style, and if so, what is it?
2. One of my lecturers says that I must not use 'I' in my essays. But what can I use it instead?

Grammar

1.   Are there any special grammatical features of academic writing?
Referencing and Plagiarism

1.   Do I really need to reference when I have put ideas from a book in my own words?
2.   How do I make reference to Smith in my essay? He is mentioned in a book by Jones which I have read. I haven't read the actual book by Smith.

Presentation Skills

1.   I get so nervous at the thought of talking in front of lots of people. What can I do about it?
2.   I'm dealing with complicated theories and ideas. How can I make sure that the listener can follow these?

Sample FAQs for Music students

1.   What is the best way of providing evidence in a music assignment?
2.   Music is all about emotions. Why should I have to write unemotionally about it?
3.   What is a good way to compare two pieces that are very different in style?
4.   What's the best way to make a proper bibliography and discography?
5.   How can I have an argument in what I write about music? I haven't got a point of view to persuade a reader about.
6.   In my assignment we are asked to write an evaluation of a musical piece. What should go into an evaluation?

ELLS on OASIS can be accessed by following the log-on instructions at: [http://oasis.mdx.ac.uk/public/ELLS01/index.html] Available until September 2007.

Bibliography

Frodesen, J. (1995) 'Negotiating the Syllabus: A learning-centred, interactive approach to esl graduate writing course design' in Belcher, D and Braine, G. (eds) (1995) *Academic Writing in a Second Language*, 331–50. New Jersey: Ablex Publishing.

Harmer, J. (2004) *How to Teach Writing*. Harlow: Pearson.

Hale, L., Lazar, G. and Odeniyi, V. (2004) 'Developing an Online Resource for Academic Writing: different voices, multiple concerns'. *Conference proceedings for writing development in higher education*. Sheffield Hallam University, May 2004.

Hyland, K. (2002) *Teaching and Researching Writing*. London: Pearson.

Irekponor, O. and Crivello, L. (2004) *Middlesex University Statistical Digest 2003/04*. Middlesex University Planning and Development Service.

McDonough, J. and Shaw, C. (1993) *Materials and Methods in ELT*. Oxford: Blackwell.

McVay Lynch, M. (2002) *The Online Educator: a guide to creating the virtual classroom*. London and New York: RoutledgeFalmer.

Nielsen, J. (2000) *Designing Web Usability*. Indiana: New Riders.

Popovici, R. and Bolitho, R. (2003) 'Personal and professional development through writing: the Romanian Textbook Project' in Tomlinson, B. (ed.) (2003).

Price, J. and Price, L. (2002) *Hot Text: web writing that works*. USA: New Riders.

Nielsen, J. (2000) *Designing web usability*. Indiana: New Riders.

Renandya, W.A. (ed.) (2003) *Methodology and materials design in language teaching: current perceptions and practices and their implications*. Anthology Series 44. SEAMEO Regional Language Centre [www.relc.org.sg].

Rogerson-Revell, P. (2005) 'A hybrid approach to developing CALL materials: authoring with Macromedias Dreamweaver /Coursebuilder'. *ReCALL* 17/1, 122–38.

Tomlinson, B. (ed.) (1998) *Materials development in language teaching* Cambridge: Cambridge University Press.

—— (ed.) (2003) *Developing materials for language teaching* London: Continuum.

Fei-Yu Chuang and Hilary Nesi

24 GrammarTalk: Developing Computer-based Materials for Chinese EAP Students

Introduction

GrammarTalk is a set of interactive grammar materials designed to help Chinese EAP students improve their formal accuracy. The syllabus for the materials was informed by our systematic analysis of a corpus of 50 essays (88,000 words) written by Chinese participants on a British pre-undergraduate foundation programme. Mismanagement of the English article system was found to be the most frequent cause of error in the students' writing, and an examination of article errors revealed five particularly problematic areas: 1) the use of bare singular count nouns for generic or non-specific reference, 2) the use of generic or non-specific noncount nouns with a redundant *the*, 3) the use of proper nouns with a missing or redundant *the*, 4) the use of generic or non-specific plural nouns with a redundant *the*, and 5) the representation of a unique thing without *the*. By examining the occurrence of these error types in context we were able to establish that our learners had particular difficulty with noun phrases for generic or non-specific reference (i.e. generic articles), the definite article with proper nouns, and the concept of the unique thing in immediate or wider situations. The identifying function of the definite article, which involves shared knowledge between the speaker/writer and listener/reader, seems to be an intrinsically difficult concept for Chinese learners of English to acquire. Some errors seemed to reflect L1 interference and could be attributed at least in part to differences between the grammar of English and the grammar of Mandarin Chinese. In particular, Mandarin differs from English in that there is no article system, count and noncount nouns are treated in the same way, plural markers are not required, and bare count nouns (a singular noun without a determiner or a plural noun without a plural marker) are used for generic or non-specific reference (Chuang 2005).

After considering these error features and their possible causes we set about designing a syllabus for our remedial materials. The target users of GrammarTalk are intermediate and advanced level learners of English who have already undergone several years of English language instruction, but who need a refresher course on some concepts and structures that are present in English but absent in Chinese (count and noncount nouns, singular and plural noun forms and the functions of the definite article). The GrammarTalk syllabus needed to re-establish understanding of the basic differences between the functions of the definite and indefinite article with reference to the concepts of definiteness/indefiniteness, specificity/non-specificity, generic reference, and shared knowledge between writers/speakers and readers/listeners. The syllabus also needed to review structures involving generic and non-specific nouns (the use of generic articles), and re-introduce the rule that unique items and qualified nouns require the definite article. We also planned to draw attention to the role of articles in idioms and in noun phrases containing proper nouns.

With this syllabus in mind we conducted some preparatory research. We reviewed the literature to discover what were considered to be the most effective ways of teaching grammar rules, examined existing pedagogical grammar materials to see how the rules were actually being taught, and elicited suggestions and comments from EAP tutors with experience of teaching Chinese learners. Our findings are briefly documented below.

Insights Drawn from Prior Studies

SLA researchers have put forward the view that explicit grammar knowledge enhances productive accuracy (Rutherford and Sharwood Smith 1985, Ellis 1994), and research evidence has lent support to this claim (for example Green and Hecht 1992, Sorace 1985). It has been noted, however, that individual learners tend to perceive and assimilate pedagogical rules in different ways, and that left to their own devices learners' reformulations may deviate greatly from the rules as they were originally taught in the classroom (Sorace 1985, Green and Hecht 1992). Schmidt (1990) observes that the learner's conscious noticing of L2 input is crucial for the conversion of input to intake, and Gass (1997) emphasises the importance of noticing in her six stage model of second language acquisition, which begins with input, apperceived input and comprehended input, and proceeds to intake, integration and output. When planning GrammarTalk we therefore chose tasks that would help learners focus on input-processing, so that they could formulate and internalise appropriate rules relating to the English article system.

Ellis (1991:235–7) favours consciousness-raising (C-R) tasks as a means of acquiring explicit grammar knowledge. C-R tasks perform five functions: 1) they direct focal attention to an L2 item, 2) they provide data or rules which illustrate or describe the item, 3) they require learners to understand the item, 4) they help to clear up any misunderstandings about the item, and 5) they encourage learners to construct explicit rules. In Ellis' view, C-R activities are concept-forming, while practice activities emphasise repeated production and are mainly behaviour oriented. Ellis insists that 'the focus of [grammar] instruction should be *awareness* rather than *performance*' (ibid:29). Thornbury (2001) points out that the main difference between C-R tasks and production activities is one of reduced expectations – C-R tasks do not expect 'immediate and consistently accurate production' (ibid:38). This accords with Rutherford and Sharwood Smith's (1985:280) view that C-R can facilitate the acquisition of L2 competence, but is not directly related to the achievement of fluency. C-R activities are designed to make learners notice the target feature and construct form-meaning mapping (Thornbury 2001) and to guide learners to discover the target language grammar for themselves (Batstone 1994).

Many studies have advocated the use of C-R tasks in grammar teaching, and different kinds of C-R tasks have been proposed (Fotos and Ellis 1991, Ellis 1991, 1993, 1997, Fotos 1994, Thornbury 2001).

For example, Ellis (1993:152–3) proposes grammar consciousness-raising and interpretation tasks. Grammar consciousness-raising tasks engage learners in explicit discussion of a target feature in order to formulate conscious representations of the feature. Interpretation tasks provide learners with enhanced structured data (such as contrastive pictures) so that they can be induced to notice a target structure, identify correct form-function mapping or notice the gap between their own production and the target form.

We concluded that GrammarTalk should employ C-R activities to actively engage learners in awareness raising and rule forming. We felt, however, that some production activities could also be usefully included, provided that they engaged the learners at a cognitive level and did not simply require mindless repetition of a given structure. Editing seems to be a particularly useful production task for our learners, because we want to encourage them to take responsibility for the editing of their own written work, and because it provides a means of initiating hypothesis testing and rule refining, essential to the later stages of integration and output in Gass's SLA model.

SLA researchers tend to write in general terms about the acquisition of L2 vocabulary and target structures. The definite, indefinite and zero article, however, are less salient to learners than most linguistic features in English text. *A* and *the* are phonologically reduced in speech, which makes them difficult to notice in classroom interaction, and although article misuse can seriously affect communicative function (unlike, for example, the omission of third person singular *s* from verbs in the present tense), the meanings conveyed through the article system are often subtle, and misuse may not lead to requests for clarification or the same sort of negotiation of meaning that may occur, for example, when a learner selects the wrong lexical item. This helps to explain why many very advanced learners of English continue to have problems with the article system. Perhaps this lack of salience also helps to explain why the English article system has been rather neglected by applied linguists, both as researchers and as course designers. Those few researchers who have specifically investigated the teaching and learning of articles have acknowledged their complexity, and the difficulties learners face in acquiring competence in this area (Whitman 1974, Master 1990, 1997, 2002, Berry 1993).

Master (1986) claims that the rules associated with article use are best acquired if they are presented to learners in a specific hierarchical sequence. His six-point schema suggests that knowledge of the article system entails the ability to distinguish between contrastive noun phrase features, which should be taught in the following order: 1) countable/uncountable, 2) definite/indefinite, 3) premodified/post-modified, 4) specific/generic, 5) common/proper, and 6) idiomatic/non-idiomatic. We decided to follow this sequence for the presentation of materials in GrammarTalk, although as our materials are designed for self-access use our learners are able, in fact, to create their own route through the activities, working in any order, as well as at their own learning pace.

The Treatment of the Article in Pedagogical Grammar Books

Seven grammar reference books in current use were randomly selected for analysis (see Table 1 below). All of them included sections on the article, although one (Active Grammar) did not relate article use to noun features (countability and number).

Fei-Yu Chuang and Hilary Nesi

Grammar book	Author(s)	Year	Publisher
A Practical English Grammar	Thomson, A.J. and Martinet, A.V.	1986	Oxford University Press
Active Grammar	Bald, W-D, Cobb, D. and Schwarz, A.	1986	Longman Group Limited
Collins Cobuild English Guides (3): Articles	Berry, R.	1993	HarperCollins Publishers
English Grammar in Use	Murphy, R.	1994	Cambridge University Press
Practical English Usage	Swan, M.	1995	Oxford University Press
Oxford Practice Grammar	Eastwood, J.	1999	Oxford University Press
Advanced Grammar in Use	Hewings, M.	1999	Cambridge University Press

Table 1. The seven grammar books selected for analysis

The remaining six books varied in the amount of detail they provided, but generally conformed to the following presentation sequence: 1) the features of the noun, 2) the functions of the definite and indefinite article, 3) the different patterns of generic articles, and 4) the use of the article with proper nouns and special groups of words. These features and their sequence are similar to those proposed by Master (1986, 1990), and accorded with our own plans for GrammarTalk.

However, although these books covered the necessary syllabus areas, their treatment of the article system did not seem to facilitate acquisition. The more recent works included a wider range of presentation styles and exercise types but all the books we examined adopted for the most part a presentation-practice model in which the learner was first introduced to grammar rules and exemplars deductively, and was then expected to practise the rules through exercises which required immediate production of the target form. These production-oriented exercises seemed to assume that L2 input inevitably led to L2 intake, and that after having been presented with rules and exemplars at the presentation stage, learners would understand the grammar point(s) and would only need to practise extensively in order to increase their production fluency, or as Ur (1988:7) puts it, 'to transfer what they know from short-term to long-term memory'. Ellis (1991) expresses doubts about the effectiveness of traditional grammar practice activities, and argues against the belief that more practice leads to greater proficiency, claiming that because of psycholinguistic constraints, practice does not guarantee the automisation of the learner's conscious grammar knowledge. Thornbury (2001) also criticises the presentation-practice model for assuming a direct link between input and output (i.e. between teaching and learning). We thought that the grammar books we examined paid insufficient attention to the apperception and comprehension stages of acquisition, and often failed to check whether learners had actually noticed and understood the target L2 features.

A further problem with many of the grammar books we examined was that their exemplars tended to be decontextualised, and employed very simple language referring to everyday topics rather than more cognitively demanding abstract concepts. Although we concede that this approach might help learners to focus on grammatical forms, we suspect that it might be counterproductive in the longer term. One reason for this is that decontextualised examples are likely to discourage the equation of form and meaning. Since article usage is often meaning-dependent, and communicative function is often expressed at levels beyond the sentence (Petrovitz 1997), the learner who only uses decontextualised sentences as productive models and only produces single sentence answers to grammar exercises may not learn what is needed to make rhetorical choices at the level of discourse. Nunan (1998:102) criticises traditional grammar materials for presenting isolated sentences for the learner to internalise 'through exercises involving repetition, manipulation and grammatical transformation'. Such materials, he argues, deny the learner 'the opportunity of seeing the systematic relationships that exist between form, meaning, and use'. Furthermore, the use of very simple language and topics does not reflect most EAP students' receptive and productive experience. As we know, academic texts frequently construct sustained and complex arguments, involving the explicit signalling of logical relations between propositions, and the marking of given and new information. The examples in the grammar books lacked many of the characteristics of academic writing, and were unlikely to encourage EAP students to consider the role of articles in the expression of complex meaning.

We concluded that although pedagogical grammars have the potential to provide self-access support for L2 writers, many of those that we examined did not provide an ideal remedy for our Chinese learners' article misuse, both because they did not have an EAP focus (in terms of language and topics) and because of the pedagogical assumptions underpinning their general design.

The Treatment of the Article in English Language Teaching Textbooks

We also examined the treatment of the English article system in nine recent EFL textbooks ranging from pre-intermediate to upper intermediate level (about the level of our Chinese learners). Details of these books are provided in Table 2 below.

Textbook	Author(s)	Year	Publisher
New Generation 3	Granger, C. and Beaumout, D.	1988	Heinemann International
Snapshot (intermediate students' book)	Abbs, B., Freebairn, I. and Barker, C.	2000	Pearson Education Limited
True to Life (upper intermediate)	Gairns, R. and Redman, S.	1998	Cambridge University Press
New Headway English Course (intermediate student's book)	Soars, L. and Soars, J.	1996	Oxford University Press
Opportunities (intermediate)	Mugglestone, P.	2000	Longman
Inside Out (upper intermediate)	Kay, S. and Jones, V.	2001	Macmillan Publishers Limited
Matters (Upper Intermediate)	Bell, J. and Gower, R.	1992	Longman
Cutting Edge (intermediate)	Cunningham, S. and Moor, P.	1998	Longman
Clockwise (pre-intermediate)	McGowen, B. and Richardson, V.	2000	Oxford University Press

Table 2. The nine EFL textbooks selected for analysis

We found that only five of the nine textbooks (*New Generation 3, Inside Out, Matters, Snapshot,* and *True to Life*) included sections explicitly dealing with the use of the definite article. These treatments were always brief, suggesting that this grammatical area did not have a very high priority for the textbook writers. Two books provided short lists of rules (*Inside Out* 'Language reference: articles' p. 28, and *Matters* 'The definite article' p. 17). Two more, *Snapshot* and *New Generation 3,* provided a small number of decontextualised gapped sentences, to give learners a (very limited) opportunity to practise article use. The fifth textbook, *True to Life,* did not deal with articles directly but provided two activities in the 'Noun groups' section (pp. 35–6) which required learners to consider article use. (One exercise asked learners to differentiate between sentences such as *He's gone to prison/He's gone to the prison*, and the other required them to use the definite article with certain adjectives to describe groups of people, e.g. *the poor*).

Because the information in the textbooks was kept short and simple it often only provided a partial account of a particular rule. For example, the following rule in *Matters* (p. 17) was useful to a certain extent, but misleadingly suggested that *the* can never be used when referring to parts of the body, transport and meals.

> The definite article is NOT used: …………..
> d) When referring to parts of the body, transport, meals, games, some expressions of time, seasons, months, etc.:
> Mandy's got *big ears*. / I'm going *by car*.
> Have you had *breakfast*? / The park closes *at night*.

Similarly *Inside Out* over-simplified the rule when giving this piece of advice (p. 28):

> You don't use articles with proper nouns such as places, people and companies.
> There was a young lady from *Niger*.
> *John Smith* had a job with *Microsoft* but now he's moved to *IBM*.

The warning appended to this rule was not very helpful, as it did not attempt to explain why certain exceptions occur:

> Exceptions are when the article is part of a name (*The United States, The BBC, The Beatles*).

Snapshot provided no rules for article use but presented a series of short sentences (either in pairs or completely decontextualised) to illustrate the article system (p. 17). Examples include:

> The definite article
> She's on a trek. *The* trek takes sixteen days.
> They went to *the* Netherlands and *the* USA.
>
> Zero article
> They went by bus.
> I'm starting school / university next week.

Although learners were invited to notice the target forms in these examples, and were thus provided with some opportunities for inductive rule formulation, the *Snapshot* authors also allowed for a more deductive approach to grammar teaching. Readers were told to discuss the rules with their teacher, and we can imagine that in some classrooms at least this would encourage a presentation-practice method of instruction.

Inside Out provided the fullest treatment of the different functions of the definite and indefinite article, although this was still fairly brief. The other four textbooks mainly dealt with article use in relation to proper nouns and special groups of words, and their coverage of concepts such as definiteness, specificity and generic reference was scanty. *Inside out* and *Matters* mentioned the patterns of generic noncount nouns and generic plural nouns, but none of the textbooks discussed the usage of different generic articles, confirming Celce-Murcia and Larsen-Freeman's (1983) claim that this is a neglected area in ESL/EFL textbooks. The results of our error analysis revealed that the students often needed to use generic/non-specific noun phrases to express generic/non-specific meaning in their essays, and the textbooks' failure to deal with this aspect of article use was therefore an important omission for EAP contexts.

EAP Tutors' Suggestions

In addition to our review of the prior literature and existing grammar materials, we also conducted a small-scale survey to elicit suggestions from EAP tutors with experience of teaching writing skills to Chinese learners. Seven tutors responded, and all of them indicated that they would welcome some new grammar materials especially written for Chinese students. Drawing on their own TEFL training and classroom experience they made the following suggestions regarding materials design.

1. The materials should include activities that encourage students to discover the patterns and rules underlining a target linguistic feature.
2. The explanation of rules should not be given directly. The materials should provide sentences/texts for students to identify rules.
3. Students should have lots of opportunities to write their own sentences once they have assimilated the form and use of a grammar item.
4. Exercises should be presented in short isolated sections that are then built upon. There should be an element of free/uncontrolled practice to improve students' writing. This should also be short.
5. There should be 'quick revision' exercises for students to return to later.
6. The materials should have an EAP focus.

The tutors' suggestions seemed to reflect a number of underlying assumptions about language acquisition. In accordance with current SLA theory, they expressed the belief that it is useful for L2 learners to formulate explicit grammar rules. They also favoured learning through discovering, and in this they concurred with advocates of C-R tasks and inductive teaching. We noted, however, that despite its current popularity no conclusive research evidence exists to support the superiority of the inductive approach over the deductive approach. The tutors thought that practice was important, but that traditional controlled grammar exercises were not sufficient to proceduralise learners' declarative knowledge and develop communicative competence. Finally they thought that grammar materials designed for the learning of general English were unlikely to meet the needs of EAP learners. This view corresponded with our own doubts about the language, topics and discourse of existing grammar practice materials.

Our Design Principles

In the light of these findings the following design principles were drawn up:
1) The materials should aim to help learners to notice and comprehend the target features with a view to helping them to formulate satisfactorily correct rules.

2)   Consciousness-raising activities (e.g. grammar consciousness raising tasks and interpretation tasks) should be employed to help learners to achieve apperception and comprehension of the target linguistic features. They should precede production-oriented activities. Production-oriented activities should serve as a means of initiating hypothesis testing and rule refining.

3)   The materials should reach a compromise between the inductive and deductive approaches by combining elements of both. Learners should be given opportunities to analyse selected language data and attempt to formulate their own grammar rules, but they should also be given opportunities to compare these rules with the correct rules, supplied in GrammarTalk, and finally to start refining these rules through productive tasks.

4)   Learners should be exposed to longer texts (of a paragraph or more) when article use depends on the discoursal context (for example in the distinction between given and new information). Decontextalised sentences could be used, however, when the use of the article relies solely on the syntactic structure or the lexical item (as, for example, in the phrase the length of the table).

5)   The materials should refer to authentic learner errors, and all texts should be authentic. We decided to take our texts from the corpus of Chinese learner writing we had previously used for error analysis, and from a corpus of proficient university student writing (the pilot corpus of British Academic Written English). Texts from both sources would have an EAP focus in terms of language, communicative purpose and information content.

6)   The operation of the program should be simple because the language and tasks would be difficult. Clues, help features and feedback should also be provided.

The GrammarTalk Materials

We prepared GrammarTalk using MS Visual Basic, and following the design principles outlined above. A wide range of different task types are employed, some more conventional (cloze, multiple choice) and others more innovative (examining concordance data, distinguishing between native speaker and learner writing, translating from the Chinese). Grammar consciousness-raising tasks are the most frequent, but a number of interpretation tasks are dispersed throughout the course. Production tasks only occur after learners have been provided with consciousness-raising opportunities.

Several small-scale pilot studies have already been carried out to refine the GrammarTalk materials, test their usability and elicit suggestions for improvements. Participants in these studies seemed to like the materials and indicated that they were very useful. We have now reached the final stage of materials development, when, with the help of an e-learning grant from the University of Warwick, we will conduct larger-scale trials with a wider range of international students. Although GrammarTalk was designed with Chinese learners in mind we will also make the materials available to learners of other nationalities, and may create alternative translation exercises in other languages. Ultimately we plan to apply the same process of error analysis, review and consultation to the development of further modules, to address other recalcitrant grammar problems. We also hope that our experience of creating GrammarTalk can inform other materials developers who wish to focus on neglected syllabus areas, and produce useful, authentic, research-based activities for their learners.

Bibliography

Batstone, R. (1994) *Grammar*. Oxford: Oxford University Press.

Berry, R. (1993) *Collins COBUILD English guides (3): Articles*. London: HarperCollins Publishers.

Celce-Murcia, M. and Larsen-Freeman, D. (1983) *The grammar book*. Cambridge, MA: Newbury House.

Chuang, F-Y. (2005) 'Addressing the grammar needs of Chinese EAP students: an account of a CALL materials development project'. Unpublished doctoral thesis. University of Warwick, UK.

Ellis, R. (1991) *Second Language Acquisition and language pedagogy*. Clevedon: Multilingual Matters.

—— (1993) 'Talking shop: second language acquisition research: how does it help teachers?' An interview with Rod Ellis. *ELT Journal* 47/1, 3–11.

—— (1994) *The study of Second Language Acquisition*. Oxford: Oxford University Press.

—— (1997) *SLA research and language teaching*. Oxford: Oxford University Press.

Fotos, S. (1994) 'Integrating grammar instruction and communicative language use through grammar consciousness raising tasks'. *TESOL Quarterly* 28//2, 323–51.

—— and Ellis, R. (1991) 'Communicating about grammar: a task-based approach'. *TESOL Quarterly* 25/4, 605–28.

Gass, S. (1997) *Input, interaction, and the second language learner*. Mahwah, NJ: Lawrence Erlbaum Associates.

Green, P.S. and Hecht, K. (1992) 'Implicit and explicit grammar: an empirical study'. *Applied Linguistics* 13/2, 168–84.

Master, P. (1986). 'Teaching the English article system to foreign technical writing students'. *The Technical Writing Teacher* 13/3, 203–10.

—— (1990) 'Teaching the English articles as a binary system'. *TESOL Quarterly* 24/3, 461–78.

—— (1997) 'The English article system: acquisition, function, and pedagogy'. *System* 25/2, 215–32.

—— (2002) 'Information structure and English article pedagogy'. *System* 30/, 331–48.

Nunan, D. (1998) 'Teaching grammar in context'. *ELT Journal* 52/2, 101–9.

Petrovitz, W. (1997) 'The role of context in the presentation of grammar'. *ELT Journal* 51/3, 201–7.

Rutherford, W. and Sharwood Smith, M. (1985) 'Consciousness raising and Universal Grammar'. *Applied Linguistics* 6/3, 274–82.

Schmidt, R. (1990) 'The role of consciousness in second language learning'. *Applied Linguistics* 11/2, 129–58.

Sorace, A. (1985) 'Metalinguistic knowledge and language use in acquisition-poor environments'. *Applied Linguistics* 6/3, 239–54.

Thornbury, S. (2001) *Uncovering grammar.* Harlow: Longman.

Ur, P. (1988) *Grammar practice activities.* Cambridge: Cambridge University Press.

Whitman, R.L. (1974) 'Teaching the article in English'. *TESOL Quarterly* 8/3, 253–62.

STELLA HARVEY AND KAREN NICHOLLS

25 From Live Lecture to Online Materials: Developing Listening Skills and Lexical and Grammatical Accuracy

Introduction

Lectures form a key element of the learning experience of our students. They provide not only subject matter, but also a wealth of language learning opportunities. Can these opportunities be enhanced by online materials? This paper describes two sets of online materials which take live lectures as their starting point and attempt to make greater use of these opportunities. The first set of materials is based on audio-visual recordings of live lectures and is designed to improve listening and note-taking skills and understanding of academic argument. The second set of materials is based on EAP tutor notes of another lecture series and is designed to develop students' lexico-grammatical knowledge within a content-relevant framework. After describing the rationale, development and use of each set of materials, we will critique them in terms of the achievement of their objectives and the comparative benefits of online and paper-based language practice materials.

Listening and Note-taking Materials

The first set of materials aims to provide realistic listening exercises which replicate the tasks that students undertake when they are on their degree courses, in other words, simultaneous listening and note taking. In addition, the materials were designed to provide a framework of graded exercises from which students could gain confidence and improve their listening skills. This would allow them to start with closely guided activities and move on to unsupported listening and note-taking tasks with sample answers. A further important goal was that the materials would be motivating enough for students to use independently outside the classroom.

The shortcomings of EAP listening and note-taking materials have been highlighted by Flowerdew and Miller (1997). They have identified four key characteristics of live lectures which were not present in the materials they analysed. The first of these is features of spoken language, including false starts, repetition, body language and facial gestures. The second is interpersonal strategies, for example, the use of 'we', rhetorical questions, checking questions like 'yeah?', and any utterance or gesture that gives some kind of personalisation on the part of the lecturer. The third element mentioned by Flowerdew and Miller is discourse structuring. They point out that in live lectures this tends to be less consistent than in textbook simulations. Moreover, the discourse extends beyond any particular lecture to previous or forthcoming lectures. Finally, they highlight integration with other media, referring to the fact that students listening to just an audio recording miss out on the integration of sight and sound. In authentic contexts, students sometimes have to look at the projections of slides, OHTs, or PowerPoint presentations and listen and take notes simultaneously. Integration of content also takes place at other times, for example, with students' independent reading or in seminar discussion.

From the outset, therefore, our goal was to use authentic lectures, in order to expose students to a more realistic, less controlled representation of a lecture. The technical implications of making a live, in situ recording are significant; however, it was hoped that the live recording would be superior to a simulation (e.g. a lecturer talking to a camera in a studio environment), which would suffer from the same weaknesses as those materials mentioned above.

A number of recordings were made of lectures from a nine-week course on 20th century British cinema and one of those was selected to be put online. In order to gain as wide an appeal as possible, the lecture on gender in 20th century British cinema was chosen. (Gender is one theoretical area which almost all students at Goldsmiths are likely to encounter.) After taking notes of the whole lecture, seven clips of about five minutes each were selected. These clips were chosen because they gave a coherent overview of the lecture. For each clip, four sets of questions were written to support students at different levels (ranging from 5.5 IELTS to near-native speakers). The aim was that students choose the level that helps them to develop most.

The first type of question is a gap-fill exercise based on a transcript of the lecture. Students watch and listen to the video and enter the missing words. This is a cognitively demanding exercise, but students can pause and rewind the video as many times as they like. On completion, they submit their answers, get a score, and can receive the correct answers. The second exercise elicits more or less the same key words, using comprehension questions. Again, students can submit their answers to get a score and receive feedback. The third exercise encourages students to take their own notes. They type into a blank note-taking space and then compare their notes to a sample answer. The fourth task involves a more analytical question about what the lecturer is doing in each clip or what her attitude to the topic is. Again, students can compare this to a model answer.

In terms of the rationale for the materials, there are two notable points. Firstly, it is clear that the materials do replicate the students' task of note taking, and use a scaffolded approach to help build confidence and improve listening. From a tutor's point of view, they were more motivating for EAP students than other materials we have for independent study, since they provide extensive practice in listening and note-taking skills with stimulating content and relevant lexis. Most of our students go on to study arts or social sciences degrees, and will have to deal with critical approaches to cultural artefacts. Most existing published EAP listening materials have only a few sections with a direct relation to our students' interests, and in a time-pressured course, direct relevance to their future studies is a key factor in motivating independent learning. Equally, it can be said that our materials address the first three elements which Flowerdew and Miller (1997) found to be missing in the textbook listening materials they analysed (Table 1).

Characteristic of live lecture	Exemplified in the video by
features of spoken language	repetition, false starts, body language
interpersonal strategies	checking questions, use of 'we'
discourse structuring – internal – external	structuring words are used, but signposting is occasionally inconsistent mentioning the topic of the next lecture
integration – sight and sound – with other media	students have to listen, watch and write not evident

Table 1. Provision of elements missing from textbook listening materials

In relation to integration, the materials do encourage students to make use of visual and audio information. However, the materials have not yet been fully integrated with other media. Ideally, therefore, they would be more fully utilised in a theme-based, integrated skills EAP course. This would combine the video lectures and listening materials with viewing the two films discussed in the lecture and readings about gender and film. The different exercises would facilitate use of such a course with students from a wide range of levels.

The other notable point concerns how students have actually used the materials. In terms of presentation, the materials have been shown to students in two ways. Firstly, in listening and note-taking classes with students on a full-time preparatory EAP course, and secondly on a four-hour per week EAP course for undergraduate students on extension degrees. In the former, the materials were presented to a group of 14 students on a nine-week pre-sessional course. This course includes content-based integrated skills strands centred on two lecture series by a non-EAP lecturer, one on the theme of postmodernism, the other on either Film or Art History. With this group, students were shown how to use the listening materials and used them in class (for about 45 minutes) for two consecutive weeks. They were not advised as to which questions they should try, but were shown all four types of question. After using the materials in class for two weeks, they were recommended to use them for independent study. The second time, the materials were presented to eight under-graduate students in their preliminary year of a four-year BA programme in either Art or Music. This year of study forms an intro-ductory year zero which feeds into the first year of the BA programmes, during which students take both introductory courses in their degree and a credit-bearing EAP course. When the materials were introduced to this group, students had been in the UK for several months and had been attending lectures and classes in their destination department. They were more used to listening to long stretches of speech and inferring meaning so, unlike the first group, they were specifically recommended to try the comprehension questions and the note-taking exercises. They were similarly shown how to use the materials, given time in class over two weeks to practise and then advised to continue to use the materials as part of their independent study.

By looking at the records that the computer software (Question Mark Perception) collects, it was clear which questions students attempted and how many times they actually used the materials independently. Analysis of the submissions showed that many students in the first group tried the same exercise several times (up to ten times in one case). Secondly, in that group many tried both the gap-fill and the comprehension questions for the same video extract. Thirdly, most of these students tended to stick to the gap-fill questions, which were perceived as the easiest. In contrast, the undergraduate students, who were advised to try the comprehension questions and note-taking exercises, did more of those than the first group. Finally, the presen-tation and use of the materials in class time for just two periods meant that most students in both groups only reached the second video clip and few went past extract 3. Even fewer attempted answers all the way through. So unfortunately, the materials did not provide sufficient additional motivation for all students to go through the remaining video clips as independent study, although some did use them a few times out of class.

In informal feedback, students reported that they enjoyed the exercises and found them useful. The guided questions received unanimously positive feedback, followed by the gap-fill exercise, whereas the note-taking exercise was less well received: 'I like gap fills and guided questions because it is clear. But I don't like the others because writings can't be properly evaluated online and I can't get feedback from computer.' Other criticisms highlighted local technical difficulties and computer-related discomforts such as head-aches.

Perhaps unsurprisingly, students have requested similar materials in a wide range of subjects, so ideally, this will be expanded across the University. However, in terms of efficiency and value for money (and production time), it is clear that the materials need to be used more systematically as the basis of an integrated skills course in which students would view the films, read texts on gender and film, and write an essay, as they would in their future studies. Furthermore, students who are shown the materials need firm recommendations about which tasks are the most appropriate for them.

An interesting additional point about these materials compared to the live lecture itself, was pointed out by one student. When asked what she had found to be the most useful experience to prepare for her MA lectures, she said that the face-to-face live lectures were best because sitting through them for an hour helped her to develop stamina. This requirement for physical stamina and extended concen-tration should perhaps be added to Flowerdew and Miller's (1997) list of considerations for the improvement of listening materials.

Lexico-grammatical Materials

While the listening materials are a composite multimedia resource, the lexico-grammatical materials form an extension of a lecture series whose content they review. In this way they integrate the target stu-dent group's experience of a live lecture with language development. As with the listening materials, their relevance to students' subject areas is a significant advantage. These materials are based on a two-term lecture series entitled 'The Enlightenment and its Legacy' out-lining the evolution of western thought from Descartes to the present day, through the rise of modernity and the emergence of postmod-ernity. This forms part of a core strand on Goldsmiths' Diploma in

Language and Contemporary Culture, a one-year pre-master's course for arts and social sciences students. The strand comprises the lecture series itself, given by a visiting sociology lecturer, a lecture feedback session with an EAP tutor and a textual analysis class also with an EAP tutor. The related assessments are two hand-in essays, i.e. one at the end of each term, and an examination essay.

Student evaluation of the lecture strand accords with the findings of Kirschner and Wexler (2002) on their content-based projects, indicating that it is highly motivating due to its stimulating and challenging material and relevance to students' proposed future studies. However there remains a need (as evidenced by expectations of Departments within the University and observations of external examiners) to improve the degree of linguistic accuracy in students' written work.[1] Hence the Diploma aims to integrate language study with the thematic content of the lecture strand. The online resources take the raw material of the lecture as the starting point. They were developed from EAP tutor notes taken during the lectures for the purpose of providing lecture feedback. They are designed to be used as an independent study resource that might also be embedded as a blended learning element. Their objectives are to provide further language study during the term and in preparation for the Diploma final examinations, to provide peripheral consolidation of the lecture strand content and recycle the substantial lexical load this generates, and to add an additional medium to the Diploma that will stimulate further interest and motivation.

The first materials to be piloted provide practice in gap-fill, word formation and word choice. In the gap-fill exercises, students must supply the correct word themselves to fit the gap. In the word choice exercise they are given a choice of two possible collocates and must choose the appropriate one. In the word formation exercise they are provided with a base form of the correct word and must change it grammatically to fit the gap. In the online version, students type in their answers, then submit them and receive feedback.

---

1   See Turner (2004) for a fuller discussion of the need for EAP to re-evaluate its approach to accuracy and precision of language.

The pilot study focused on the usefulness of the exercises in terms of language development and recycling of the thematic content of the lecture programme, as well as their affective dimension. The pilot group consisted of ten Diploma students, all East Asian. While firm conclusions cannot be drawn from such a restricted sample, some interesting patterns and issues presented. The most salient of these was the disparity between the students' positive evaluation of the exercises themselves, and their doubts about the benefits of doing them online. As Table 2 shows, a clear majority agreed that the exercises were useful and enjoyable and that they would like to do more of the same. However, the majority disagreed that it was preferable to do the gap-fill and word choice exercises online rather than in paper-based form, while in the case of the word formation exercises opinion was divided equally.

This exercise was useful.	Agree	Disagree
Gap-fill	9	1
Word choice	8	2
Word formation	10	0
I enjoyed doing this exercise.	Agree	Disagree
Gap-fill	8	2
Word choice	8	2
Word formation	8	2
I would like to do more of this type of exercise	Agree	Disagree
Gap-fill	8	2
Word choice	8	2
Word formation	9	1
It is better to do this type of exercise online than on paper.	Agree	Disagree
Gap-fill	4	6
Word choice	4	6
Word formation	5	5

Table 2. Student evaluation of online lexico-grammatical materials

This discrepancy was explored further in the follow-up focus group. The discussion took as its starting point one student's comment on the pilot session feedback form which expressed her ambivalence towards the online exercises by characterising them as a form of game. The focus group clarified this ambivalence: the exercises were enjoyable but problematic because they entailed an element of trial and error, which made it possible to find the right answer simply by luck. A suggested improvement was to introduce a time limit. However, a counter-argument put forward by another student highlighted the motivating effect of the trial and error element – it allows the possibility to keep trying until you get the right answer.

Another key point that emerged from the focus group was that while most participants agreed that the online materials were potentially useful for independent study, specifically for review purposes, they emphasised that they were no substitute for class study. This response suggests a perceived element of threat that possibly contributes to the ambivalence towards the online format – that the trials might have been a precursor to losing class time.

Other critical points made of the online resources were:

- lack of an answer key
- frustration arising from the lack of opportunity to discuss with a tutor issues not covered in the online feedback
- physical discomforts associated with computer use
- difficulties operating the computer (one student claimed to be unable to operate any machine other than the telephone)
- no possibility of the teacher giving feedback for online materials.

Overall, however, the response to the first pilot is encouraging. Some of the criticisms highlighted above can be easily addressed. An answer key can be provided, and queries not covered by the online feedback could be resolved by an online forum or in the classroom if the materials are used as a blended learning element. As with our listening materials, it is more difficult to address the issue of students who experience significant difficulties or discomfort when using a computer – or who simply dislike the medium. The possibility of the students annotating the same paper where the exercises are printed is clearly an advantage of paper-based format. What seems to be required is clarification of the intended purposes of the online materials so that students realise they are additional to, not a substitute for, their paper-based equivalent, and know how to use them in the most effective way.

From the perspective of the EAP tutor developing these online materials, there are also some reservations. The most significant of these relate to local technological constraints. In principle, the technology should be adaptable to the type of activity the tutor wishes to produce. In reality, it is the tutor who must adapt to what the technology is able to do. The process is also time-consuming: identifying the most appropriate technology and most effective ways of creating the materials entails considerable trial and error, while the actual creation of the online materials is laborious. Another constraint on the creation of materials for use as an independent study resource concerns the need to produce questions with a limited number of potentially correct answers and to predict all valid possible alternatives. The classroom setting affords the opportunity to discuss alternatives, doubts and ambiguities and is thus more flexible.

Conclusion

These materials have addressed the shortcomings of existing listening materials, crucially incorporating characteristics of authentic live lectures and combining subject specificity with language focus. Our experience has indicated that both sets of materials would benefit from more embedding, as well as more explicit instruction on their best use. For further investigation, the comparative benefits and drawbacks of paper-based and online materials need more extensive probing. It may also be worth exploring what impact cultural factors have on students' online learning strategies, and whether these have any bearing on the ambivalence towards the game element.

Bibliography

Flowerdew, J. and Miller, L. (1997) 'The teaching of academic listening comprehension and the question of authenticity'. *English for Specific Purposes* 16/1, 27–46.

Kirschner, M. and Wexler, C. (2002) 'Caravaggio – a design for an interdisciplinary content-base EAP/ESP unit'. *Journal of English for Academic Purposes* 1/2, 163–83.

Turner, J. (2004) 'Language as academic purpose'. *Journal of English for Academic Purposes* 3/2, 95–109.

IAN MCGRATH

26 Textbooks, Technology and Teachers

Introduction

This paper deals with relationships: the relationship between text-books and teachers, textbooks and technology, and textbooks, technology and teachers. Centrally, however, it concerns the impact of technology. What part does technology now play in learning materials? Do we still need textbooks? Do we even need teachers and, if so, what kind of teachers?

Textbooks and Teachers

Doubts about textbooks and their effect on teachers were voiced some 25 years ago by Brumfit (1979:30), who expressed the view that 'even the best textbooks take away initiative from teachers by implying that there is somewhere an "expert" who can solve problems' for teachers and learners. This notion of taking away initiative, resulting in teacher dependence and even deskilling, has since been elaborated by a number of other writers, among them Richards (1993) and Shannon (1987, cited in Richards 1998). A related but rather different argument was put forward by Allwright (1981), who presents two perspectives on the role of materials and the teacher-textbook relationship: either teachers are seen as deficient, with the textbook being a form of insurance against their limitations, or they are seen as having expertise which is different from but complementary to that of the materials writer. Preferring this latter perspective, he concludes that 'the management of learning is far too complex to be satisfactorily catered for by a pre-packaged set of decisions embodied in teaching materials' (1981:9).

As alternatives to the textbook, Brumfit and Allwright made rather similar proposals. Brumfit (1979:30) envisaged 'resource packs, sets of materials with advice to teachers on how to adapt and modify the contents', while Allwright (1981:9) conceived of a 'guide to language learning' for learners and 'ideas books' and 'rationale books' for teachers, supported by learner training and an appropriate focus within teacher training, all within a framework of the cooperative management of learning by learners and teachers – effectively a process syllabus. Almost 25 years on, we still have textbooks (or 'coursebooks', as they have rather tellingly come to be known), and the arguments for and against them continue to run.

My own survey of the literature (McGrath 2002:10–11) found the following commonly referred to reasons for valuing coursebooks. For both teachers and learners:

1) a coursebook is a map, which shows where one is going and where one has been
2) it provides language samples (at best, samples of authentic language use)
3) it offers variety.

For learners:

4) a coursebook defines what is to be learned and what will be tested
5) it reinforces what the teacher has done and makes revision and preparation possible. It thus offers support for learning outside class.

For teachers:

6) a coursebook provides a structure for teaching
7) it saves time. To prepare materials from scratch for every lesson would be impossible
8) it offers linguistic, cultural and methodological support
9) it is easy to keep track of what has been done (helpful when reporting to the Head of Department or briefing a substitute teacher)

10) coursebooks can serve as an input to professional development.

Though these points appear to constitute a convincing pragmatic argument for coursebook use, a clear distinction needs to be made between coursebook-*led* teaching and coursebook-*based* teaching (McGrath 2002). While acknowledging that 'some teachers stick to textbooks slavishly', Harwood (2005:152) points out that there is also evidence to show that many teachers do adapt materials, exploiting them as resources or, in Harmer's words, as 'proposals for action, not instructions for use' (Harmer 2001:8, cited in Harwood ibid).

Harwood's primary concern in this paper, however, is with EAP textbooks and whether these reflect applied linguistics research, particularly corpus-based research. With one exception, the textbooks surveyed did not stand up well to analysis based on this criterion. This leads him to conclude that though textbooks can provide a long-term syllabus and structure and make a teacher's life easier, they must meet certain general criteria: for instance, there should be no inherent tension between pedagogical soundness and product marketability, the textbook should be the product of research and dialogue, and teachers and learners must be able to judge content accuracy. The same requirements might also be made of general English coursebooks.

Textbooks and Technology

In the form of computers to support linguistic research, technology is a relatively recent phenomenon. As an aid to teaching and learning, with or without coursebooks, it has been with us for some time, as Howatt (1984) illustrates: Palmer experimented with the gramophone during his years in Japan in the 1920s; English by Radio was first broadcast in 1943; tape recorders became available for classroom use in the 1950s and audiovisual courses for French teaching, in which tape-recorded dialogues were synchronised with filmstrips, were pioneered in the early 1960s by CREDIF, a research centre at the

École Normale Supérieure de St Cloud near Paris. Language labora-
tories, first developed in America in the 1940s and relatively common
there by 1960 (Stack 1960), were used extensively in Britain in the
late 1960s to support the oral-structural-situational approach, the
European version of American audiolingualism. The unwieldy audio-
tapes were in due course succeeded by cassettes; video became available in the form of pre-recorded tapes and as an option for teachers
and learners to produce their own recordings and now we have CD-
ROMs, DVDs and the Internet.

In assessing the value of these developments, it may be helpful to
reflect on Ventola's (2005) comment, that CD-ROMs and VCDs may
simply be a new way of packaging old material. In producing
materials in these forms, does the underlying motivation appear to be
commercial, i.e. a recognition on the part of the publisher that, to stay
competitive, producing such materials is a necessity, even when for
this element of the total package costs may exceed income? Or are
writers and publishers enthusiastically seizing the opportunities
offered by the new technology to create something innovative in terms
of content or pedagogy – for example in the form of additional, out-
of-class learning opportunities? The reality, of course, is that publishing houses are commercial enterprises and for existing courses the
repackaging option will be the cheaper. Nevertheless, there is some
evidence in the new generation of courses that the technology is being
used for the benefit of teachers and learners.

The new generation of courses

The table below lists the components of two coursebook packages
(recent publications or new editions) from each of four major publishers. The purpose of the table is not to provide a comparison
between courses or publishers but rather to present a cross-section of
where ELT coursebook publishing is now, specifically in relation to
the use of linked technology. The course packages surveyed were as
follows:

Cambridge   *face2face* (1)   *Interchange*[1] (2)
Longman   *Cutting Edge* (3)   *Total English* (4)
Macmillan   *Straightforward* (5)   *Inside Out* (6)
Oxford   *New English File* (7) *New Headway* (8)

	C		L		M		O	
	1	2	3	4	5	6	7	8
Student's book	√	√	√	√	√	√	√	√
Teacher's book	√	√	√	√	√	√	√	√
Teacher's resource pack		√			√	√		√
Workbook (various versions)	√	√	√	√	√	√	√	√
Audiocassettes	√	√	√	√	√	√	√	√
Audio CDs	√	√	√		√	√		√
Lab audio CDs		√						
Videocassettes		√				√	√	√
DVD		√		√			√	
Teacher's Guide to video						√		
Tests		√			√	√		√
CD-ROM	√	√					√	√
Linked website	√	√	√	√		√	√	√
Other website resources (T)	√	√			√	√	√	√
Other website resources (S)							√	√

Table 1. Content of coursebook packages

So what is new about this latest generation of resources? Firstly, teachers are offered more *integrated* resources. Teachers' books are reconceptualised as resource packs or additional resources are separately packaged. These may now include photocopiable activities, supplementary materials for mixed groups, and warm-up activities (*New English File*). Further resources for teachers include teachers' guides to videos (*Inside Out* contains guidance and worksheets), custom-

---

1   3rd edition.

isable texts (*face2face*), customisable tests on CD (*Inside Out*), and websites either linked to specific courses (Oxford sites include articles, downloadable worksheets and activities, and discussion groups) or of general interest to teachers (e.g. Macmillan's onestopenglish. com). Secondly, learners are also provided for. There are CD-ROMs to accompany students' books (*face2face*) or workbooks (that for *English File* includes video extracts and activities, interactive grammar quizzes, vocabulary banks, pronunciation charts, and listen and practise audio material; the workbook for *Inside Out* comes with either an audio cassette or an audio CD). Learners also have access to parallel websites designed specifically for them (e.g. *New English File*). And thirdly, a variety of linked resources are available which can either stand alone or be used in combination with specific courses. These include OUP's Business Resource Books, which can be used in conjunction with *English File*, the Headway pronunciation course and interactive practice material on CD-ROM, and Macmillan's bilingual 'Companions' – lists of words/phrases with pronunciation, translation (Dutch/French/German) and contextualisation, which can be used alongside *Inside Out*.

Overall, this is an impressive picture. The teachers' resource packs and the materials for learners, some of them interactive, are not only reminiscent of the ideas put forward by Brumfit and Allwright, they go even further. 25 years ago, who would have dreamed of website resources linked to courses or freely available general website resources for teachers and learners? And more is being offered almost daily. For instance, whiteboard software is available to accompany the two Cambridge titles, and learners can register for free e-lessons with Macmillan.

Does more mean better?

There is, nevertheless, still a niggling doubt. In essence it is that expressed by Brumfit and Allwright, but here voiced by Littlejohn (1998:190):

[...] the use of published materials is now more widespread than ever before [... and] materials [...] have evolved into much more complex objects. In the early days textbooks contained mainly readings, perhaps with some questions and sentences to translate. Now materials frequently offer complete 'packages' for language learning and teaching, with precise indications of the work that teachers and students are to do together. The extent to which materials now effectively structure classroom time has thus increased considerably.

Is there any substance to Littlejohn's claim that the increasing complexification or 'completeness' of coursebook packages has led to a reduced role for the teacher because materials 'now effectively structure classroom time'? Are materials-led classrooms more likely now than was the case previously ? A key factor in the answer to these questions is whether the technology associated with textbooks extends or restricts the choices of learners and teachers. Does the technology offer an *alternative* means of catering for different learning styles, and therefore an enhancement of the learning materials, or is it used to provide *additional*, optional materials for independent, out-of-class learning? Or is it *integral* to the learning experience? The decision to make audiorecordings an integral part of a course, on the grounds that students need to be exposed to a variety of examples of spoken English, does not seem particularly controversial. However, if the recordings, in whole or in part, are not suitable, the decision not to make use of them leaves a vacuum which can only be filled by the teacher (or learners) providing replacement materials. Given the predictable effort involved, it seems likely that even in resource-rich environments teachers will take the easy option of using what is provided, even when this is not entirely suitable. If, on the other hand, the recordings are conceived as an alternative or addition to the core materials then the decision not to use them is just one of the many pedagogical decisions teachers are expected to make, based on their knowledge of their students' needs. We may conclude that the concept of a technologically-enhanced and integrated learning experience may sound very attractive, but too close an integration could indeed lead to the situation of which Littlejohn warns.

At the heart of the debate about textbooks is not so much the nature or quality of the textbook (and the materials associated with it) but the locus of control for what happens in classrooms. In the scenario depicted by Littlejohn, control has effectively passed to materials packages. This is, of course, in stark contrast to Allwright's proposals, which placed responsibility for decision-making firmly in the hands of teachers and learners – although these found little favour at the time because the resources and guides for learners and teachers were not available. For thinking teachers with a full-time teaching load, the preferred option has been somewhere between these extremes: to base their teaching on a textbook, where an appropriate book existed, while still exercising judgement over what to use from this book and how to adapt or supplement it (Cunningsworth 1995, McGrath 2002).

Two developments pose a threat to this middle-way solution, in which the textbook is treated as the spine of a course but not its entire body. One, as we have seen, is the development of integrated coursebook packages. The apparent completeness of these packages may, as Littlejohn fears, lead to teachers losing control. For self-directed teachers, the other problem, paradoxically, is represented by, on the one hand, the variety of material within such packages and, on the other, the availability of a hugely increased range of non-textbook material (particularly on the Internet), which may be more relevant or more appealing than that provided as part of a coursebook package. In itself, more does not mean better. Increased choice brings its own challenges: in this case, the challenge of weaving together materials from different sources into a course which has coherence for learners.

Technologically-enhanced materials packages: some issues

The development of technologically-enhanced materials packages thus raises a number of issues.

1) The design of the packages: either these are carefully integrated and intended to be teacher-proof, with the teacher expected to function largely as a manager of resources and learners, or they are presented as a set of resources from which teacher and learners can select, and which can be adapted and supplemented as necessary.

2) The fit between package and teacher: while skilled teachers can deploy materials in ways that meet the needs of their students, the flexibility or otherwise of the materials becomes a problem when teachers are inexperienced, untrained, lacking in self-confidence, or lazy, or when alternative resources are not easily available. In such situations, it may be argued, teacher-proof materials are more desirable. One consequence, however, is that teachers may simply allow themselves to be led by the materials, abdicating responsibility for course and lesson planning and, in effect, for student learning.

3) The evaluation of complex packages: despite a steady growth in the literature on materials evaluation, anecdotal evidence from teachers suggests that coursebook evaluation still tends to be informal, with the focus largely on the coursebook itself, a focus reflected also in the literature. User-friendly evaluation schemes are needed which take into account the media-specific characteristics of each of the potential components of a coursebook package, and institutions and teachers must take these seriously enough to make use of them. Until then, the glossy will continue to seduce the unwary. Key considerations in the evaluation of such packages must be the extent to which the materials lend themselves to flexible use, the characteristics of the teachers who will use them, and the availability of pedagogic guidance and support.

4) Practical constraints: access to hardware and technical assistance in maintaining hardware and troubleshooting is needed, as is time for teachers to familiarise themselves with non-book materials and prepare lessons using these resources.

5) Teacher (and student) attitudes and competence: teachers and students may have different attitudes towards the technological components, and may not have the necessary competences to handle them. This is the issue to which we now turn.

Technology and Teachers

Impact of technology on language learners (and therefore teachers)

Technology has had an impact not only on the form of learning materials, but also on the students who come to the UK for courses. Potentially, these students have been exposed to a wide range of multimedia in and outwith schools and universities (though this does not mean that they know how to use it effectively or critically). Inevitably, these prior learning experiences will colour their expectations. Overseas teachers, who come to the UK for English-language courses and methodology courses may also have certain expectations. A number of overseas countries have in the last few years introduced information and communication technology (ICT) competences as a requirement within initial teacher education (ITE) and for practising teachers. In Hong Kong the amount of lesson time in which ICT is to be used has even been specified. Such teachers may therefore not only expect that ICT will play a significant part in their learning experience in the UK but also that their UK-based teachers will demonstrate levels of competence similar to those they have been required to acquire in their own country. As a consequence of these differences in prior experiences, a class of adult learners in the UK is now likely to contain individuals who differ not only in their expectations of how they will learn and the skills of their teachers, but also in terms of their own technical competence.

Technology and the teacher

Two assumptions are generally made about ICT: it can enhance the learning experience and it is a support for the teacher. For these assumptions to be valid, certain conditions must be met. These include familiarity with the software available, the ability to make judgments as to what will best serve specific teaching objectives and confidence and creativity in the use of the technology.

At this point, it may be helpful to refer to official standpoints on ICT competences. Section 4.4 of the UCLES CELTA syllabus, which deals with the selection, evaluation and adaptation of materials and resources, refers to computer and other technology-based resources. However, the associated learning outcomes are limited in the extreme. Successful candidates are expected merely to 'develop a *basic* working knowledge of *some* commercially produced and non-published materials and classroom resources for teaching English to adults' (italics added). The corresponding section of the DELTA syllabus (section 3) makes reference to 1) knowledge and effective use of published and non-published resources and materials 2) the ability to evaluate and select materials and resources for different purposes and contexts and 3) the ability to adapt, develop and create materials. However, specific reference to ICT is made only in one sub-section (3.4, italics added):

> demonstrate their *understanding of the role* of a wide range of technical aids and media, *including ILT* (Information and Learning Technology), and *make effective use of these, if appropriate*, in their work on the course for classroom teaching, for preparing materials and for classroom research

By contrast, the requirements of the Teacher Training Agency (TTA) for Qualified Teacher Status (QTS) in the UK are much more rigorous.[2] Trainees must pass an online test, which covers skills (researching and categorising information, developing and modelling information, presenting and communicating information) and software (word processor database, presentation, browser). They must also 'know how to use ICT effectively, both to teach their subject and to support their wider professional role', and 'use ICT effectively in their teaching'. These standards are further specified and amplified by evidence criteria. Space does not permit fuller comparison of the UCLES ELT and QTS sets of standards, but it will perhaps be clear that in relation to ICT, the UCLES requirements (even at DELTA level) are less stringent than those for QTS – an initial qualification.

---

2   For further information see [http://www.tta.gov.uk/php/read.php?sectiionid=275&articleid=1932] and guidance handbook at http://www.tta.gov.uk/php/read.php?sectionid=160].

ELT teachers are required only to demonstrate awareness in relation to the role of technical aids and media, including ICT, and make effective use of these 'if appropriate'. The stipulation, mentioned earlier, that teachers use ICT 25% of the time, hardly inspires faith in purposeful resource use and one can therefore see the point of the phrase 'if appropriate'. Nevertheless, to leave it to teachers' discretion not to use ICT provides no guarantees that they can and if we accept that ICT can enhance the learning experience, then this is hardly desirable. In this sense, the requirements imposed by TTA for QTS seem preferable.

Textbooks, Technology and Teachers: present and future

A detailed and helpful overview of technological developments can be found in Derewianka (2003). Though the purpose of Derewianka's paper is not to stimulate discussion of the relationship between teaching (as traditionally practised) and learning, the evidence which it provides of increasingly sophisticated technological support for learning is a compelling argument for a reconsideration of the balance within a course between time allocated to face to face interaction between a teacher and a class of learners and time allocated to individual learners interacting with electronic resources – and with each other using these resources. Some readjustment of the balance between classroom activity and individualised technologically-supported self-access need not, of course, entail less face-to-face contact with teachers, in that this could free up time for more teacher-supervised self-access work. However, Derewianka (2003:211) describes

> commercial multimedia packages that allow students to work through units of work at their own pace, with the program offering feedback, tracking their progress, diagnosing their needs, providing focused, intensive practice in weak skills, adjusting the level and difficulty of the exercises, assessing achievement and keeping records.

On the face of it, such 'adaptive environments', as she refers to them, not only seem to call into question the need for a textbook – but even a teacher. That is not my own conclusion, but it does, I think, serve to highlight the challenge facing teachers, and the institutions in which they work, in an increasingly technological age. It seems to me that we have now reached a point at which we need to rethink the organisation of learning environments. As various forms of technology have become available, we have incorporated them into classroom teaching or perhaps made them available as optional elements within self-access centres. If, for certain aspects of language learning, interaction with other students is unnecessary, why should we continue to group students together in classes, simply because that is what we have always done and they expect? If technology *can* provide a learning experience that is more effective than is possible in a whole-class environment, shouldn't we be offering this as one component within a planned framework of activities?

Conclusion

I draw three conclusions from the above discussion.
1) It is probably no longer appropriate in our field to talk about textbooks or coursebooks. What we now have are teaching-learning packages. The printed materials that form part of that package will continue to be important, I think, because books are convenient. Although on-line menus seem to offer students the same kind of flexibility to move around text pages as they have with books, they still seem to prefer to download. In short, the life of the textbook (as a form of teaching-learning support) has been extended as a consequence of its reconceptualisation as the core of an integrated package, though the nature of that integration merits further careful consideration. Equally important is the fact that the new generation of coursebook packages include

technologically-based learning (and not just teaching) materials which can facilitate and enliven independent learning.

2)   However, the new packages represent an even greater challenge than the traditional textbook since the teacher has a responsibility not to teach the package but to teach a unique group of learners. Teachers who in the past have accepted that learners are their first responsibility have had to be needs analysts and syllabus designers, as well as providing guidance on learning how to learn. Now that the resources available are much more diverse, such teachers must be capable of fulfilling a number of additional roles. They must be able to plan, research, evaluate and select ICT-enhanced learning experiences. They must also, of course, be capable of using ICT resources and, perhaps, producing materials (PowerPoint slides being an obvious, example), as well as providing learner training for both classroom-based and independent learning.

3)   Within ELT, there as yet seems to be insufficient recognition of how demanding these additional roles are. Teacher certifying bodies such as UCLES and Trinity College, London have an important role to play in encouraging the development of these competences and the provision of such support by specifying more exacting standards of ICT competence. Moreover, observation and anecdotal evidence indicate that on a personal level individual teachers in many institutions are not getting the necessary support. If teachers are now expected to be capable of autonomous decision-making in relation to a wider range of learning resources, then they need not only access to training but also encouragement and appropriate support within the institutions in which they work.

Bibliography

Allwright, D. (1981) 'What do we want teaching materials for?' *ELT Journal* 36/1, 5–18.

Brumfit, C. (1979) 'Seven last slogans'. *Modern English Teacher* 7/1, 30–1.

Cunningsworth, A. (1995) *Choosing your coursebook*. Oxford: Heinemann.

Derewianka, B. (2003) 'Developing electronic materials for language teaching' in Tomlinson, B. (ed.) *Developing materials for language teaching*, 199–220. London: Continuum.

Harmer, J. (2001) 'Coursebooks: a human, linguistic and cultural disaster?' *Modern English Teacher* 10/3, 5–10.

Harwood, N. (2005) 'What do we want EAP teaching materials for?' *Journal of English for Academic Purposes* 4/2, 149–61.

Howatt, A. (1984) *A history of English language teaching*. Oxford: Oxford University Press.

Littlejohn, A. (1998) 'The analysis of language teaching materials: inside the Trojan Horse' in Tomlinson, B. (ed.) *Materials development in language teaching*, 190–216. Cambridge: Cambridge University Press.

McGrath, I. (2002) *Materials evaluation and design for language teachers*. Edinburgh: Edinburgh University Press.

Richards, J. (1993) 'Beyond the textbook: the role of commercial materials in language teaching'. *RELC Journal* 24/1, 1–14.

—— (1998) 'Textbooks: help or hindrance in teaching?' in Richards, J. *Beyond Training: perspectives on language teacher education*, 125–40. Cambridge: Cambridge University Press.

Shannon, P. (1987) 'Commercial reading materials: a technological ideology, and the deskilling of teachers'. *The Elementary School Journal* 87/3, 307–29.

Stack, E. (1960) *The language laboratory and modern language teaching*. New York: Oxford University Press.

Ventola, E. (2005) 'New challenges for English language teaching materials and the classroom'. Paper presented at joint BALEAP/

SATEFL conference on New Approaches to Materials Development for Language Learning. Edinburgh, 15–17 April, 2005.

Coursebook packages

Cunningham, S. and Moor, P. *Cutting Edge*. Harlow: Longman.
Hall, D. and Foley, M. *Total English*. Harlow: Longman.
Kay, S. and Jones, V. *Inside Out*. Oxford: Macmillan.
Kerr, P., Clandfield, L., Jones, C. and Scrivener, J. *Straightforward*. Oxford: Macmillan.
Oxenden, C. et al. *New English File*. Oxford: Oxford University Press.
Redston, C., Warwick, L., Young, A. and Clementson, T. *face2face*. Cambridge: Cambridge University Press.
Richards, H. Hill, J. and Proctor, S. *Interchange*. Cambridge: Cambridge University Press.
Soars, L. and Soars, J. *New Headway English Course*. Oxford: Oxford University Press.

Notes on Contributors

OLWYN ALEXANDER was the main organiser of the BALEAP/ SATEFL conference 2005. She is a Teaching Fellow at Heriot-Watt University, Edinburgh, and is involved in the design and development of materials for academic English courses delivered to overseas students studying applied science and business degrees.

RICHARD BAILEY is a senior lecturer in the English Language Centre at Northumbria University. He teaches on the centre's EAP programmes. His research interests include student writing and academic literacy development in higher education.

CATHY BENSON works at The University of Edinburgh, where she teaches EAP and General English, contributes to masters courses in Language Teaching and Applied Linguistics and post-graduate supervision, and designs and runs teacher education courses. Her research interests include academic writing, pedagogical description, and learners' acquisition of grammar.

ROBERT BERMAN, who has lived in the UK, New Zealand, and recently Canada, is an Associate Professor of the Iceland University of Education, where he teaches English and TEFL to prospective teachers. Robert's main research interests are second language writing and language transfer.

ANDY BLACKHURST works in the Research and Validation Division at University of Cambridge ESOL Examinations, and has particular responsibilities for the IELTS exam. His special interests include East Asian Learners, and the ethics of test usage.

ERIK BORG is currently researching writing in Fine Arts and Design while working for his PhD at the University of Leeds. Until recently, he was Senior Lecturer in the English Language Centre of Northumbria University, where he oversaw the Pre-Master's programme and taught on the MA Applied Linguistics.

IAN BRUCE is a lecturer in Applied Linguistics at the University of Waikato, Hamilton, New Zealand. His main research interest is in the area of genre constructs and their application to EAP curriculum and task design.

SANDRA CARDEW teaches at the University of Essex where she is currently Academic Director of the Bridging Year. Her other responsibilities include an MA module on materials design, which is her main area of professional interest. She was also Chair of the BALEAP Working Party on Teacher Training in EAP.

FEI-YU CHUANG works at the University of Warwick, where she is responsible for the development of electronic EAP materials, and contributes to MA and short courses in the areas of Computer Assisted Language Learning and multimedia materials design and development. Her main research interest is in CALL and Educational Technology.

LYNN ERREY is a Principle Lecturer in Teaching and Learning and academic conduct officer at Oxford Brookes University. She manages the MA TESOL and teaches Psycholinguistics on the undergraduate programme, as well as developing EAP materials for pre-sessional international students. Her main research interests are academic literacy and materials development.

SIÂN ETHERINGTON is a lecturer at the University of Salford where she works on in-sessional and pre-sessional EAP programmes and is leader of the MA TEFL and Applied Linguistics programmes. Her research interests are in student and teacher beliefs and attitudes, academic writing and SLA.

PAUL FANNING is an ELT lecturer at Middlesex University, working partly on undergraduate and postgraduate programmes in the School of Arts, and partly on in-sessional EAP in the Language Centre. His main interests are in developing innovative EAP grammar materials and in psychological aspects of Second Language Acquisition.

BOB GILMOUR works at Newcastle University. He is the English Language Materials Online (ELMO) Project Leader and Programme Leader for two Language Centre programmes. He also teaches EAP and on the MA in Applied Linguistics for TESOL. His main interests are video, CALL and online learning.

JACQUELINE GOLLIN is Deputy Director of Studies at IALS, The University of Edinburgh, where she has been involved in a wide variety of teacher training courses as well as tuition and supervision on Masters courses. Her particular interests include discourse perspectives on grammar, and the teaching and learning of grammar.

After twelve years at Middlesex University as founder and Head of English Language and Learning Support, LYNNE HALE is now an independent consultant and educational entrepreneur specialising in language, communication skills and Action Learning. Her research interests include how techniques from the Arts can be used to stimulate imagination and enhance learning.

STELLA HARVEY is a lecturer at Goldsmiths University of London. She teaches EAP courses to international and home students, coordinates the pre-master's Diploma in Language and Contemporary Culture, and teaches a BA module on Cross-cultural Communication. Her main research interests are content-based language development and academic literacy.

BRUCE HOWELL works at the University of Reading, where he teaches EAP classes, and contributes to individual tutorial support. He also organises pre-sessional assessment, and develops and administers

TEEP (the Test of English for Educational Purposes). His main research interest is in EAP testing.

GILLIAN LAZAR works for English Language and Learning Support (ELLS) at Middlesex University. She teaches EAP/Academic Literacies classes to home and international students, delivers individual support to students and co-ordinates online academic support. Her research interests include materials writing, online learning, using literature in ELT and teaching figurative language.

JOAN MCCORMACK works at the University of Reading and is involved in teaching and materials writing for EAP courses. Her current research interests include the use of sources extended writing, and speaking in the academic context.

IAN MCGRATH is an Associate Professor in TESOL at the University of Nottingham. His research relates primarily to professional development and teacher autonomy and he is currently involved in HEFCE-funded projects concerned with the development of online materials to support e-tutors in HE and English teachers in China.

MARTIN MILLAR teaches study skills, EAP, and International Relations on two of Oxford Brookes' foundation courses, and English language and linguistics modules to undergraduates enrolled in a range of fields. His research interests include student progression, language attitudes and descriptive linguistics.

HILARY NESI is a Reader in the Centre for English Language Teacher Education at the University of Warwick, and is project director for the BASE and the BAWE corpora and coordinator of the MA in English Language Teaching and Multimedia. Her interests include academic genre analysis and EAP materials development.

KAREN NICHOLLS is a lecturer in EAP at Sheffield Hallam University. Her main responsibilities are coordinating the university's pre-sessional course, and teaching in-sessional courses. Her main research interests are in the development and use of e-learning materials, and investigating the expectations and responsibilities of students and institutions.

DIANA RIDLEY has taught and conducted research projects in the field of EAP since 1993. She currently works at the University of Sheffield where she coordinates a teacher training module for research students and is exploring the potential of e-learning to enhance the delivery of research training.

HANIA SALTER-DVORAK is director of Polylang, the University Wide Language Programme at the University of Westminster, where she teaches EAP and Arabic. Her research interests include Authorship and Intertextuality in Academic Writing, and Interlanguage Pragmatics.

PETER SERCOMBE is currently a senior lecturer at Northumbria University where he teaches Applied Linguistics. Among his other academic interests, he researches issues of language contact and code-switching.

JOHN SLAGHT is an EAP teacher, tester and author working at the University of Reading. His main research interests include the development of topic-based language tests, the link between language needs and test development, and student perceptions of assessment methods and their significance.

ANN SMITH is a tutor at the Centre for English Language Education at Nottingham University. She has extensive experience in EAP and teacher training and in Asia, Canada and Britain. Her interests include methodology, materials development including case-based teaching, and cross-cultural communication.

ALISON STEWART teaches English at Tokyo University of Foreign Studies in Japan. She has recently completed a PhD on teacher professionalism, and is currently working on a study of the teaching community of an on-line business writing program. She is also involved in EAP materials development for Japanese students.

FRED TARTTELIN is a senior lecturer at the International Centre for English Language Studies, Oxford Brookes University. He is a programme manager, personal tutor and teaches on pre-sessional EAP courses. Current research interests include mature students' approaches to learning foreign languages, and learner training for international students on short courses.

HUGH TRAPPES-LOMAX is Deputy Director at IALS, University of Edinburgh, where he is Programme Director of the MSc in Language Teaching and teaches courses on grammar and discourse analysis. He is interested in the description of languages for teaching (and other applied) purposes.

PAUL WICKENS works at Oxford Brookes University, where he teaches on the International Foundation Diploma, BA in Language and Linguistics and the MA TESOL for which he co-ordinates the off-campus cohort. His main research interests are in E-learning, corpus linguistics and systemic functional linguistics.

JOHN WRIGGLESWORTH works at the University of Portsmouth, where he teaches academic English to Home and International students. His main interests are in systemic functional linguistics, genre, blended learning, and assessment. He is currently working on a discipline-specific writing project for business undergraduates.